ESSENTIALS
OF
MANAGEMENT

thirdedition

Joseph L. Massie
University of Kentucky

PRENTICE-HALL, INC., ENGLEWOOD CLIFFS, NEW JERSEY 07632

Library of Congress Cataloging in Publication Data

MASSIE, JOSEPH L
  Essentials of management.

  (Prentice-Hall essentials of management series)
  Includes bibliographical references.
  1.–Industrial management. 2.–Management.
  I.–Title.
HD31. M335–1979   658   78-23326
ISBN 0-13-286351-0
ISBN 0-13-286344-8 pbk.

Prentice-Hall Essentials of Management Series
Stephen P. Robbins, **editor**

Editorial/production supervision: Marian Hartstein
Interior and cover design: Christine Gadekar
Manufacturing buyer: Harry P. Baisley

© 1979 by Prentice-Hall, Inc., Englewood Cliffs, N.J. 07632

*All rights reserved. No part of this book
may be reproduced in any form or
by any means without permission in writing
from the publisher.*

10 9 8 7 6 5 4 3 2 1

Printed in the United States of America

Prentice-Hall International, Inc., *London*
Prentice-Hall of Australia Pty. Limited, *Sydney*
Prentice-Hall of Canada, Ltd., *Toronto*
Prentice-Hall of India Private Limited, *New Delhi*
Prentice-Hall of Japan, Inc., *Tokyo*
Prentice-Hall of Southeast Asia Pte. Ltd., *Singapore*
Whitehall Books Limited, *Wellington, New Zealand*

FOREWORD

With the rapid growth in recent years of courses in such areas as personnel, organizational behavior, production, decision science, labor relations, and small business management, there has developed an increased need for a viable alternative to the standard 500- or 600-page, casebound textbook. The Essentials of Management Series has been designed to fill that need. The Series consists of brief, survey books covering major content areas within the management discipline.

Each book in the Series provides a concise treatment of the key concepts and issues within a major content area, written in a highly readable style, balancing theory with practical applications, and offering a clarity of presentation that is often missing in standard, full-length textbooks. I have selected authors both for their academic expertise and their ability to identify, organize, and articulate the essential elements of their subject. So, for example, you will find that the books in this Series avoid unnecessary jargon, use a conversational writing style, include extensive examples and interesting illustrations of concepts, and have the focus of a rifle rather than that of an encyclopedic shotgun.

The books in this Series will prove useful to a wide variety of readers. Since each covers the essential body of knowledge in a major area of management, they can be used alone for introductory survey courses in colleges and universities or for management development and in-house educational programs. Additionally, their short format makes them an ideal vehicle to be combined with cases, readings, and/or experiential materials by instructors who desire to mold a course to meet unique objectives. The books in this Series offer the flexibility that is either not feasible or too costly to achieve with a standard textbook.

Stephen P. Robbins
Series Editor

CONTENTS

3
MORAL AND SOCIAL DIMENSIONS OF MANAGEMENT

27

4
INTERNATIONAL MANAGEMENT AND ITS ENVIRONMENTAL DIMENSIONS

38

PART
2

FUNCTIONS IN THE MANAGEMENT PROCESS

51

5
DECISION MAKING AND POLICY FORMULATION

53

6
STAFFING AND ORGANIZING

66

11

THE BEHAVIORAL SCIENCES IN MANAGEMENT 135

12

QUANTITATIVE METHODS OF ANALYSIS 155

13

MANAGEMENT INFORMATION SYSTEMS AND COMPUTERS 172

PART

APPLICATIONS OF MANAGERIAL FUNCTIONS IN OPERATIONS 189

14

APPLICATIONS IN BUSINESS OPERATIONAL AREAS 191

15

MANAGEMENT OF PUBLIC ORGANIZATIONS 221

PART

5

DYNAMICS OF MANAGEMENT 237

16

MANAGEMENT AND CHANGE 239

PREFACE

This book summarizes the essential elements of management. Its primary aim is to provide the reader with a synthesis of the traditional and newer quantitative and behavioral approaches to the subject of management by focusing attention on basic concepts and techniques of analysis. It proposes a framework for integrating the contributions of the various disciplines interested in the study of management; yet, it encourages a critical attitude toward all administrative thought, with the hope that the reader will reach a synthesis of his own.

The author adopts the view that management must be based on interdisciplinary study. Important advances have recently been made in economics, accounting, sociology, social psychology, statistics, and mathematics in areas directly related to management. These areas have been emphasized in this book, and the traditional, functional framework has been condensed.

This second edition was expanded by the addition of three chapters on basic subjects that increased in importance in the decade of the 60s: international and comparative management, information systems and computers, and the role of management in a rapidly changing world. Since the behavioral contributions had been most extensive, the chapter on this disciplinary foundation in this third edition was completely rewritten. This third edition also responds to an additional need that became evident in the 1970s; a new chapter focuses on the unique aspect of not-for-profit organizations, especially public administration, and the role of women in management is emphasized throughout. However, the original purpose of the book remains the same—to provide a concise, organized summary of management for a reader who needs an introductory framework for the broad subject of management. The original framework has been retained, while the text has been updated by the addition of the many contributions made during the last two decades. The fact that most chapters needed only minor changes supports the proposition held by many users of the previous editions that the original text included essentials of lasting importance.

The reader will find that several techniques have been used to present as much useful information as possible in this volume. The index, for example, includes many of the terms one must know in order to understand the meaning of management. These terms appear in **boldface type** in the text where they are first used. Tables and charts are frequently used to summarize important information that would otherwise require many pages to present.

The author hopes that this volume will be a stimulating and provocative experience for the reader and will prompt further study in order to secure a more comprehensive knowledge of the field of management.

With this end in view, references have been provided at the end of each chapter. The reader will find in these books a more elaborate treatment of the subjects and more extensive bibliographies for further study.

As a summary of the essentials of management, this book will prove useful to a wide variety of readers. It will be understandable to the lay person who has had no formal education in management. It will be helpful to students in various management courses who feel the need for a concise integration of subjects covered in other books. It will be of particular help to students in "case" courses who need some references to concepts and techniques of analysis to apply in specific situations. In addition, it will provide a useful summary of ideas for the person who is in, or hopes to be in, a managerial position.

The author gratefully acknowledges contributions of several doctoral students at the University of Kentucky: Thomas Barnes, Mary Joyce, and Sridhar Kadaba. Also, thanks go to the reviewers of new chapters in the third edition. I also wish to express my appreciation to Mrs. Rachael Massie who represented the author in the final stages of the production of this book while he was out of the United States.

Special appreciation is extended to colleagues who contributed chapters: James L. Gibson, Professor, University of Kentucky for work on Chapter 10 of the original edition; Marc Wallace, Jr., Associate Professor, University of Kentucky, for the completely new Chapter 11 on "The Behavioral Sciences in Management"; Martin Solomon, Director of the Computing Center, University of Kentucky, for his work on Chapters 12 and 13, "Quantitative Methods of Analysis" and "Information Systems and Computers"; Lawrence X. Tarpey, Professor, University of Kentucky, for the marketing portion of Chapter 14; Lawrence Lynch, Assistant Professor, University of Kentucky, for the new chapter on "Management of Public Organizations"; and John Douglas, Glos Professor of Business, Miami University, for work on Chapter 16, "Management and Change." Finally, the support and feedback from the users of the first two editions was essential to the improvements in this third edition.

J.L.M.

1

BACKGROUND OF MODERN MANAGEMENT

The study of modern management begins with a broad look at the nature and scope of the field, then proceeds to examine the functions that managers are called upon to perform. Chapter 1 discusses these functions and raises several questions concerning the place of management in our modern-day society.

Although management is a relatively new discipline, it has developed rapidly. The history of managerial thought provides perspective for those who wish to benefit from yesterday's contributions. Chapter 2 summarizes the contributions of the most important authorities who have laid the foundations upon which present management students can further advance the discipline.

More and more, the philosophical foundations, including moral and ethical issues, are viewed as necessary frameworks for management thought. A manager must develop some philosophical framework within which to think and act. This framework helps in separating the important from the unimportant. Chapter 3 provides this basis of philosophical thought and focuses attention on the importance of setting clear and definite objectives. These objectives then become the foundation for all the manager's actions.

The study of management in the 1970s spread rapidly across national and cultural boundaries as a result of the rapid development of international business. A recognition of the impact of environmental factors by contingency theories has resulted in numerous comparative studies which tend to reduce the ethnocentric tendencies of managers who previously had little contact with other cultures. Chapter 4 concentrates on the environmental factors important to multinational companies and to managers of domestic companies who increasingly feel the need to adapt their approaches to the varied cultural forces of the complex modern world.

NATURE AND IMPORTANCE OF MANAGEMENT

◁══ **IDEAS TO BE FOUND** ══▷
IN THIS CHAPTER

- Definition of management
- Functions of management
- Management as an art, science, profession
- Management development
- Leadership
- Organizational development

Management is universal in the modern industrial world. Every organization requires the making of decisions, the coordinating of activities, the handling of people, and the evaluation of performance directed toward group objectives. Numerous managerial activities have their own particular approach to specific types of problems and are discussed under such headings as farm management, management of health delivery systems, college management, government management, marketing management, production or operations management, and others. All have elements in common. This book summarizes some of the essential concepts and techniques of management that are fundamental to various applications.

Management has become more important as labor has become more specialized and as the scale of operations has increased. Technological developments have continually created new challenges. The complexities of human relationships constantly challenge those who perform managerial functions. The dynamics of management, therefore, should be characteristic of any study of its theory and practice.

Because of the increasing importance of management, and because of the new challenges it faces, many researchers in various disciplines have concentrated their attention on parts of the subject. The result is that managerial approaches to such subjects as psychology, economics, and accounting have helped to improve the thinking in relation to the overall field of management. Research on subjects important to management since World War II offer renewed hope to those who must face the complexities that confront the operating manager. On the other hand, managers face new challenges to established doctrines and dogmas as the result of research which requires them to adapt their approaches.

In the last decade, certain fundamental changes in society have altered the relative opportunities in management. In the past, management developed in the industrial and business sector. In the 1970s, opportunities developed more rapidly in the following ways:

1. *Post-industrial society*—Service-oriented organizations now are the dominant and most dynamic parts of the economy.
2. *Growth in the public sector*—Although the profit-oriented firms remain important in the U.S., public agencies, Health Maintenance Organizations (HMO's), and non-profit associations are increasing at a more rapid pace.
3. *Women in management*—The role of women as managers has increased in the 1970s and this new factor has made a significant impact on management thinking.

MEANING OF MANAGEMENT The chief characteristic of management is the integration and application of the knowledge and analytical approaches developed by numerous disciplines. The manager's problem is to seek a balance among these special approaches and to apply the pertinent concepts in specific situations which require action. The manager must orient himself to solving problems with techniques tailored to the situations; yet, he must develop a unified framework of thought that encompasses the total and integrated aspects of the entire organization.

What, then, is management, and what does it do? In general usage, the word "management" identifies a special group of people whose job it is to direct the effort and activities of other people toward common objectives. Simply stated, management "gets things done through other people." For the purpose of this book, **management** is defined as the *process* by which a cooperative group directs actions toward common goals. This process involves techniques by which a distinguishable group of people (managers) coordinates activities of other people; managers seldom actually perform the activities themselves. This process consists of certain basic functions which provide an analytical approach for studying management and is the subject of Part 2 of this book.

4

The concept of management has broadened in scope with the introduction of new perspectives by different fields of study (the subject of Part 3). The study of management has evolved into more than the use of *means* to accomplish given *ends*; today it includes moral and ethical questions concerning the selection of the right *ends* toward which managers should strive.

Harbison and Myers[1] offer a threefold concept for emphasizing a broader scope for the viewpoint of management. They observe management as (1) an economic resource, (2) a system of authority, and (3) a class or elite.

1. As viewed by the economist, management is one of the *factors of production* together with land, labor and capital. As the industrialization of a nation increases, the need for management becomes greater as it is substituted for capital and labor. The managerial resources of a firm determine, in large measure, its productivity and profitability. In those industries experiencing innovations, management must be used more intensively. Executive development, therefore, is more important for those firms in a dynamic industry in which progress is rapid.

2. As viewed by a specialist in administration and organization, management is *a system of authority*. Historically, management first developed an authoritarian philosophy with a small number of top individuals determining all actions of the rank and file. Later, humanitarian concepts caused some managements to develop paternalistic approaches. Still later, constitutional management emerged, characterized by a concern for definite and consistent policies and procedures for dealing with the working group. As more employees received higher education, the trend of management was toward a democratic and participative approach. Modern management can be viewed as a synthesis of these four approaches to authority.

3. As viewed by a sociologist, management is *a class and status system*. The increase in the complexity of relationships in modern society demands that managers become an elite of brains and education. Entrance into this class is based more and more on education and knowledge instead of on family or political connections. Some students view this development as a "managerial revolution" in which the career managerial class obtains increasing amounts of power and threatens to become an autonomous class. Some observers view this development with alarm. Others point out that as the power of managers increases, their numbers expand, so that there is little need to worry about this tendency toward a managerial autoc-

[1]Frederick Harbison and Charles A. Myers, *Management in the Industrial World* (New York: McGraw-Hill Book Company, 1959), pp. 21-86.

racy. A broad view of management requires that the student consider this larger perspective of the place of management in society.

These three perspectives are not the only important ones for the manager to recognize. An industrial manager would argue that the technological viewpoint is of prime importance. A psychologist would emphasize the needs of the human being and adjustment to organizational pressures. The theologian would concentrate on the spiritual implications of managerial actions. A politician would look to what is feasible and acceptable.

Many chief executives and educators contend that the most important perspective of top executives should be based on a "liberally educated outlook on life." The total concept of management requires an understanding of the meaning of liberal education and its relationship to management functions. A **liberal point of view** is not merely the sum of a finite number of narrow approaches. Its emphasis is on freedom to choose from the widest range of possibilities by discovering new possibilities, and by recalling possibilities previously developed but forgotten. The liberally oriented executive continues to expand his horizons with utmost freedom in an effort to strive toward an ultimate in life. Because management must be concerned with ends as well as means, it is clear that it must maintain a broad perspective, unfettered by specialized restrictions. The paradox of management is that it is based on identifiable and rigorous frameworks of concepts, but at the same time it continues to strive toward breaking out of any set discipline. This paradox makes management an extremely interesting subject; it also makes any attempt to summarize it in a short book a presumptuous task. Yet there is a need for the development of better thinking by managers, and a student must take a first step before attempting a second. The basic approaches summarized in this book should provide ideas for this first step and should challenge the reader to supplement this knowledge with new ideas from further study and experience.

FUNCTIONS
OF
MANAGEMENT

One way to view the process of management is to identify the basic functions which together make up the process. These functions will be discussed in greater detail in Part 2 and will serve as elements for all applications of management concepts. These functions are basic to managerial activities at all levels from the immediate supervisor to the chief executive. They are fundamental in all types of cooperative endeavor, including business firms, government agencies, and benevolent institutions. They form the core of activities in various applications such as marketing, manufacturing, financing, and public agencies.

Different authorities offer different names for the key functions of management; however, there is general agreement on most of the actual duties of a manager. In this book, the following seven functions will be used to describe the job of management:

1. *Decision making*—the process by which a course of action is consciously chosen from available alternatives for the purpose of achieving a desired result.
2. *Organizing*—the process by which the structure and allocation of jobs are determined.
3. *Staffing*—the process by which managers select, train, promote, and retire subordinates.
4. *Planning*—the process by which a manager anticipates the future and discovers alternative courses of action open to him.
5. *Controlling*—the process that measures current performance and guides it toward some predetermined goal.
6. *Communicating*—the process by which ideas are transmitted to others for the purpose of effecting a desired result.
7. *Directing*—the process by which actual performance of subordinates is guided toward common goals. Supervising is one aspect of this function at lower levels where physical overseeing of work is possible.

All these functions are closely interrelated; however, it is useful to treat each as a separate process for the purpose of spelling out the detailed concepts important to the whole job of the manager. At times it may be desirable to consider several functions jointly in order to show their close interrelationships. For example, communicating and controlling must be considered together in systems planning; organizing, communicating, and staffing may be viewed together in studying organization behavior.

A list of management functions is merely a useful analytical device for stressing the basic elements inherent in the job of management. At times it might be desirable to identify subfunctions for purpose of emphasis. For example, each of the above seven functions assumes that management has a certain set of objectives. In this book, objectives are considered in Chapter 3 as the foundation for the performance of the seven functions. Recently, motivation of human beings has received special attention from behavioral scientists; it might be considered a subfunction of staffing and directing. Motivation will receive special attention in Chapter 11 as part of one of the disciplines which contribute to management thought. Other terms, such as leading, coordinating, evaluating, and integrating, have been used in lists of managerial functions, but they have the defect of being too general and vague for inclusion here as basis for an analytical study of the job of management. It should be obvious that the seven functions stated above do relate to what might be called "leadership"; however, for our purposes, it is important to distinguish between leadership and management.

Leadership involves personal qualities which enable one person to induce others to follow. These qualities are particularly important to the directing function of management. Styles of leadership are important to the study of management, but management is a more comprehensive concept than leadership. Development of a manager can be achieved through academic study. The essence of leadership is interpersonal and action-oriented, and therefore can best be developed in practice.

DEVELOPING FUTURE MANAGERS The need for managers will increase with the development of more complex enterprises. Rapid growth of knowledge useful to management will demand a higher quality of managers. Greater effort is being given to the development of persons who can better perform managerial functions. This book directs attention to the essentials of developing future managers. It provides some of the available knowledge useful to future managers and indicates the attitude and point of view of good managers.

Executive development programs have long been a useful means for supplying the needed manager personnel. More recently, attention has been given to **Organizational Development** (OD), which includes the process of reeducation and training to increase the adaptability of the organization to environmental requirements. Organizational development thus is a broad subject area of management, since its focus is on group adaptations rather than personal leadership qualities.

The characteristics of a good manager may be described in broad terms of initiative, dependability, intelligence, judgment, good health, integrity, perseverance, and so on. The trouble with this broad approach is that it is not very useful in describing how a given individual can develop into a better manager. Two more useful approaches provide conceptual help to those aspiring to managerial positions.

One approach, suggested by Robert Katz,[2] is to explain the *skills* which can be developed. In this approach three skills are fundamental: (1) technical, (2) human, and (3) conceptual. **Technical skills** relate to the proficiency of performing an activity in the correct manner and with the right techniques. This skill is the easiest to describe, because it is the most concrete and familiar. The musician and the athlete must learn how

[2]Robert L. Katz, "Skills of an Effective Administrator," *Harvard Business Review* (January-February 1955), pp. 33-42.

to play properly and must practice their skills. The executive, likewise, develops skills in such areas as mechanics, accounting, selling and production that are especially important at lower levels of an organization. As he rises to more responsibility, other skills become relatively more important. A second required skill involves **human relationships.** The executive deals with people and must be able to "get along" with them. Human relations concentrates on developing this skill of cooperating with others. However, if colleagues notice that the executive has read a book on "how to win friends" and is consciously attempting to manipulate them, trouble develops. A third skill involves **conceptual ability:** to see individual matters as they relate to the total picture. This skill is the most difficult to describe, yet is the most important, especially at higher levels of an organization. Much of this skill can be learned, and is not "just born into a person." Conceptual skill depends on developing a creative sense of discovering new and unique ideas. It enables the executive to perceive the pertinent factors, to visualize the key problems, and to discard the irrelevant facts.

A second approach to analyzing factors important in developing managers is suggested by Charles E. Summer.[3] He emphasizes knowledge factors, attitude factors, and ability factors. *Knowledge factors* refer to ideas, concepts, or principles that are conscious, able to be expressed, and accepted because they are subject to logical proof. *Attitude factors* relate to those beliefs, feelings, desires, and values that may be based on emotions and that may not be subject to conscious verbalization. Interest in one's work, confidence in one's mental competence, desire to accept responsibility, respect for the dignity of one's associates, and desire for creative contribution are some of the attitudes that can be acquired by proper education. *Ability factors* are too often treated as being unaffected by environment. Executive development depends upon attention to four major ability factors: skill, art, judgment, and wisdom. These ability factors are abstract, but they direct one's thinking to factors that can be developed by the individual who takes the trouble to consider them.

The basic proposition of this book is that the development of managers can best be achieved through a directed effort in the study of the subject of management. True, some people may be born leaders; others may be able to learn as apprentices while working with a mature manager; others may become successful managers with education in the law, engineering, medicine, and so on. Yet, these leaders with innate abilities, varied practices, or education could more rapidly become superior managers if they acquired the necessary knowledge and attitudes in the most efficient manner—some formal recognition of the complex role of man-

[3]Charles E. Summer, *Factors in Effective Administration* (New York: Graduate School of Business, Columbia University, 1956).

agers. Furthermore, in modern complex organizations the demand for managers is so great that reliance on elite leaders results in a deficiency in the supply of managers. Organizations have been increasing in number and size, with the result that the number and the quality of managers required are much greater than ever before. Thus, in the modern world the need for more and better managers is greater than the available supply. This book is a contribution toward increasing the supply of professional managers.

ART, SCIENCE, AND PROFESSION   Discussions about management usually raise the question of whether management is primarily an art, a science, or a profession. The proper answer to this question depends first upon a clear understanding of the meaning of the three key terms: art, science, and profession.

The emphasis in any activity that is classed as an **art** is on applying skills and knowledge and accomplishing an end through deliberate efforts. If this idea of art is applied to managerial activity, it is clear that management is an art. **Science**, on the other hand, involves seeking new knowledge through the use of a rigorous method of collecting, classifying and measuring data, setting up hypotheses, and testing those hypotheses. In the last century, management has given increased attention to its scientific aspects. In Part 3, we shall summarize some of the sciences that contribute new knowledge to the field of management. In any case, art and science are complementary concepts.

The question of whether management is a profession is complicated by the fact that management is a broad subject. Parts of the subject may have professional characteristics and other parts may not. The following **criteria of a profession** will help identify those parts which may be considered to be professional:

1. A profession is based on a proven, systematic body of knowledge, and thus requires intellectual training.
2. A profession maintains an experimental attitude toward information, and thus requires a search for new ideas.
3. A profession emphasizes service to others, and usually develops a code of ethics that requires that financial return not be the only motive.
4. Entrance into a profession is usually restricted by standards established by an association that requires its members be accepted by a group composed of people with common training and attitude.

Whether management is an art, science, or profession is not merely an academic question. It raises issues concerning the future development of the discipline. Management, in its applied aspects, is an art for getting things done through others, guided to a great extent by practitioners. Since World War II, the interest of other disciplines in management problems and management's interest in the findings of other disciplines have resulted in a trend toward seeking scientific validation of management precepts. Part 3 of this book concentrates on these disciplinary foundations and summarizes the scientific approach of management. Management itself may not be a science, but it gradually is employing the approaches and the contributions of a variety of sciences.

The place of management in modern society has forced a new look at its professional status. In Chapters 2 and 3 it will be clear that the moral and social climate has created new challenges for management. To answer the challenges, managers need more intellectual training; they must stress creativeness and search for new ideas; they must consider ethics and service to society; and they must organize associations with definite standards for membership.

During the last decade, society increasingly has challenged the ethical bases of many management decisions, and thus has stressed the need for professionalism. The consumer movement led by Ralph Nader, disclosures of briberies in foreign operations, the campaign for equal rights for women, affirmative action programs against racial discrimination, the Watergate scandal, and many other developments point toward increased emphasis on the ethical dimensions of management. The narrow view of management as striving only toward efficiency, profitability, and effective human relations seems obsolete. Clearly, the trend is toward requiring managers to consider ethical issues, service to society, and other characteristics of a profession.

THE STRUCTURE OF THIS BOOK Part 1 of this book consists of four chapters that provide the historical background of management thought and the philosophical and social setting in which management activities take place. Part 2, also consisting of four chapters, offers the essentials of the seven managerial functions, which form the central theme of managerial activities. In these chapters, the reader will find some of the basic concepts that are useful in all management applications. These concepts should be considered as first approximations. The modern manager will do well to recognize that the subject of management is developing rapidly and that new ideas are being formed. This fact should be exciting and promising; it surely should not be discouraging or frustrating.

Part 3 consists of five chapters and directs attention to the disciplinary foundations upon which managers can build a better understanding of their functions. Each of these disciplines presents a definite point of view that expands the horizons of management and provides techniques and knowledge useful to managers in carrying out their functions.

Part 4 consists of two chapters that concentrate on important operational activities. These chapters include concepts and analytical devices of special importance to particular areas of operations. Each of the sub-areas of management has developed unique methods of applying the general concepts of management. Marketing managers use key terms of special significance to them; financial managers apply economic and accounting concepts in handling money and other resources; operations managers focus on the production and manufacturing aspects of operations; public administrators have developed unique approaches to fit organizations in the public sector with a non-profit orientation.

Part 5, the final chapter, concentrates on the dynamic nature of management and the requirements for the decade of the 1980s.

REFERENCES

DALE, ERNEST, *The Great Organizers.* New York: McGraw-Hill Book Co., 1960.

DRUCKER, PETER, *Management.* New York: Harper and Row, 1974.

LEAVITT, H. J., W. R. DILL, and H. B. EYRING. *The Organizational World.* New York: Harcourt Brace Jovanovich, 1973.

MCGUIRE, JOSEPH, *Contemporary Management.* Englewood Cliffs, N.J.: Prentice-Hall, Inc., 1973.

MASSIE, JOSEPH L. and JOHN DOUGLAS, *Managing: A Contemporary Introduction* (2nd ed.). Englewood Cliffs, N.J.: Prentice-Hall, Inc., 1977.

2

DEVELOPMENT
OF
MANAGEMENT
THOUGHT

⟸ IDEAS TO BE FOUND ⟹
IN THIS CHAPTER

- Early thought on management
- Appearance of management as a distinct discipline
- Contributions of the pioneers of scientific management
- Early attempts to state management universals
- Development of research in the behavioral sciences
- Modern concentration on quantitative methods
- Contingency theories

The concentrated study of management, as a separate and distinct field of endeavor, is a product of the last century. Most writers agree that the origin of this young discipline was the work performed by Frederick W. Taylor and his associates during the scientific management movement that developed around 1900. In this chapter, the review of the development of the thinking about management will provide historical perspective for an understanding of the concepts discussed in later chapters.

PRESCIENTIFIC MANAGEMENT ERA   Problems of administration were of interest to students of government even in ancient Greek and Biblical times. The Bible, for example, explains organizational problems faced by Moses in leading his people. Histories of the Roman Empire contain information on how administrative problems were handled.

In spite of the fact that administrative problems received attention in ancient times, no important managerial tools of analysis developed until the end of the Dark Ages, when commerce began to grow in the Mediterranean. In the thirteenth and fourteenth centuries, the large trading houses of Italy needed a means of keeping records of business transactions. To satisfy this need, the technique of *double entry bookkeeping* was first described by Pacioli in 1494. The roots of modern accounting, therefore, were planted four centuries before they were to form an important field of knowledge for the modern manager.

Not until after the rise of the capitalistic system did students rigorously give attention to the field of economics. In 1776, Adam Smith wrote *The Wealth of Nations*, in which he developed important economic concepts. He emphasized the importance of *division of labor*, with its three chief advantages: (1) an increase in the dexterity of every workman; (2) the saving of time lost in passing from one type of work to the next; and (3) the better use of new machines. The development of the factory system resulted in an increased interest in the economics of production and the entrepreneur.

In the Middle Ages (and even until recently in many countries) the family unit was the basic production organization. A skilled craftsman taught his sons a trade, and the family was known by its particular trade and skill. Modern surnames such as Carpenter, Goldsmith, Butcher, Farmer, and Taylor are evidence of this development. Production functions were not distinguished from social functions; there was still no need for separate attention to managerial activities. The inventions of the eighteenth century initiated a change which Toynbee later called the Industrial Revolution. Production moved from the home to a separate installation—the factory—where machinery was concentrated and labor employed. In the early stages of the Industrial Revolution, owners of factories directed production but generally did not distinguish between their ownership functions and their management duties.

Some of the first factory owners concentrated on improving methods of production and introduced concepts that proved fundamental to modern manufacturing methods. Before 1800, Eli Whitney and Simeon North developed the concept of **interchangeability of parts** in the manufacture of pistols and muskets. This concept led to the producing of parts to close tolerances, thus making possible the exchange of one part for another without fitting or further machining. In 1796, Matthew R. Boulton and James Watt, Jr., organized the Soho Foundry, in which product components were standardized, cost records kept, and management of the factory improved.

In the early nineteenth century, the need for larger aggregations of capital to support factory operations resulted in increased applications of a special legal form of organizing a business. The **corporation,** as a separate legal entity, could sell shares of stock to many individuals and thus raise large sums of capital. Stockholders then became so numerous that all could not actively manage a business. By the middle of the nineteenth century, general incorporation acts made it possible for many businesses to use this legal form of organization at a time in which technological developments were forcing an increase in the size of the manufacturing unit. If the family fortune was insufficient for the family owners to expand, the corporation provided a means by which capital could be secured from owners who were not managers. The distinction between the function of owners and the function of managers became clear. This distinction set the stage for students to concentrate on the management process as a separate field of study.

The social evils of the Industrial Revolution received wide attention in the early nineteenth century. In England, social reformers sought legal regulation of employment practices in the Factory Acts of 1802, 1819, and 1831. One reformer also became a pioneer in management. Robert Owen, as manager of a large textile firm in New Lanark, Scotland, concentrated on the improvement of working conditions and on the development of a model community. The social impact of modern productive methods became an important interest of such men in operating management.

By 1832, scientists and other persons not directly related to ownership of manufacturing firms began to consider improvements in management. In that year Charles Babbage, a mathematician and a teacher, wrote *On the Economy of Machinery and Manufactures*, in which he applied his principles to the workshop. This early work introduced the idea of using scientific techniques to improve the managing process. Such developments before the twentieth century were, however, exceptional and did not include any integrated effort to study management. The social, legal, technical, and economic environment had not provided the necessary conditions for concentrating on management improvements. By the end of the nineteenth century, the stage was set for a group of people to tackle management problems in a systematic manner.

CLASSICAL MANAGEMENT

By 1886 the American Society of Mechanical Engineers was an established professional society, holding meetings at which leaders presented technical papers. In that year Henry R. Towne, President of Yale & Towne Manufacturing Company, presented a paper, "The Engineer as an Economist," and made a plea to the society to recognize management as a separate field of study.

At the time that Towne's paper was presented to the ASME, Frederick W. Taylor was an operating manager at the Midvale Steel Works. He had progressed from the level of worker in the plant—where he had been able to observe the accepted practices of the time—and had ob-

15

tained an engineering degree in 1883 by studying evenings at Stevens Institute of Technology. With his strong will and keen powers of observation, he rebelled against the restriction of production that he called "soldiering." Taylor noticed that managers were supposed to "pick up" their management skill through trial and error. "Rules of thumb" were their only guides. Above all, he argued that too much of management's job was being left to the worker. He felt that it was management's job to set up methods and standards of work and to provide an incentive for the worker to increase production. Two of Taylor's specific contributions resulted from this thinking: (1) experiments with Maunsel White led to the development of high-speed cutting steel that trebled production; (2) interest in motivating the worker to greater effort led to a piece-rate system of wage payment based upon a definite time standard.

Taylor would have been remembered for his early work in providing specific techniques for managers; yet his contributions leading to his recognition as the "father of scientific management" were two books written after he had resigned as a practicing manager: *Shop Management* (1906) and *The Principles of Scientific Management* (1911).

Until his death in 1915, Taylor expounded his new philosophy, stressing that the core of scientific management was not in individual techniques but in the new attitude toward managing a business enterprise. The essence of **scientific management** was in four general areas:

1. The discovery, through use of the scientific method, of basic elements of man's work to replace rules of thumb.
2. The identification of management's function of planning work, instead of allowing workmen to choose their own methods.
3. The selection and training of workers and the development of cooperation, instead of encouraging individualistic efforts by employees.
4. The division of work between management and the workers so that each would perform those duties for which he was best fitted, with the resultant increase in efficiency.

Scientific management was an innovation and, as such, generated tremendous opposition. During Taylor's lifetime and in spite of the support of such other leaders as Louis Brandeis, James Dodge, and Henry Towne, opposition to change retarded the spread of its basic ideas. Public opposition was demonstrated before special Congressional committee hearings in 1912. At these hearings, Taylor's testimony in defense of his ideas contained some of the most lucid explanations of the central ideas of this first stage of management as a separate and identifiable discipline.

Taylor was a major contributor to scientific management, but by no means was he alone. Henry L. Gantt, a contemporary and associate of

Taylor, joined in the attack on existing management practices and emphasized the psychology of the worker and the importance of morale in production. Gantt devised a wage payment system, which stimulated foremen and workers to strive for improvement in work practices. He developed a charting system for scheduling production that remains the basis for modern scheduling techniques.

Other leaders in the scientific management movement had independently developed improved techniques of management before being influenced by Taylor. Frank Gilbreth made studies in applying principles of motion economy and is considered to be the originator of motion study. Starting in the construction industry, he revolutionized the techniques of bricklaying and later applied his new approach in a variety of industries. His wife, Lillian Gilbreth, not only helped her husband develop his ideas but also contributed to a new dimension in her writings on the psychology of management. Both Gilbreths took an analytical approach and stressed the importance of giving attention to minute details of work. This approach was to become an important characteristic of all scientific management.

Morris L. Cooke and Harrington Emerson were among the founders of scientific management and are important for their applications of the philosophy to a wider group of activities. Cooke demonstrated the applicability of scientific management in nonindustrial fields, especially in university operations and city management. Emerson concentrated on introducing new ideas to the Santa Fe Railroad and later developed what he termed twelve principles of efficiency.

Scientific management's effect on unemployment rapidly became a national and social issue. Dedicated disciples of the movement took an aggressive mechanical view of production and immediately created opposition by organized labor. The result was that the spread of scientific management was not as great as it could have been.

By 1924, when the first International Management Congress was held in Prague, scientific management had become international in scope. Henri Fayol had previously led a French movement in the improvement of work at the administrative level of organization. Lenin had seen the advantages of the techniques of scientific management and introduced the ideas in Russia.

During the 1920s and 1930s, scientific management fell into the hands of "efficiency experts," who concentrated on the mechanical aspects of production. Critics of the movement pointed out that this approach neglected the elements of the psychological needs of workers and the sociological aspects of cooperation. They also observed that scientific management, by concentrating on the details of the shop, had neglected improvements at higher levels of the organization. During these decades, some management thinkers and practitioners attempted to remedy this defect by formulating generalizations deduced from their understanding of what management should be. A number of books attempted to collect these universals and state them as tight and complete prescriptions.

Lyndall Urwick, a British consultant, Ralph C. Davis, a college professor, James D. Mooney and Allan C. Reiley, industrial executives, and many others expounded their views concerning the principles of organization and management. These views were considered authoritative and were widely quoted as basic readings for the education of managers. Later, they served as points of departure for students who were intellectually skeptical of the universality of the observations when applied to actual business cases. Thus the groundwork was laid for a multiple attack on the study of essentials of management.

BEHAVIORAL AND QUANTITATIVE APPROACHES TO MANAGEMENT

In the last fifty years, many disciplines have been active in making contributions to the development of management thought. The fields of public administration and business education have felt, more than any others, the impact of the diversified attack on current practices and past thought by disciplines that previously had little to offer the practicing manager. Barriers to communication among these disciplines were pierced by joint research and the publication of findings in both academic journals and popular periodicals. The streams of thought, together with their principal exponents, that have contributed to this development appear in Figure 2-1. A partial integration of these streams has been attempted by some of their exponents as they developed interests in fields outside their major discipline (indicated by arrows and repetition of their names in the fields in which they have made important contributions).

One of the earliest and clearly most important events in this trend of interdisciplinary activity in the study of management was the Hawthorne Experiment, conducted between 1927 and 1932 at a plant of the Western Electric Company. Elton Mayo, a Harvard sociologist, and a team of social scientists conducted a series of experiments and worked with management in an attempt to explain variations of productivity in the plant. Physical factors, such as lighting and working conditions, were the first aspects to receive attention, but psychological factors emerged as the more important.

An early contributor to the psychology and sociology of management, Mary Parker Follett, attempted to interpret classical management principles in terms of the human factors. She proposed four principles as guides to management thinking:

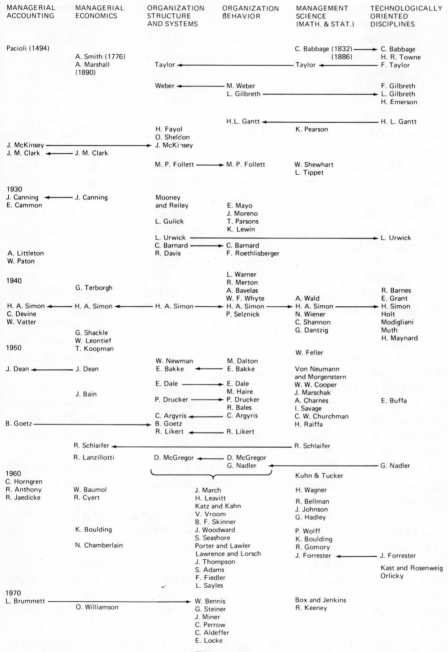

Figure 2-1
Contributors to Interdisciplinary Streams of Management Thought*

*Arrows indicate cross-disciplinary interchange resulting in partial integration of thought; organization structure and organization behavior show as the merging of two central streams.

1. Coordination by direct contact of the responsible people concerned.
2. Coordination in the early stages.
3. Coordination as the reciprocal relating to all the factors in the situation.
4. Coordination as a continuing process.

Central to the thinking behind these principles was the idea that management must continually adjust to the total situation. Follett observed that conflict is usually present in management situations and offered a process for resolving it. The manager must handle conflict by (1) domination, (2) compromise, or (3) integration. The first two never satisfy everyone, but integration can achieve a new approach to the problem that will satisfy all parties. In order to achieve integration (1) the differences must be brought into the open; (2) a "re-evaluation" must be made by all parties; (3) all parties must anticipate the responses of the others and seek a new position that suits not only the parties but the relationship among the parties. In other words, each party should avoid the limitations of his own position and seek a new, integrated position acceptable to all.

Later, behavioral scientists developed new approaches to the study of management. Kurt Lewin developed theory and research under the heading of "group dynamics." His study with small groups led him and his followers to concentrate on the advantages of group participation and increased interaction among members of a group.

More recently, psychologists have improved the validity and reliability of tests used for the selection and placement of individuals in industrial and government organizations. Other recent developments in the behavioral sciences will be summarized in a later chapter. It is clear that the modern manager has access to new techniques that have scientific basis, thus eliminating the need to depend solely on intuition and guesses.

Much of the modern development in management can be traced to the theoretical work of a practicing executive, Chester I. Barnard, who in 1938 published a classic in management literature, *The Functions of the Executive*. In this work he introduced the concepts of informal organization, decision making, status, and communications that became important topics for management consideration. His influence on the thinking of other leaders with regard to new developments cannot be overemphasized.

Concurrent with the developments in the behavioral sciences were other developments, quite separate and independent, that affected management. Economics, the basic discipline of business for a century, began to direct its attention to business decisions. New meanings of old economic principles began to have practical implications for the manager.

Accounting, too, took on a new outlook. It no longer looked only to past transactions but began to offer answers to problems dealing with the future. In the early 1920s J. O. McKinsey developed budgeting as a basic tool for management's use. Although McKinsey died at an early age, he was able to develop budgetary theory as a college professor, expand its use through a consulting firm that he founded, and apply it in practice as Chairman of the Board of Marshall Field & Company. In a short period of time, both economics and accounting became basic fields of study for the manager.

Modern developments in management have promised help to the manager in still another area that has long caused management worry, that is, how to handle uncertainty. Here, the maturing of the field of statistics proved to be of great help. After W. A. Shewart had applied statistical theory to the area of quality control during the early thirties, the use of statistical samples expanded and enabled the manager to estimate probabilities with mathematical accuracy in other types of problems. Recently the manager has been offered a way of using this same approach in handling problems about which his information is very uncertain.

With the availability of electronic computers, the manager now can deal with theoretical questions in a more definite and rigorous manner. This new hardware permits him to state his theory in terms of a clearly definable model and to handle the constants and variables of his problem with more precision. New mathematical tools of analysis, such as linear programming, which G. B. Dantzig developed in the late 1940s, enable the manager to find the best answers to problems of resource allocation, which he previously had to approximate through application of judgment and experience.

Other developments in quantitative analysis are being brought forth by researchers and are rapidly being adopted by practicing managers. In fact, the approach of a team of specialists, working together to frame quantitative techniques for making decisions on companywide issues, has led to the creation of a new analytical profession called **operations research** (OR). The limits of operations research are ill-defined, because its applications are continually breaking out of previously conceived frameworks and deal with a wide range of problems including defense systems, outer space, and management. **Management science** is a term of more recent origin and refers more specifically to application of quantitative techniques to management problems. The terms tend to be used interchangeably yet OR is more general and theoretical in its orientation while management science is more application- and problem-oriented to management.

This short survey of management should make it clear that the subject is faced with growing pains. These pains result from the continuous process of having to accommodate new ideas that spring from many new sources. Management thought, therefore, continually requires re-

statement and consolidation. One of the leaders in this modern development of progressing from one fruitful stream of thought to another is
Herbert A. Simon. Trained as a political scientist, he was faced first with
problems of public administration. These problems led to questions of
organization, and his publication in 1947 of *Administrative Behavior*—a
book that proceeded to challenge the existing thought on the subject and
became a classic in the field. Concurrently, economic questions were
central to topics of his interest, and thus he presented research in that
discipline. However, psychological aspects of organization and economics
became so important that he intensively began to handle specific issues in
that discipline. Throughout his research, he felt the need for the rigorous
tools of mathematics and statistics. His techniques, therefore, employed
these basic tools together with experimentation on the applications of
computers in management research. His approach, thus, has been interdisciplinary and can be categorized primarily as involved with "decision
making," a term that he has been influential in establishing as a major
subject for management attention. Others in management thinking are
finding it necessary to take a similar interest in many disciplines.

The development of management thought has accelerated and diversified to an extent that defies comprehensive treatment in a single volume. Table 2-1, however, summarizes the pioneers in disciplines closely
related to management and identifies their contributions. Figure 2-1
shows the major disciplines that have contributed techniques and ideas to
the field of management and identifies the chief contributors to the trend
of cross-disciplinary exchange resulting in recent integration of two central
streams.

Table 2-1
**Pioneers in Management and Their Contributions
(chronological by birth date)**

Name	Chief Publications	Major Contributions
Henri Fayol (1841-1925)	*Administration Industrielle et Generale* (1916).	Stressed that the theory of administration was equally applicable to all forms of organized human coopera- tion.
Harrington Emerson (1853-1931)	*Efficiency as Basis for Oper- ation and Wages* (1900). *The Twelve Principles of Effi- ciency* (1912). *The Scientific Selection of Employees* (1913).	Studied the Sante Fe Rail- road and promoted "scientific management" in general usage.

Table 2-1 (cont'd.)

Name	Chief Publications	Major Contributions
Frederick W. Taylor (1856-1915)	*A Piece-Rate System* (1895). *Shop Management* (1903). *On the Art of Cutting Metals* (1906). *The Principles of Scientific Management* (1911).	Father of Scientific Management. Developed high-speed cutting tools. Introduced time study to industry. (See text discussion.)
Karl Pearson (1857-1936)	*On the Correlation of Fertility with Social Value* (1913). *Tables for Statisticians* (1914). *Tables for Statisticians* (1933).	Developed basic statistical tables and early statistical techniques, including the chi-square test and the standard deviation concept.
Henry L. Gantt (1861-1919)	*Work, Wages, and Profits* (1910). *Industrial Leadership* (1916). *Organizing for Work* (1919).	Emphasized relation of management and labor. Stressed conditions that have favorable psychological effects on the worker. Developed charting techniques for scheduling.
Max Weber (1864-1920)	*The Theory of Social and Economic Organization* (translated by Henderson & Parsons in 1947). From Max Weber: *Essays in Sociology* (translated by Gerth and Mills in 1946).	The foremost pioneer in the development of a theory of bureaucracy.
Frank Gilbreth (1868-1924)	*Concrete System* (1908). *Motion Study* (1911).	Searched for "the one best way." Introduced motion study to industry.
Mary Parker Follett (1868-1933)	*Dynamic Administration* (edited by Metcalf and Urwich) (1941).	Led in practical observations about the value of human relations to the basic principles of organization.
G. Elton Mayo (1880-1949)	*The Human Problems of an Industrial Civilization* (1933). *The Social Problems of an Industrial Civilization* (1933).	Stressed the importance of human and social factors in industrial relationships. Questioned the overemphasis on technical skills at the expense of adaptive social skills. Led a team of researchers in extensive studies at the Hawthorne plant of Western Electric Company.

Table 2-1 (cont'd.)

Name	Chief Publications	Major Contributions
Chester I. Barnard (1886-1961)	*The Functions of the Executive* (1938). *Organization and Management* (1948).	Leader in stressing sociological aspects of management. Concentrated on the concept of authority, the importance of communication, and informal organizations in management.
Kurt Lewin (1890-1947)	*Resolving Social Conflicts* (1948). *Field Theory in Social Science* (1951).	Developed research and theory of group dynamics.
Ronald A. Fischer (1890-1962)	*Statistical Methods for Research Workers* (1925). *The Design of Experiments* (1935).	Pioneer in the use of statistical methods in research. Made valuable contributions to the design of experiments.
Walter A. Shewart (1891-1972)	*The Economic Quality Control of Manufactured Products* (1930).	Applied theory of probability and statistical inference to economic problems at Bell Laboratories. Developed statistical control charts.
F. J. Roethlisberger (1898-)	*Management and the Worker* (with W. J. Dickson) (1939). *Management and Morale* (1941). *A New Look for Management* (1948).	Made a comprehensive report on the Hawthorne experiment. Led in experimental research on human factors in management.
Peter Drucker (1909-)	*The New Society* (1949). *The Practice of Management* (1954).	Developed concept of management by objectives. As a consultant and writer, popularized new developments in management.
G.B. Dantzig (1914-)	*Maximization of a Linear Function of Variables Subject to Linear Inequalities* (1947).	Developed the basis for practical applications of linear programming.
Claude Shannon (1916-)	*The Mathematical Theory of Communication* (1948).	Laid the theoretical foundation for information theory.
Herbert A. Simon (1916-)	*Administrative Behavior* (1947). *Models of Man* (1957). *Organization* (with J. March) (1958).	See text for summary.

**OVERVIEW OF SHIFTS
IN FOCUS IN
MANAGEMENT THOUGHT**
The development of management thought over the last hundred years has not been a single continuous stream from one source but has been a process of integrating ideas from a number of streams, as indicated in Figure 2-1 and Table 2-2. Furthermore, during this development the focus of attention has shifted from one stream to another. (1) From 1900 to 1930, the major focus was on the physical factors as viewed from industrial engineering and economics. (2) Between 1930 and 1960, the focus shifted to the human factors affecting productivity, with supporting efforts from managerial accounting and classical concepts of personnel and finance. (3) During the 1960s, as a result of reports prepared for the Ford and Carnegie Foundations, emphasis was placed on achieving precision through the use of quantitative methods (mathematics and statistics) and the behavioral sciences (psychology, sociology, anthropology). Computers and systems thinking developed rapidly during this decade as techniques for management. (4) The trend in the 1970s has focused on organizational behavior (built on the behavioral approach) as almost synonymous with management. In the last decade *contingency* theories, that is, theories of

Table 2-2
Disciplinary Bases for Management

Discipline	Special Emphasis
Industrial Engineering	Measurement and analysis of physical factors in achieving efficiency.
Economics	Allocation of scarce resources with orientation to future.
Financial Accounting	Recording, reporting, analyzing, and auditing of past transactions.
Public Administration	Formation of a rational hierarchy for the accomplishment of activities.
Legal Profession	Development of a consistent course of action based on precedents to achieve stability, order, and justice.
Statistical Methods	Employment of probability theory to infer facts from samples and to handle uncertainty.
Mathematics	Construction of models which state explicitly one's assumptions, objectives, and constraints.
Psychology	Scientific investigations concerning human needs, perceptions, and emotional factors.
Sociology	Study of interrelationships within and among human groups in society.
Anthropology	Cultural variations and discoverable patterns of behavior from history and environment.

management which are dependent upon the environmental situations in which they are applied, received major attention. The classical approach of a single universal theory of management has given way to a number of contingency theories. Legal aspects, cultural considerations, and the emerging field of public administration have received new emphasis.

This overview of the historical development of management indicates two concurrent, opposing trends over time: first, periodically, specialists in one or two streams of thought have attempted to narrow management topics to their particular stream of research, e.g., the current emphasis on organization behavior; yet, second, new demands by society on management have continually expanded the scope of management to include new streams of thought, e.g., the present attention to the environment, legal and ethical issues, and information systems. Thus, the remainder of this book is a summary of the terms and issues used by several of the narrow academic streams, while recognizing the expanding scope and integration of management in practice.

REFERENCES

FILIPETTI, GEORGE, *Industrial Management in Transition.* Homewood, Ill.: Richard D. Irwin, Inc., 1949.

GEORGE, CLAUDE S., *The History of Management Thought* (2nd ed.). Englewood Cliffs, N.J.: Prentice-Hall, Inc., 1972.

MERRILL, HARWOOD, ed., *Classics in Management.* New York: American Management Association, 1960.

METCALF, HENRY C. and L. URWICK, eds., *Dynamic Administration.* New York and London: Management Publications Trust, Ltd., 1941.

URWICK, L., ed., *The Golden Book of Management.* London: Ryerson Press, Newman Neame, Ltd., 1956.

WREN, DANIEL, *The Evolution of Management Theory.* New York: Ronald Press, 1972.

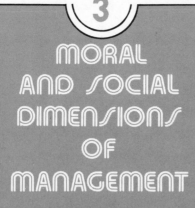

3

MORAL AND SOCIAL DIMENSIONS OF MANAGEMENT

⟸ **IDEAS TO BE FOUND** ⟹
IN THIS CHAPTER

- Social responsibilities of management
- Ethical propositions in management
- Values
- Philosophy of management
- Multiple objectives
- Management by objectives (MBO)

The emergence of management as a distinct and identifiable activity has had an important impact on the society within which it developed. So, too, society, with its institutions, customs, and value systems, has molded the foundations upon which management has formed its framework of thought. In recent years, the attention of businessmen, philosophers, scientists, and the general public has been directed to issues concerning responsibilities of management, ethical and legal practices of managers, and the entire set of value systems of the business community. In this chapter, we shall consider the cultural setting within which managers make decisions and the moral framework for their philosophies of management. We then point out the fundamental role of objectives in a firm.

MANAGEMENT AND SOCIETY

Management first evolved as the part of an economic system that allocated the resources of land, labor, and capital in a way to maximize material returns to satisfy the wants of human beings. Its primary orientation is still economic; yet, as a result of its increasing importance in society, it

27

has become a social institution. Its decisions and actions now have widespread impact on other social institutions, and, therefore, management cannot escape social issues.

The growth of the large corporation, with its professional managers, has changed the nature of society through its effect on competitive forces and the ownership of private property. With its increased power in society, it has been forced to concern itself with the nature of its social responsibilities. Management must make decisions involving moral issues and must adapt itself to the social forces that affect it.

Among the many social institutions that have affected the value systems of management, the following four are particularly important: (1) the family, (2) the educational system, (3) the church, and (4) the government.

Within the patterns of values formed by these institutions, the executive must resolve issues of social responsibility. During the 1970s consumerism with its emerging spokesmen and new laws, environmentalists with their increased emphasis on pollution and on threats to health and the quality of life, and political disclosures of Watergate, activities of the CIA, and bribery of executives by multinational firms forced increased attention on managers' social responsibility. Legally, executives are representatives of stockholders or a governmental agency; yet they have responsibilities to employees, consumers, suppliers, and the general public. Conflicts of ethical concepts necessarily develop.

Four schools of thought relative to social responsibility offer a framework for managers in viewing social responsibility. (1) *Profit maximization as socially desirable:* Many agree with Milton Friedman and Theodore Levitt that executives can make their best contribution to society if they focus on profit maximization. This school argues that if managers attempt "to do good" for society they will do a poor job in performing the role for which they are best fitted and will usurp the responsibility of government and social institutions which have clear roles in promoting public welfare. (2) *No long-run conflict between corporate and social responsibility:* A second school argues that the executive finds that he must assume responsibility for community and social development because his organization's profits depend upon such activities as aid to education, community development, and social welfare. In short, the executive should be socially responsible because it pays! (3) *Improvement of one's own organizational behavior best leads to social betterment:* This third school focuses on social improvements *within* one's own organization through attention to motivation, leadership, communications, power equalization, and worker satisfaction. The emphasis in this school is on a social consciousness within the organization where the manager can be effective in achieving improvements. (4) *Management as trustee:* The fourth school represents the opposite extreme from the profit maximizer; it takes the view that managers should act voluntarily as trustees of the public interest. In this view, large corporations have such increased power that their responsibilities transcend the boundaries of their own organizations. The strategic position of these large organizations requires special consciousness of social obligations. Regardless of which school is followed, the manager must develop some strategy concerning (1) how his company will adjust to external factors and (2) what impact his organization will have on its environment.

The social issues faced by modern managers are numerous and complex. Here we can list only a few as a sample to indicate the scope of subjects requiring managerial policies.

1. Policies regarding racial discrimination in its employment practices. For example, how should a firm attempt to comply with laws and court decisions on civil rights?

2. Policies toward labor unions. For example, what importance should management give to guidelines by the President's economic advisors, to the mediation and conciliation services, to efforts by unions to narrow "management prerogatives," and to problems of unemployment?

3. The willingness by business to accept "voluntary" restraints. For example, in helping the country meet its balance of payments problems, how far should management go in voluntarily restricting its overseas investment?

4. Adjustments by management to controls over exports to certain countries. For example, what guides can be established to comply with public policy concerning sale of goods to countries that have been designated as unfriendly or enemies?

5. Recognition of responsibilities to developing countries. For example, how should a large company conduct itself in small developing countries in which large purchases of raw materials have a large impact on the economic and social development of those countries?

6. Policies toward support of educational institutions. For example, should a corporation contribute to public and private educational institutions when the return on the "investment" is only indirect?

7. Involvement of management personnel in political campaigns and organizations. For example, should a corporation seek to cement ties with a particular political party?

8. Marketing policies promoting products that create health, safety, and other social problems. For example, should corporation executives be concerned with overuse or misuse of its products to ultimate social detriment—as with tobacco, liquor, drugs, weapons, and so on?

9. Operating policies that impose social costs. For example, should manufacturing operations aim at minimizing costs to the firm when they increase the costs to society in greater air pollution, water pollution, urban congestion, or unemployment?

10. Involvement in the community and in the family life of employees. For example, should management become involved in community planning, marital counseling, or religious activities?

11. Policies of providing opportunities for women in roles traditionally unavailable to them in the past.

The orientation of management has broadened in the last several decades. Initially, scientific managers focused at the shop level on how to operate efficiently. Later, the focus was on organization behavior at all levels within the organizations. More recently the scope has broadened from **micro-management** (operations within the organization) to **macro-management** (interactions between the organization and its environment). Thus a manager must develop understanding of matters affecting numerous social issues such as those listed above. Furthermore, a manager in modern society must develop some philosophical foundation for his own value system.

VALUE SYSTEMS AND MANAGEMENT

Management is confronted with two general types of propositions: those of a factual nature, which accurately describe the observable world, and those of an ethical nature, which assert that one course of action is better than another. According to this classification, a **factual proposition** can be tested and proved to be *true* or *false*, but an **ethical proposition** can only be asserted to be *good* or *bad*. Ethical matters pertain to what conditions "ought to be." The ethical elements of a proposition are subject to varying opinions and value judgments. To date, no philosophical system has been developed that can be called a "science of ethics." The problem is that there is no way to *prove* ultimate values. Value systems can be constructed only if we assume what is good; for example, one school of thought may assume that "happiness" is an ultimate good, and another school may assume that custom and tradition determine "right."

Management must meet problems involving varying mixtures of factual and ethical elements. A useful approach is to segregate the factual elements from the ethical ones and to use different methods for handling each group. A great part of the remainder of this book involves methods by which the factual elements can be analyzed. In this section, we concentrate on the ethical elements.[1]

[1]Also, most recent advances in the behavioral sciences have been **descriptive** (studying what *is*) while managerial policies and strategies require a **normative** orientation (determining what *should* be).

Chester I. Barnard has described **moral behavior** as "governed by beliefs or feelings of what is right or wrong regardless of self-interest or immediate consequences of a decision to do or not to do specific things under particular conditions."[2] The difficulty concerning moral propositions is that varying standards may be used. A number of the generally accepted virtues, such as happiness, lawfulness, consistency, integrity, and loyalty, may in a specific situation conflict with one another. For example, a manager who attempts to use integrity and loyalty as his standards may experience conflict if he discovers wrongdoing on the part of a superior. Should he remain loyal to his superior, or should he maintain his integrity? Managers typically face moral dilemmas in their decisions and actions. Wayne A. R. Leys illustrates the moral conflicts faced by management in a diagram (see Figure 3-1) in which moral standards surround action but in which the standard at one arrow conflicts with the standard at the opposite arrow.

Two approaches to moral questions will illustrate some philosophical treatments of what is good or what "ought to be." One theological approach considers that certain ultimate values are matters of **natural law.** Under this view, certain actions are always wrong because they break some basic intuitive law. If one of these laws is "Thou shalt not kill," then a strict interpretation of this law would make killing wrong under all conditions. Self-defense, capital punishment, abortion, or "killing for what is right" would be considered to be wrong because they violate the natural law. An opposing viewpoint is often referred to as **situational ethics.** Under this approach, the question of whether an action is right or wrong depends upon the total situation in which the action occurs. This view holds that an action under one set of circumstances and in one environment would be right, whereas the same action under another set of circumstances and in another environment would be wrong. In an organization, a subordinate may face a situation in which his superior orders him to do something that is for the good of the organization but that may conflict with the interests of others to whom the subordinate has a responsibility. Does an order by a superior absolve the subordinate of blame, in the event that an action is detrimental to society or is outright illegal? Managers often must face dilemmas of this type.

David Riesman describes changes in societies by distinguishing three types of men according to their source of moral direction: (1) the tradition-directed type, (2) the inner-directed type, and (3) other-directed type. The *tradition-directed* type conforms to the culture and social order in which he lives. Society presents unchanging relationships that are accepted as right. In this society, little effort is directed toward changing the status quo, because it is considered wrong to break traditions. The

---

[2]Chester I. Barnard, "Elementary Conditions of Business Morals," *California Management Review*, vol. I, no. 1 (1958), p. 4.

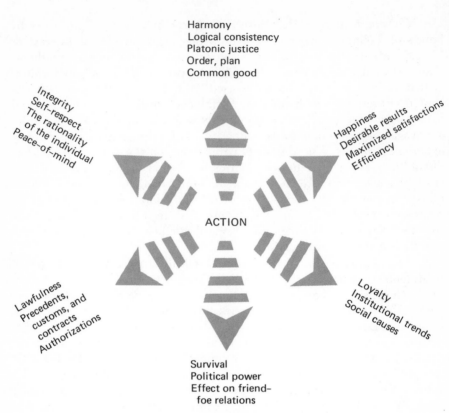

Figure 3-1
Conflict of Six Kinds of Moral Values.

From Wayne A. R. Leys' "The Value Framework of Decision Making" in Sidney Mailick and Edward H. Van Ness, eds., *Concepts and Issues in Administrative Behavior* (Englewood Cliffs, N.J.: Prentice-Hall, Inc., 1962).

inner-directed man receives his source of direction early in life from his elders and develops a "psychological gyroscope" that keeps him on his moral course. If he should get off course, he tends to feel guilt. The *other-directed* man receives his source of direction from his contemporaries and changes his concepts of what is right through a socialized sensitivity to the actions of others. Riesman describes the change in direction from the tradition-directed type of the Middle Ages, to the transitional inner-directed type of the nineteenth century, to the other-directed type of modern man.[3]

Closely related to Riesman's thinking, yet more directly pertinent to management's moral dilemma, is William H. Whyte's description of the

[3]David Riesman, *The Lonely Crowd* (New Haven, Conn.: Yale University Press, 1950).

organization man.[4] Whyte sees a major shift in American ideology, from the rugged individualism of the nineteenth century to the social orientation of the twentieth century. He describes this shift as a change in ethics, from what Max Weber called the Protestant Ethic to what Whyte calls the Social Ethic. The **Protestant Ethic** emphasized the quest for individual salvation through individual efforts, thrift, and competitive forces. The **Social Ethic** emphasizes that moral good is determined by pressures of society against the individual. Recent social issues, such as sexual permissiveness, the public right to information, and the personal right to privacy, raise many problems for practicing managers.

The philosophical background for managers is, of course, much too vast to cover in a short summary. Nevertheless, a study of management without a recognition of its cultural and philosophical heritage would be particularly naive. The enlightened manager of the late twentieth century should consider the vast quantity of literature that has developed over the past 3000 years. From an understanding of the provocative comments by leading philosophers and reflections by current practitioners in management, the individual manager must develop his philosophy of management for his own particular firm.

PHILOSOPHY OF MANAGEMENT

Executives in a specific firm operate with some type of philosophy, regardless of whether they have studied their philosophical heritage. Furthermore, they may not consider consciously the broad structure of ideas that influence their decisions, let alone make explicit the elements of this philosophy to others. If they attempt to write down the basic elements, their statements tend to appear vague and general. Even though it may be difficult to verbalize these basic ideas, the attempt to understand the moral issues involved in managerial activities provides a broad framework that gives meaning to day-to-day actions.

Philosophies differ among firms. One philosophy might be good for Firm A but not useful to Firm B. In this connection **philosophy of management** refers to those general concepts and integrated attitudes that are fundamental to the cooperation of a social group. These concepts and attitudes evolve into the particular way in which the firm perceives itself. Generally, the philosophy of a given firm can be learned only through close and continuous association with it. It is uniquely determined for the individual firm and is affected by a group of factors that, together, may be called the concept of the firm. The **concept of the firm** is the total of how

[4]William H. Whyte, *The Organization Man* (New York: Simon and Schuster, Inc., 1956).

the firm got where it is, the place it occupies in the industry, its strengths and weaknesses, the viewpoints of its managers, and its relationship to social and political institutions.

THE ROLE OF OBJECTIVES IN MANAGEMENT

Human beings attempt to be purposive; that is, they try to act in a manner that will enable them to reach certain goals. **Rational behavior** can be defined in terms of whether actions are conducive to the achievement of predetermined goals. To the extent that management is rational, it directs its actions toward objectives. The realization of objectives is the target toward which decisions and actions are oriented.

Personal versus Organizational Objectives

Individual members of a cooperative group have their own personal ideas of what results they want to achieve. The needs of individuals are important as bases for their motivation. People will cooperate as long as the goals of a group are consistent with their ideas of their own goals. The individual has many goals: some tend to conflict; some are more important to him than others; some are short run and some are long run.

A cooperative group must maintain a set of objectives that is common to the members of the group. The organizational objectives are nonpersonal; yet they must remain consistent with the personal objectives of individuals in the organization. If an individual is to accept organizational objectives, he must feel that achieving the organizational goals will satisfy, or at least not conflict with, his own personal goals. Although an organization is composed of a number of different persons, each with his own set of goals, organization goals must serve as common denominators for the entire group. Some organizational goals will conflict with the goals of the individual; however, an individual usually has a wide "zone of indifference" and will continue to cooperate unless he becomes convinced that the conflict is fundamental.

Hierarchy of Objectives

Organizational objectives give direction to the activities of the group and serve as media by which multiple interests are channeled into joint effort. Some are ultimate and broad objectives of the firm as a whole; some serve as intermediate goals or subgoals for the entire organization; some are specific and relate to short-term aims. Moreover, there is a hierarchy of objectives in an organization: at the top, the entire organization aims in a given direction; each department, in turn, directs its efforts toward its own sets of goals; each subdivision of each department has its own meaningful aims. Each of the subgoals should be consistent with, and contribute toward, the goals of the next higher level. For example, it is generally assumed that a corporation has the broad objective of maximizing profit. To aid in achieving that overall goal, it is necessary to define more meaningful subgoals for individual departments. The marketing department may have goals in terms of a certain increase in total sales and its subdivisions may be given goals in definite geographical areas or in specific product lines. The production department may state its goals in terms of minimizing production costs, and its subdivisions may be given subgoals for particular types of costs. Other departments in turn have goals redefined for them so that they can visualize exactly their part in striving for the company's broad goal of maximizing profits.

Although economists have assumed, for analytical reasons, that profit making is *the* goal of a business enterprise, in fact management has many objectives. All these objectives form hierarchies for cooperative action; yet organizational goals often tend to conflict. For example, growth may be considered an objective that is measured in terms of sales, market share, acquisition of assets, and so on. At times, growth may be achieved by accepting new orders that are "unprofitable," for the sake of achieving a competitive edge over another firm. Management should be conscious of this conflict so that it can make basic decisions as to which goals are considered most important. In times of poor business conditions, the mere survival of the firm may be a most important goal. Profitable business may be turned down if acceptance would mean that the finances of the firm would be strained to the extent of bankruptcy. If the corporation attains a dominant position in an industry, an important goal may be the minimization of attack by the Department of Justice on antitrust grounds. The management of a firm may set as its goals the retention of present personnel and the minimization of the chance of a proxy fight by a group of stockholders. Stability of operations and security of jobs for employees may be additional objectives. Finally, service to the government and society may be not only a public relations statement but also an actual basic goal of the organization.

Management by Objectives (MBO)

After recognizing the relationship between personal and organizational objectives and the multiplicity of organizational objectives, with the resulting conflicts, it is clear that the job of using objectives in an organization is no simple task. Good management must develop a way in which objectives can be used to focus the attention of individual members of the organization on objectives that are meaningful to them. A useful approach, suggested by Peter Drucker,[5] and popularized by George Odiorne,[6] is **management by objectives (MBO)**.

In MBO, an executive must narrow the range of attention of each person in the organization to focus on *definite* and *measurable* results that have a clear meaning for each individual. Each part of an organization can contribute toward companywide objectives if it clearly sees its own specific goals and can determine, through measurement, how well it is doing. The selection of the proper factors to be measured is an important decision, because usually that which is measured is that which receives attention.

The key to MBO is the mutual relationships between the superior and the subordinate in setting realistic objectives for the subordinate. Odiorne suggests that this meeting should establish objectives in three major categories: routine objectives, problem-solving objectives, and innovative objectives. For each of these categories, agreement should be reached for three levels of achievement: pessimistic (absolute minimum), realistic (normally expected), and optimistic (ideal). In the last decade many organizations have developed elaborate processes for MBO, with varying degrees of success. However, the basic idea of MBO is fundamental—clear targets should be set by superior and subordinate at all levels of the organization.

The overall objectives of a **firm** generally are established by top management; yet, it is desirable for each subordinate manager to have a voice in setting his own objectives. If each manager is to understand the relationship of his own organizational objectives to the broader objectives of the company, he will need to participate in the goal-setting process. If he is involved in establishing his objectives, he will feel that the objectives are proper once they are set and will tend to accept them more readily. In this way, each part of the organization will strive in a joint effort toward the recognized organizational objectives.

Objectives may be set as ideals or as realistic expectations. Whether the objective is idealistic or realistic, it should be stated in definite terms of results. The statement "reduce costs" sounds fine, but it is vague and lacks precision. Even if a manager is conscientious and sincerely strives toward this vague objective, he never knows whether he has reached "the objective." The statement "produce at costs 10 percent less than last year" is better because it states the specific results desired.

Clearly defined objectives lay the foundation for the performance of the various functions of management. These objectives are the product of the moral and social systems surrounding the manager. Management, therefore, must be concerned with questions of philosophy, which help it

[5]Peter F. Drucker, *The Practice of Management* (New York: Harper & Row, Publishers, 1954).

[6]George Odiorne, *Management by Objectives* (New York: Pitman Publishing Co., 1965).

make value judgments in its day-by-day activities. Throughout the discussion in Part 2, the reader should remain conscious of the central role of objectives in managerial actions.

REFERENCES

CHEIT, EARL F., ed., *The Business Establishment*. New York: John Wiley & Sons, Inc., 1964.

DAVIS, KEITH and ROBERT L. BLOMSTROM, *Business and Society: Environment and Responsibility* (revised). New York: McGraw-Hill Book Co., 1975.

EELLS, RICHARD and CLARENCE WALTON, *Conceptual Foundations of Business* (3rd ed.). Homewood, Ill.: Richard D. Irwin, Inc., 1974.

GALBRAITH, JOHN K., *The New Industrial State*. Boston: Houghton Mifflin Co., 1971.

JACOBY, N. H., *Corporate Power and Social Responsibility*. New York: Columbia University, 1973.

LEYS, WAYNE A. R., *Ethics for Policy Decisions*. Englewood Cliffs, N.J.: Prentice-Hall, Inc., 1952.

SELEKMAN, BENJAMIN M., *A Moral Philosophy for Management*. New York: McGraw-Hill Book., 1959.

SMITH, GEORGE ALBERT, JR. and JOHN B. MATTHEWS, *Business, Society, and the Individual* (2nd ed.). Homewood, Ill.: Richard D. Irwin, Inc., 1967.

INTERNATIONAL MANAGEMENT AND ITS ENVIRONMENTAL DIMENSIONS

During the last two decades, management has developed rapidly in the international sphere. Business firms have expanded across national boundaries. Emerging nations have invited management specialists to advise them in economic development. International organizations, such as the International Labor Organization and the United Nations, have promoted interchange of ideas about managerial approaches. Cultural exchanges among university professors have broadened the horizons for research in management. These developments are the result of (1) the improvements in transportation and communications, (2) the growth of regional economic cooperation, e.g., the European Community (EC), (3) the relative attractiveness of foreign markets for mass produced goods, and (4) an increased intellectual awareness of a need for international understanding. As a result, the subject of management has expanded and has faced new basic questions. Is international management different from domestic management? If there are differences, how can these differences best be studied?

This chapter will outline the topics of unique interest to international business and will concentrate on the environmental factors which affect management in different countries. The chief objective will be to encourage readers to seek a better understanding of management in societies different from their own so that they can better interrelate their awareness of these other cultures with an increased understanding of their own environment and its impact on managerial thought.

COMPARATIVE MANAGEMENT

Each society shares a common cultural heritage with other societies, but each has a unique culture of its own. Figure 4-1 shows the overlap of cultural characteristics as the intersection of the different environmental factors. The shaded portion represents common cultural characteristics which support common management propositions. The unshaded areas represent unique environmental factors which might dictate different managerial concepts and techniques for individual societies. Of course, the number of possible circles or societies might be made very large. Figure 4-1 shows only three circles, or societies; in fact, a variety of cultures or circles might be advisable for a single country such as India, Malaysia, or the United States. For example, in the United States it might be necessary to distinguish the cultures of various regions: Appalachia, Brooklyn, Texas,

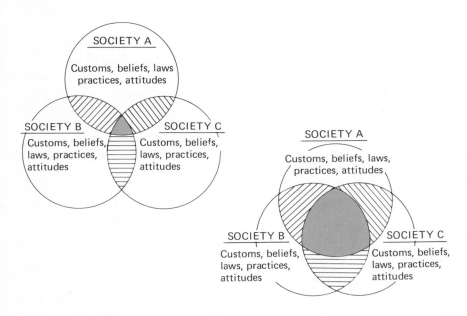

Figure 4-1
Cross-cultural Comparisons of Three Societies. (Shaded area represents the intersection—common elements—of environmental factors supporting a common management approach.)

etc. A great deal of research is needed to validate a proposed managerial principle that would be basic in all cultures.

Chapter 1 outlined the basic managerial functions. Management, in all societies, must perform these functions in some manner. However, the concepts, analytical techniques, and approaches for performing them may differ under varying environmental conditions. The study of management in differing countries, therefore, involves a comparative, analytical process of identifying each of the relationships among functions, or elements, of the managerial process, as well as each of the environmental determinants. For example, one could take each element of the planning function and compare its execution under the environmental conditions in each country of the world. In this study, it would be useful to identify each element of these environmental conditions, e.g., attitude toward time, government planning, inflation, etc.

In order to facilitate comparison, the environmental determinants could be grouped under four headings: educational, sociological-cultural, legal-political, and economic. Table 4-1 provides a framework for this analysis of the relationships of managerial functions as they relate to the groups of environmental constraints. A study of the body of this table will reveal some of the topics that relate the environmental factors to the functions of management. This framework enables us to seek systematically those relationships of managerial functions and environmental determinants that are necessary for a general theory of management. Furthermore, the framework will be valuable in the development of a better understanding of management within individual countries.

The study of management in different countries indicates a divergence of managerial approaches resulting from varying environmental conditions. Is there a trend over the last few decades toward convergence of these approaches, caused by the increasing interactions between cultures, i.e., are managerial skills transferable across national boundaries? One view is that the intersection shown in Figure 4-1a has been getting larger, as illustrated by the change between Figures 4-1a and 4-1b. This view results in the optimistic observation that the differences in the environmental constraints are decreasing and that a common set of managerial propositions is becoming more generally relevant. For example, international firms with a common set of western cultural determinants can increasingly employ the same set of managerial propositions in all countries in which they operate.

An opposing view stresses the unchanging characteristics of many of the cultural constraints. In this view, it is argued that the managerial process employed under one set of environmental factors (say, in the United States) may not be relevant under another set of environmental factors (say, in an oriental country). In this view, there is little hope for a universal set of managerial propositions that will be applicable under all

Table 4-1
Environmental Factors Affecting
Managerial Functions

	Environmental Factors			
Managerial Functions	Educational	Sociological-Cultural	Legal-Political	Economic
Setting Objectives	Technical and Higher Educational Systems	Role of Religion; View of Management; Goals and Values Important in Culture	Government Influence/ Regulations	Fiscal and Monetary Policies
Policy Formulation and Implementation	Educational Match with Requirements	Attitude toward Management and Managers	Political Stability	Economic Stability
Research and Development	Scientific Orientation	Acceptance of Change	Government Support: Financial Investment	View of Risk-Taking and Progress
Production and Procurement	Supply of Engineers and Technicians	Attitude toward Efficiency	Government Support; Defense and Other Government Contracts; Industrial Zoning	Availability of Resources; Adequate Infrastructure
Finance	Specialized Training in Accounting and Economics	View of Savings and Investment	Tax Reliefs; Subsidies; Financial Restrictions	Central Banking System; Foreign Aid and Private Investment
Marketing	Literacy Level	Attitude toward Material Possessions	Import-Export and Foreign Exchange Regulations	Market Size; Degree of Competition; Per Capita Annual Income; Price Stability
Planning and Innovation	Technical Capability for Budgets, Schedules, and Basic Policies	View of Time and Change; Use of New Knowledge and Statistical Data; Population Growth	National Planning by Central Government	Inflationary-Deflationary Tendencies

Table 4-1 (cont'd.)

Environmental Factors

Managerial Functions	Educational	Sociological-Cultural	Legal-Political	Economic
Organization	Functional Specialists, and Type of Education	View of Authority; Group Decision-Making; Interorganizational Cooperation	Predictability of Legal Actions; Political Influence	Division of Labor; Factor Endowment
Staffing	Educational Level	Interpersonal Cohesion, Class Structure and Individual Mobility	Status of Management Vis à Vis Government; Labor Laws	Labor Union Influence, Attitude toward Unemployment
Direction, Supervision, Motivation	Management Development	View of Achievement; Dedication to Work; Language Barriers to Communication	Tolerance of Bribes, Fraud, and Tax Evasion	Worker Participation in Management; Use of Monetary and Fringe Benefit; Incentives
Control	Ability to Use Feedback for Corrective Action	Attitude toward Scientific Method	Accounting Data, Reports for Government Regulation	Private Property Rights; Quotas

sets of environmental conditions. However, this view would not ignore the possibility of focusing on the intersection in Figure 4-1 and, to use Margaret Mead's phrase, "stripping the cultural baggage" from the management concepts which have developed in the western countries.

Regardless of which view one might take, the comparative approach to management, using the relationships of managerial functions and environmental factors, offers promise for improving management in all countries. Probably some intermediate position between these views is most useful; that is, some external factors, such as educational level and legal regulations, might be subject to change in order to accommodate managerial approaches from other countries, while other external factors, such as religion and long-standing social customs, might resist change and force the use of managerial approaches that differ from those used widely under other environmental conditions.

The management process, as suggested by Mary Parker Follett, is dependent upon the "total situation." In Follett's view, the management process is a social process in which evoking, interacting, integrating, and emerging are basic elements. Evoking is related to the leader's duty to draw out from each individual his fullest possibilities: interacting is related to the reciprocal behavior of individuals with their environment; integrating is related to finding the significant elements in a situation and reaching a new level for resolving conflicts; emerging is related to the changing situation. The comparative approach studies the social process under various conditions with the goals of (1) identifying those management approaches which can be transferred from one society to another, (2) searching for new and better management techniques, and (3) improving management within the environmental constraints of a given country.

THE IMPACT OF ENVIRONMENTAL FACTORS ON MANAGEMENT

This volume cannot discuss in depth all environmental factors and their effects on management in each and every country. However, it does illustrate this relationship by comparing managerial approaches in several countries and by pointing out the impact of external factors on management techniques.

The very subject of management is viewed differently among countries. Moreover, there are subtle variations in word meanings even when experts translate from one language to another. For example, in the German language *Unternehmer* is the key term relative to management; it refers to one who leads on the basis of his ownership and to one who is "called" to leadership. In Germany a manager is viewed as a lower level person whose position is clerical and who carries out routine administrative duties. In French *entrepreneur* means a risk taker, one who promotes a business activity. (In French, discussing the concept of management requires the use of several different terms [*direction, gestion, cadre*], none of which alone includes the total meaning of management as defined in this book.) In Chinese *kung tou* means "head of workers" and implies that the person is merely a special type of worker. When the concept of professional management, as used in this book, is expressed in other countries, the initial problem is to recognize semantic difficulties and to select terms that will convey proper meanings.

The *formal education* of the manager differs widely among nations; there can be few generalizations made concerning worldwide trends in management development. For example, South Africa, the most industrialized nation in Africa, has fairly extensive in-company training programs and offers graduate courses and MBA degrees for its indigenous white population; however, it offers little training to nonwhites. France, on the other hand, subordinates the status of business to the professions of law and teaching. In South Korea, the ratio of college students to the general population is twice that in England and there are fairly extensive undergraduate and postgraduate programs in business administration. In many countries, especially among those that foster traditional or conservative managers, antieducational biases are often strong and quite effective. In Belgium, however, if quick promotion is expected, a university degree is paramount. Often, though, the only vehicle to upper levels of management is social position or some form of engineering-technical degree.

Another variable that influences management is the *economic* environment. Under a socialist economic system, such as that in Czechoslovakia, the effectiveness of the manager is often hampered by the unrealistic demands and restrictive attitude of the Central Planning Commission. In Yugoslavia, however, a modified socialist economic system is utilized; this system is essentially democratic self-management, based on a pricing system which reflects market conditions. Many times the international manager must function in an atmosphere of chronic inflation and/or political instability. Such is the case in Brazil and Argentina. In Singapore and Malaysia many large firms are foreign-owned and must function in an area of extreme economic diversity. The international manager must be ever cognizant of his function and must adapt to his economic environment. Foreign aid, inflation, political instability, rapid economic expansion, labor shortages, and entrenched governmental bureaucracies are often real and critical factors determining his economic existence.

The *legal* aspects often reflect salient variables affecting the management function. In Yugoslavia the enterprise is relatively autonomous and functions within its own bylaws (statutes) under which its organization and function are determined. In Argentina the government regulates rates of exchange, duties, labor laws, salary increases in collective bargaining, fringe benefits, and numerous other areas. In some cultures personal contracts are sufficient and the suggestion of a written contract would be regarded as a faux pas. Others have a taste for secrecy that results in a minimum of financial records. Secrecy is a major element in the business life of a Chinese businessman, who often prefers to retain most of his financial facts in his memory. This tendency makes income tax collection quite difficult. In bureaucratically controlled economies, graft is often widespread and accepted. Some governments are too unconcerned or too weak to regulate bribery, monopolies, cartels, or collusion.

Socio-cultural factors are most significant. These are often the most powerful factors, hence they tend to be the ones over which the manager has the least control. The cultural milieu is often so heterogeneous that management functions must be sufficiently adaptable to reflect this environment. India, for example, is a country of many nationalities, religions, and languages. The society is based on a hierarchical system reflecting the informal caste strata which often precipitate role conflicts between individuals of different castes. The French, on the other hand, are secretive in financial dealings and react to change slowly. Thus many French firms are reluctant to publish financial statements and decentralize from the Parisian area which has traditionally been the economic and cultural center of the country. The management function itself in some cultures is carried on by specific minorities. In India certain castes carry out this function; in South Africa business has traditionally been assigned to the English, Dutch, and Jewish minorities.

International management, therefore, functions in an environment that is diverse, often contradictory, and ever changing. The one thing that all international managers would probably agree on is that their environment requires special knowledge and attention beyond the general scope of management.

INTERNATIONAL MANAGEMENT

Since World War II, one of the major changes in management has been the growth of international operations. Originally, international business was chiefly a matter of international trade; that is, raw materials were imported by the developed countries from the less developed ones and finished products were exported through various marketing channels to other countries. The essential subjects for attention at this stage were those covered in international economics, such as the law of comparative advantage, foreign exchange mechanisms, and marketing channels. While these subjects are still very important, they are normally covered by other disciplines and do not necessarily involve specific problems in the managerial process.

Stages of Internationalism

Despite the long and interesting history of international trade, until recently little attention has been paid to management aspects. Some early companies such as the East India Company and the Hudson Bay Company operated as political subdivisions of colonial powers long before management became a separate discipline.

A second stage of international development involved international finance and investment. Those countries with available capital sought to invest funds outside the home countries. These investments were treated strictly from the financial viewpoint and involved the flow of funds through banks, investment firms, and governments. The management of the operations was chiefly within national boundaries, with the flow of goods treated solely as imports and exports.

Beginning in the twentieth century, however, some large firms entered a third stage, in which the management of overseas operations was controlled by subsidiaries which handled all international business. These subsidiaries were treated as appendages to the parent company and served chiefly as export agencies. The countries outside the home nation view these business operations as efforts by foreigners to gain profits from their economies while providing only minimal employment for local people and without contributing to the local economies. The headquarters of these subsidiaries were usually located in the home country, with only warehouses, service offices, and sales agencies located in other countries. Management functions were handled as they were in the domestic company.

A fourth stage in the development of international companies (immediately after World War II) was seen in the appointment of vice-presidents of international operations as members of the domestic companies. The vice-president of a firm acted as contact and liaison with the various subsidiaries involved in international manufacture and trade. This was the first time that management began to recognize the unique problems of international operations.

A fifth stage saw the evolution of a global company in which the overseas operations were integrated into a single organizational structure. This stage developed during the 1960s and resulted in the forming of divisions in foreign countries to handle not only sales but also production, personnel, and finance. It was at this stage that international management emerged as a separate field of study, concentrating on management problems of a multinational nature. The emergence of this fifth stage was directly related to the formation of regional trade groupings of countries, such as common markets and free trade areas, which created markets large enough to warrant separate production and distribution organizations. Thus the managerial problems of the multinational company became a separate area of study; they will receive our attention in the next section.

In addition to the different types of organization for foreign operations, two special cases of international business firms deserve mention. One type is the company organized in a particular country for legal, tax, or political reasons. This type of firm chooses as its headquarters a small country which offers special advantages to firms seeking locations for legal headquarters. The differences among these firms are usually based on legal rather than managerial grounds. Another kind of international firm is evolving from the growth of several distinct companies in different countries which maintain a loose coalition but do not necessarily have common overall policies. The managements of these companies tend to operate as domestic firms with no centralized policies or organizational structure.

THE MULTINATIONAL COMPANY

A recent development in world business is the multinational or global company—a corporation which maintains world headquarters in one country but performs production, marketing, finance, and personnel functions within many nations. Although some of these companies were started early in the twentieth century, their importance as major factors in the international business world became evident only after World War II. Chief reasons for their development are: (1) the corporate form of organization with its infinite life and legal recognition as a separate entity; (2) the vastly improved systems of communication and transportation which facilitate global strategies; (3) the concentration of capital funds in advanced countries; (4) the rapid growth of markets in many countries, together with the maturing of markets in the home country; and (5) the creation of larger regional markets through common market and free trade agreements.

A great number of the multinational companies are American in origin, e.g., the automotive giants, electrical manufacturers, oil producers and refiners, and a variety of producers of consumer goods, but there are a sizeable number based in Western Europe, e.g., Unilever, Royal-Dutch Shell, Philips, Nestlé, Ciba. The management of these companies have numerous advantages, but they also face many problems different from those faced by purely domestic firms.

The chief advantages of the multinational firm are: (1) the access to organized capital markets and the resulting size of their investment potential; (2) the means by which management personnel can be recruited, formally trained, and developed; (3) the advanced stage of their accounting techniques, which provide controls and comparisons not available in many countries which operate on a less scientific basis; (4) the greater possibility of applying the law of comparative advantage and thus shifting procurement and production to low-cost areas; and (5) the power over governments wielded by their size and their impact on the entire economies of individual, small countries.

New problems and policy issues emerged with the growth of multinational operations. Since some of these problems are unique to this new form of organization, we shall discuss these in some detail.

First, a multinational company, by its very definition, finds itself a citizen of more than one nation and, therefore, must reconcile its loyalty to more than one sovereign power. It must at times cope with basic conflicts among foreign policies of several countries to which it has obligations. Embargoes by one country against another may create obstacles; one country may prohibit the sale of goods to a second country in which the company operates; to honor the laws of one country may force disastrous unemployment in the second. Every country attempts to enforce some of its laws extraterritorially; the U.S. antitrust laws restrict the American company's action in other countries; tax treaties or the lack of them cause double taxation or havens for avoiding taxation. Political activity may be difficult to avoid in many governmental situations; a multinational manager tends to become involved in the activities of local governments, and these activities may be opposed to the political position in the company's parent country.

A second policy issue unique to the multinational firm is the attempt to maintain coordinated policies consistent with its global strategy; at the same time, it must operate in different societies with different customs, languages, religions, and legal systems. Policies which may be desirable for one country may create international incidents with other countries. Different wage levels and labor practices may be required for each country in which the company operates. Variations in laws and tax systems prevent the establishment of consistent policies for all countries.

The employment of local nationals in management of a local plant is a third policy question that causes many headaches. Whereas the multinational company must attempt to identify with the society in which it operates and thus has many reasons to lean toward the use of local nationals, it may find that the quality of management is difficult to maintain or that a good local manager, with his different cultural background, may not fit in with the overall management policies of the multinational corporation.

There has been a trend toward decentralization in multinational operations as a result of national conditions which differ to such a great extent as to make it impossible to maintain centralized policies and decision making. This fourth issue at times creates a centrifugal force which pulls against a unified strategy. Once a manager has been delegated large powers of operations in a given country, it is difficult to replace him, even if his performance does not reach the standards of the company as a whole. Variations resulting from decentralization make transfer of management personnel more difficult. Furthermore, well trained managers in the parent firm may not view a transfer to an undeveloped country as the best means of promotion to top levels of management. Although American and British managers are accustomed to moving among countries, some nationalities—e.g., the French—often view a managerial position in another country as undesirable.

The growth of international business and multinational corporations has increased the importance of comparative approaches to management thought. Furthermore, the foreign aid programs have increasingly recognized that improved management is a critical factor in helping less developed nations to achieve their economic and social goals.

Propositions
for Intercultural Studies
in Management

This chapter has introduced a large number of environmental variables which have a significant impact on management functions. Management pertinent to differing environments needs propositions to help meet the challenges of the present diversity in the world. On the basis of the preceding analysis, the following can be concluded:

1. The management process is interdependent with its environmental setting. While the management functions must somehow be performed in all societies, the managerial approach most applicable in obtaining optimum performance is contingent on individual environments.

2. Improvement in management practices in a given country may depend on (a) changing elements in the cultural environment, (b) adapting managerial techniques to the given environment, or (c) changing some environmental variables *and* some functional approaches to management.

3. The amount of diversity in environments provides strong arguments for decentralization of authority in international companies which operate in more than one culture.

4. Research should seek management concepts which are stripped of cultural biases; a first step in this process is to identify, with the help of the comparative method, one's own cultural bias and to refrain from making value judgments about a differing managerial approach until one understands the reasons for the difference.

REFERENCES

BARNET, R. J. and RONALD E. MULLER, *Global Reach*. New York: Simon and Schuster, 1974.

BLOUGH, ROY, *International Business in Its Environment*. New York: McGraw-Hill Book Co., 1966.

DANIELS, J. D., E. W. OGRAM and L. H. RADEBAUGH, *International Business: Environments and Operations*. Reading, Mass.: Addison-Wesley Publishing Co., Inc., 1976.

FARMER, R. and BARRY RICHMAN, *Comparative Management and Economic Progress*. Homewood, Ill.: Richard D. Irwin, Inc., 1965.

FAYERWEATHER, JOHN, *Facts and Fallacies of International Business*. New York: Holt, Rinehart and Winston, Inc., 1962.

ROBOCK, S. H., K. SIMMONDS and JACK ZWICK, *International Business and Multinational Enterprises*. Homewood, Ill.: Richard D. Irwin, Inc., 1977.

SERVAN-SCHRIEBER, J. J., *The American Challenge*. New York: Atheneum Publishers, 1967.

VERNON, RAYMOND and L. T. WELLS, *Manager in the International Economy* (3rd ed). Englewood Cliffs, N.J.; Prentice-Hall, Inc., 1976.

WEBBER, ROSS A., *Culture and Management*. Homewood, Ill.: Richard D. Irwin, 1969.

PART

2

FUNCTIONS IN THE MANAGEMENT PROCESS

One way to view the subject of management is to concentrate on it as a process. Typically, this process involves certain functions that a manager performs which, if identified and described, will increase one's understanding of the subject. This approach has the advantages of focusing attention on the fundamentals important to management and of furnishing a framework into which all techniques and generalizations can be fitted. Most of the classical writers on business management use this functional or process approach. The reader will find that the seven functions discussed in this book will provide an introduction to many of the terms used in more advanced books.

To many specialists in management, the subjects of the next four chapters are *the* essentials of management. To these classical writers, this entire book should be built around the functions of management. Here, these functions will serve as a most important framework for introducing management concepts; Parts 3 and 4 will provide perspectives of new developments and practical applications of the basic concepts.

Several cautions about the interpretation of the seven functions should be kept in mind. First, the sevenfold breakdown is used purely for analytical purposes; it does not mean that these functions are distinct and separate steps with no overlaps. Each function focuses attention on certain parts of the total management job and is closely interrelated with all other functions. Second, the functions should not be used as a "cook book" indicating what a manager thinks about in everyday actions. For example, a manager does not say to himself that he is organizing at one time, controlling at another, and directing at another. Third, the order in which the functions are discussed does not indicate the chronological order in which the functions are performed. All these functions are more or less continuous processes.

The managerial process is a complex social activity. Many executives have become experts in handling the process in practice but never have studied it analytically. When asked how they do it, they can only answer that they do it but cannot explain how. The academic study of management, however, must take some systematic approach in breaking the complexity into parts so that the process can be better understood and taught to persons who have not the opportunity to learn by trial and error. The functional approach, described in this part, has proved successful for a number of years; it is useful even when other systems of education, such as the case method, are used.

This book takes several approaches for explaining the essentials of management. Part 2 outlines the conceptual framework by analyzing the functions of the management process. Part 3 views the process from an interdisciplinary perspective and indicates how economics, accounting, the behavioral sciences, quantitative methods, and computers contribute to the performance of the seven functions discussed in Part 2. Part 4 considers areas in which these functions are applied and in which concepts and analyses of the preceding basic disciplines can be employed.

Part 2 is based on the foundation laid in Chapter 3. Within the environmental and ethical situation, the manager develops a philosophy of management and sets objectives toward which the organization is to head. In Chapter 5, the process of decision making is summarized to indicate the continual importance of choosing among alternatives. Policies are seen to be bridges between basic objectives and day-by-day decisions. Chapter 6 describes the process of organizing and staffing and how the structure and group behavior of human beings can aid in coordination and cooperation. Planning and controlling appear as essentials for all management in Chapter 7. In Chapter 8, the importance of communication in group effort receives attention and the process of directing actual performance appears as a most essential function of a manager.

5

DECISION MAKING
AND
POLICY
FORMULATION

⟸ **IDEAS TO BE FOUND** ⟹
IN THIS CHAPTER

- Steps in the decision-making process
- Committees and group decisions
- Some ideas from small group research
- Nature and meaning of policy
- Some policy issues

Most managers' duties involve making decisions of one kind or another. The other six functions could be discussed under the broad heading of decision making; therefore, we shall begin our survey of managerial functions with this activity. A manager is oriented toward making decisions rather than toward performing the actions personally; the actions are carried out by others. Thus a manager can be viewed as a specialist in the art of decision making. Furthermore, he concentrates on a particular type of decision making, referred to as policy formulation.

In Part 3 we shall concentrate on some of the specific approaches to decision making that have been developed in economics, accounting, mathematics, and other disciplines, and that have contributed to this research. In this chapter, we offer an overview of the basic elements of the decision-making process.

DECISION MAKING BY INDIVIDUALS

All human beings make decisions that affect their own actions. Managers are chiefly concerned with making decisions that will influence the actions of others. Thus, the decision-making process of management is affected by the environment of the decision makers and the role that they assume.

The product of the process is a **decision** that can be defined as a course of action consciously chosen from available alternatives for the purpose of achieving a desired result. Three ideas are important in this definition. First, a decision involves a *choice*; if there is but one possible course of action, no decision is possible. Second, a decision involves mental processes at the conscious level. The logical aspects are important; yet, emotional, nonrational, and subconscious factors do influence the process. Third, a decision is purposive; it is made to facilitate the attainment of some objective.

In the last several decades, research on the decision-making process has indicated that decision behavior is quite complex and variable; any summary of this behavior should be viewed as a first approximation of "the real thing." However, for convenience, the decision-making process may be described in five steps:

1. A good decision depends on the maker's being consciously aware of the factors that set the stage for the decision. Past actions and decisions provide the structure for current decisions. The environment of the maker determines many factors that must be accepted as being out of the control of the maker. Predetermined objectives provide the focus for a current decision. Many decisions seem to be simple at first glance merely because the maker fails to comprehend the number of factors that impinge on the situation. Broad education and experience may tend to complicate the task of decision making by increasing awareness of the number of factors involved. Confusion is not uncommon *nor* unhealthy at this stage; however, the decision maker must recognize the impossibility of considering all the facts and the need to develop a selective approach for keeping the most important and relevant facts in mind. The decision maker's mind may be saturated with facts about the situation and yet, by concentrating on the key aspects, avoid factual indigestion. It is at this stage that creative ability is put to the test. If time is available, the decision maker may find that allowing the facts to "simmer" for a while will provide opportunities for sudden insights. This gestation period can be planned and directed so that the decision maker will increase the probability of recognizing an idea when it does come to mind. This first step in decision making too

often is neglected; however, no group of high-powered techniques will substitute for an attempt to lay a good foundation for *understanding the situation*.

2. A good decision is dependent upon the *recognition of the right problem*. Too often, a decision maker is so intent on jumping to the right answer as to fail to look first for the right question. If current operations appear to be proceeding nicely, the good manager will not relax and assume that there are no problems. One of a manager's key duties is to search for problems. In this search, however, it is important to avoid creating problems or consuming time in handling insignificant problems.

The proper definition of the right problem depends on use of the concept of the **limiting factor**. Out of the maze of problems and facts, the manager seeks to frame an understanding of the problem by seeking a definition that will strike at the heart of the issue and provide residual answers to lesser problems. A key problem has the characteristic of being closely related to a series of other problems. The most damaging proof of a poor decision is to change the factor that has received attention, only to find that the problem remains.

The search for the correct questions in decision making depends upon the ethical problem of determining the end to be sought. A decision is rational if it selects means that lead to desired ends. It is useful, therefore, to try to differentiate between means and ends; yet, in reality, an end for one decision is a means for another. For example, one may wish to select a job (means) to obtain money (end), yet want the money (means) to buy a new auto (end). The auto, in turn, becomes a means for transportation or prestige (end), and so forth. This continuous process, viewed as a **means-end chain**, is a pattern showing the hierarchy of ends that, at any level, serve as instruments for attaining an end at the next higher level.

3. *Search for and analysis of available alternatives* and their probable consequences is the step most subject to logical and systematic treatment. Various disciplines offer many ideas (discussed in Part 3) of practical help to the manager, such as mathematical models, the theory of probability, and the economist's concept of incremental revenue and cost.

The use of logic is the key to this step. The study of logic involves the way in which the human mind passes from premises to propositions based on the premises. A **premise** is a statement of the relationship between a cause and a consequence. The process of decision making involves the consideration of a number of these "if we do A, then B will result" statements. If we classify the consequences into "desired" and "undesired," we then can develop some framework in which the premise can be weighted.

The premise is the fundamental unit of consideration in decision making. First, it is desirable to recognize the premises upon which an approach is based. Concealed premises may provide traps for reasoning. Second, we need to test the validity of our premises. We must anticipate whether the consequence will actually follow from the cause. Third, we should distinguish between value premises and factual premises. The test of the validity of a factual premise is observable and measurable; a value premise can only be asserted to be valid. If this distinction can be made clearly, we can concentrate objectively on handling the factual premises and consciously on recognizing the value judgments upon which the decision will rest. Every executive must make value judgments that are open to errors not subject to scientific study. One manner of handling these judgment errors is to recognize their existence and to understand the probable biases. Goals can be ranked by the decision maker and included in the conscious determination of alternatives and consequences. The good executive will not stop with a consideration of factual premises but will recognize that the job requires using value premises. Such an executive will attempt "to get the feel of the situation," that is, to make value premises in order to deliberately assess them.

This step of searching and analyzing alternatives and consequences is often delegated to staff executives. The staff concentrates on providing a framework of explicit premises that the line executive uses in selecting the best solution. One writer refers to this step as the design stage of decision making. No framework can possibly include *all* premises; therefore, any framework will tend to lead toward certain conclusions. Studies of the optimum number of alternatives that can be handled by a human being show that usually more than seven alternatives tend to confuse rather than help. Some individuals have the mental capacity to handle ten alternatives; others should break problems into the simplest form of two alternatives—"do or don't do." It may be desirable to include among the alternatives such possibilities as postponing action or leaving action to someone else.

4. Even in the best-designed framework of alternatives-consequences, the crucial step remains—the *selection of the solution*. At this stage, the ranking of preferences is important. The executive who must make decisions quickly may wish the best solution but may settle for only a satisfactory one; often the theoretically best decision may be only slightly better than a number of satisfactory ones. It may be feasible to maintain a large "zone of indifference," with no need for spending additional time to find the "best." In fact, the cost of

refining the decision-making process so that the "best" can be determined is itself a factor in determining the "best."

5. Finally, a decision must be *accepted by the organization*. The entire process is directed toward securing action. If others are affected, the decision must be communicated to them; they must be motivated to implement the decision; furthermore, control provides information for future decisions.

These five steps form a framework for the decision-making process; however, the techniques used in the process may vary, depending upon the type of executive decision making employed. Two types of decisions can be distinguished: (1) by initiation and (2) by approval. In the first type, the maker originates the process; in the latter, the decision maker receives recommendations that are approved, disapproved, or sent back for futher study. The qualities needed by executives in initiating decisions are different from those needed in approving recommendations. When decision by approval is used, group interactions become more important; however, most management decisions involve some degree of interchange among different managers, and so we now turn to decision making by groups.

DECISION MAKING BY GROUPS

In a cooperative endeavor, one person may appear to have *made* the decision but in fact may have performed only one step in the process. Executives usually make decisions in a social environment. *A* may provide a fact; *B* may provide a premise; *C* may provide a value judgment; *D* may supply one complete alternative; *E* may supply a second alternative. Even if all are not present at the time of the final choice, each has had a definite part in the process. In fact, organization may be viewed as an interrelationship of decision centers. Cooperative decision making is a process by which a group attempts to develop a composite organization mind.

In large firms facing complex problems, decisions emerge from a series of meetings in which executives jointly approach problems. These group meetings may be called conferences, committees, boards, task forces, or merely staff meetings.

A **committee** may be defined as any group interacting in regard to a common, explicit purpose with formal authority delegated from an appointing executive. Some of the disagreement among managers about the use of committees is a result of a failure to discriminate among the purposes to which a committee can be assigned. Thus a critical factor in successful use of committees is the explicit statement by the appointing authority as to its expected functions. In making this statement the appointing authority should identify which of the following **purposes of committees** he is assigning in each case:

1. For fact-finding, investigation, and *collecting information*.
2. To avoid the appearance of arbitrary decisions and to *secure support* for a position.
3. To *make a decision*—a choice among alternatives.
4. To *negotiate* between conflicting positions taken by opposing interests.
5. To *stimulate* human beings to think creatively, to generate ideas, and to reinforce thoughts advanced by others.
6. To *distribute* information—to brief members of an organization on plans and facts.
7. To *provide representation* for important elements of an organization.
8. To *coordinate* different parts and subgroups of an organization toward common, overall goals.
9. To *train* inexperienced personnel through participation in groups with experienced members.

As the reader will notice in considering the above purposes, committees may be involved in any or all of the basic five steps of the decision process. Furthermore, formal committees constitute only one of many possible forms of group decision making. As a result the manager must develop an understanding of these possibilities in order to answer satisfactorily several important questions:

1. Should group decision making be used extensively in the organization? At what stages?
2. What types of problems are best tackled by groups?
3. If groups are used, how should the meetings be conducted?

Operating executives usually have strong opinions on the answers to these questions; however, these opinions range all the way from outlawing any idea of group decision making to continual use of groups in all steps.

Whether to use a committee or some other group method of decision making is a question that can be approached by looking at the following advantages:

1. A decision can be approached from different viewpoints by individual specialists on a committee.

2. Coordination of activities of separate departments can be attained through joint interactions in meetings.

3. Motivation of individual members to carry out a decision may be increased by the feeling of participation in the decision-making process.

4. Committees provide a means by which executives can be trained in decision making.

5. Committees permit representation of different interest groups.

6. Group discussion is one method of creative thinking; a fragmentary idea by one member may create a chain reaction in the minds of others present.

The disadvantages of committees, however, are:

1. Considering the value of the time of each individual member (as measured by his salary), committees are costly.

2. The length of time required to make a decision by a committee makes its use inadvisable if a decision must be made promptly.

3. Group action may lead to compromise and indecision.

4. A superior line executive present at a meeting may make the decision individually, with subordinates attempting to appear competent by proposing ideas they believe will make a good impression.

5. Committee decisions may be reached by a method in which no one is held responsible for a decision; "buck passing" may result.

Some problems lend themselves better to committee action than do others. Any decision requiring deliberation by a group of specialists tends to encourage the committee approach. Often the conclusions of a committee are said to be advisory, the actual decision being made by a single line officer. In practice, if the members have maintained close contact with the appointing authority, the "advisory" committee report becomes the action basis for the decision.

A decision involving implementation by several departments requires some means by which the departments become involved in the decision making. Committees are means by which each department can obtain the benefit of comments from other departments. The joint decision made in a committee tends to be a balanced decision that takes into account interactions of different viewpoints. Planning decisions lend themselves to committee work, whereas implementation of orders tends to be clearer when made by a single line executive. Committees are extremely weak if forceful, immediate action is needed.

Many criticisms of committee activities are not inherent in the committee concept but result from a lack of thought about how to handle a group in the process of making a decision. Typically, if advance thought is given to a meeting, the chairman often assumes that Robert's Rules of Order will provide the "best way" to handle the meeting. The business executive tends to conduct meetings formally when the meeting involves high-level executives. Often the result is that the meeting does not engage in actual decision making but merely supplies information about a final report of a decision that has been made previously (either by a single member or by an informal group that had met prior to the formal meeting). Because group interactions are time-consuming, business executives make use of formal devices, such as agenda for the meeting, minutes of the secretary, and motions and votes on motions, to expedite the business of the group.

Research on small groups has indicated several **principles of group participation** that provide guides for group interaction.[1]

1. The physical layout, size of group, and general atmosphere are important factors determining the effectiveness of problem solving. For example, a meeting located in the boss's office will be entirely different from one held in a "neutral" conference room. If the committee has only three members, it may not have enough "interaction"; if the committee has thirty members, it is not possible for each member to participate freely.

2. Threat reduction is an important objective in the planning for group action so that the group will shift from interpersonal problems to group goals. Any tendency to put a member "on the spot" or to force him to "take sides" will increase the debating society feeling and will result in an increase of tension.

3. The best group leadership is performed by the entire group and is not the job of the "chairperson," "secretary," or other formal leader. A group that functions well tends to function informally, with no single person providing all the leadership. Leadership may shift, and different types of leaders may evolve. One member may serve as the social leader, another may serve as "questioner," another may act as "clarifier" or "summarizer," and so forth.

4. Goals should be explicitly formulated by the group. The group should refrain from being "fenced in" by predetermined rules. The objective is to increase the involvement of each member in the decision-making process.

5. An agenda should be formulated by the group but should be changed as new goals develop from new needs. Preplanning for meetings should retain *flexibility* so that the group maintains its ability to meet issues as it perceives them.

[1]J. R. Gibb, G. N. Platts, and L. F. Miller, *Dynamics of Participative Groups* (St. Louis, Mo.: Swift and Co., 1959).

6. The decision-making process should continue until the group formulates a solution upon which it can form a *consensus*. If the group action results in a minority opinion, the group has failed to maximize its effectiveness. In a group that emphasizes this principle, there is no formal voting. Discussion continues until no one in the group can add any improvements to the solution.

7. Any group should be made aware of the *interaction process* by which the group arrives at solutions. In this manner, the skill of being a member of a group becomes a distinguishable skill that the executive can develop. This principle leads to the idea that group actions are important subjects for study; continual evaluations should be made of group processes.

There is great need for improvement of group-decision processes in all types of organization. The above principles offer a definite viewpoint that may be helpful in crystallizing thought about group decision making.

Decisions vary as to their complexity and importance, whether they are made primarily by individuals or by groups. The more complex and important a decision, the greater the need for useful decision rules. The complexity of a decision increases as the number of variables to be considered increases, as the degree of uncertainty increases, and as more value judgments are required. The importance of a decision increases when more decisions are dependent on it, when more subordinates are involved, and when the financial consequences are more critical. The next section discusses one type of important and complex decision, generally referred to as a policy decision.

POLICY FORMULATION

Nature of
Policy Decisions

Policy is an understanding by members of a group that makes the actions of each member of the group in a given set of circumstances more predictable to other members. A policy is a guide for making decisions. If a decision provides help for decisions in other situations, it is said to be a **policy decision**, because it sets a precedent and provides some guide for decision making in the future. Policy decisions provide a range of freedom within which subordinates can make single-shot decisions. Table 5-1 clarifies the meaning of policy by defining related terms that should not be confused with it.

An important characteristic of policy is that it provides a guide and a framework for subordinates' decisions, Therefore, strong and clear policies encourage the delegation of decision making; they do not predetermine decisions. For example, top management might establish a financial policy

Table 5-1
Policy and Related Terms

Policy:	An understanding by members of a group that makes the actions of each member more predictable to other members. Policy is a guide for making decisions.
Rule:	A statement of precisely what is to be done (or not done) in the same way every time, with no permitted deviation. Rules allow no range for decision making; policy encourages decision making by offering guides.
Law:	A statement of an order that is invariable under given conditions. Laws are rigid statements by external authority, providing a framework for policy formulation.
Creed:	A belief or faith that lacks precision but serves as a foundation upon which policies develop.
Procedure:	A system that describes, in detail, the steps to be taken in order to accomplish a job. Procedures emphasize details; policies concentrate on basic general approaches.
Strategy:	A concept of the direction the organization should take in light of the external environment, particularly the actions of competitors, when considering risks, uncertainty, and changes in the environment.

that subordinates must obtain approval for all expenditures over $500. This clear policy would eliminate subordinates' decisions involving large sums of money, but it also clearly states the range (0-$500) in which subordinates may make their own decisions without worrying about whether they have the right to make them. Good policies provide definite and clear direction by top management and at the same time allow subordinates to make their own decisions within clearly stated limits.

The usual source of policies is the top management of the firm. Policies may (1) *originate* at the top by executive deliberation, (2) be *imposed* from outside the firm by a trade association or the government, (3) be formulated on *appeal* from a subordinate as a result of a specific problem not covered by previously set policies, or (4) be *implied* from consistent actions of subordinates and known by top management but not explicitly stated. Policies may apply to the entire firm or they may relate to only one department. Generally, policy decisions are considered to be the more important decisions of a firm; yet many important decisions have no policy implications. For example, a decision to build a $10 million plant would be important, but it would not set a precedent or be a general guide to future decisions.

A good policy has the following characteristics:

1. It is related to an objective of the firm and is explained to all persons to whom it is to apply.
2. It is stated in understandable words and placed in writing.

3. It prescribes limits and yardsticks for future action.
4. It is subject to change but relatively stable.
5. It is reasonable and capable of being accomplished.
6. It allows for discretion and interpretation by those responsible for carrying it out.

Many firms require that policies not only be in writing but be organized in a policy manual. This practice helps keep subordinates informed of policies that apply to a given situation. Of course, if a policy has been formulated but has not come to the attention of a subordinate, it cannot be effective. An oral policy can be generally known and applied, but it runs the risk of being overlooked or misinterpreted.

Policies are important to management, but they have the following limitations:

1. They are formulated by top management to relieve subordinates of the necessity of rethinking the factors upon which the policy was based. In short, a policy eliminates thinking about repetitive matters. If subordinates develop the habit of referring to company policy as the only reason for their actions, they may use policies as crutches and defeat the intent of the policies.
2. Policies provide stability and direction to the action of members of the firm; yet, if a policy remains in existence long after conditions have changed, it can have the effect of opposing progress.
3. If policies are not stated in broad and definite terms, they may tend to encourage subordinates to avoid responsibility for their own decisions.

Policy Issues   Business problems are often discussed in terms of current policy issues. A policy that works for one firm may not work for another. Some business policies apply to the entire company and may cover long periods of time. Several general policies receiving attention in recent years are:

Diversification   Large companies often guide their activities into many different lines of business to avoid having all their eggs in one basket. Among other reasons, diversification is employed to: insulate the company against violent fluctuations in the sales of a single product; give the company growing room (in those cases in which the current share of the market in one industry is looked upon with disfavor by the Justice Department); follow up discoveries made in a research and development program which provide new knowledge in areas not previously considered to be of company interest.

Many companies decide against a diversification policy. They reason that diversification can lead a company into areas in which they have little knowledge or experience and in which competitors have strong advantages.

Vertical Integration　　　　Some companies strive to operate at all stages of production, from the raw material to final sales to consumers. An integration policy gives more security to the source of supply for raw materials and more control over the quality of parts and supplies used in production. In some industries, such as oil and steel, the manufacturing processes dictate that a single company handle the product at different stages in order to attain economical operations.

Search for Niches　　　　A firm may concentrate on looking for those areas of operation that are overlooked by its competition. This policy stresses the development of those operations in which the firm has a comparative advantage and avoids trying to "beat a competitor in his own backyard."

Departmental policies may apply to personnel matters, marketing guides, financial questions, or any other operational phase of the business. The following are several illustrations of some personnel policies.

Nepotism　　　　Should the company avoid hiring persons who are closely related to present employees? The purpose of an antinepotism policy is to curb favoritism; however, should a company refuse to hire the best applicant for a job because she is the daughter of a man working in another plant of the same company?

Racial Discrimination　　　　A current policy issue involves the manner in which the company views the hiring of different races and nationalities. Such policies are directly affected by the social customs and legal decisions of the time. Affirmative action programs have focused on elimination of racial discrimination.

Mandatory Retirement at　　　　The increase in the length of human
a Given Age　　　　life has caused the retirement policy issue to receive increased attention. A mandatory retirement policy has the advantage of providing openings for aggressive young people and of preventing older people from remaining on their jobs past the age at which they are effective. On the other hand, individuals differ as to their physical and mental capacities at a given chronological age; some men at age 70 can provide great service to a company, whereas others, at the same age, are quite feeble. Federal laws have restricted the use of the policy of mandatory retirement.

In summary, decision and policy making are duties central to management. We shall see in the next three chapters that other functions of management involve decisions of different types. We turn now to two of these that relate to the structure of the relationships among positions in the firm and to the manner in which the human element is added to the structure, that is, organizing and staffing.

REFERENCES

CHURCHMAN, C. WEST, *Prediction and Optimal Decision*. Englewood Cliffs, N.J.: Prentice-Hall, Inc., 1961.

HAYNES, W. WARREN and JOSEPH L. MASSIE, *Management: Analysis, Concepts and Cases* (3rd ed.). Englewood Cliffs, N.J.: Prentice-Hall, Inc. 1975.

JONES, M. H., *Executive Decision Making* (rev. ed.). Homewood, Ill.: Richard D. Irwin, Inc. 1962.

MILLER, DAVID W. and MARTIN K. STARR, *Executive Decisions and Operations Research* (2nd ed.). Englewood Cliffs, N.J.: Prentice-Hall, Inc., 1969.

MOORE, P. G. and H. THOMAS, *The Anatomy of Decisions*. Middlesex, England: Penguin Books, 1976.

SIMON, HERBERT A., *The New Science of Management Decision*. New York: Harper & Row, Publishers, 1960.

SIMON, H. A., *Administrative Behavior* (3rd ed.). New York: The Macmillan Company, 1976.

6

STAFFING AND ORGANIZING

Two functions of management, organizing and staffing, are so closely related that they are often discussed together without any distinction between them. **Organizing** focuses attention on the structure and process of allocating jobs so that common objectives can be achieved; **staffing** pertains to the people in the jobs. In other words, organizing is job-oriented; staffing is worker-oriented. Organization deals not only with both organizing and staffing but also with the *relationship* between the two.

Problems of organization have confronted men ever since they started to work together on the simplest projects. The increasing dependence of people on one another and the concentration of people have increased the importance of organization in modern society. The development of organization theory, therefore, has received greater attention in recent years than ever before. The early pioneers of management thought concentrated on the organizing function and developed a theory which *prescribed* the manner in which jobs should be grouped in the structure. This theory will be called the **classical theory of organization**. More recently, students in the behavioral sciences have focused attention on interactions in organizations. The latter group has concentrated on *describing* how human beings actually work together. **Organization Behavior (O.B.)** concerns individuals in organizations and will be discussed in Chapter 11.

In recent years, the trend has been to concentrate on scientific research in organization behavior and to describe organization as a system of human relationships. The concepts resulting from this research comprise **modern organization theory.**

Organization has been defined in many ways, depending on the viewpoint from which the subject was observed. Today, numerous approaches to problems of organization exist, chiefly because different assumptions have been made and different definitions used. For our purpose, **organization** will be defined as the structure and process by which a cooperative group of human beings allocates its tasks among its members, identifies relationships, and integrates its activities toward common objectives. It will be observed that this definition involves the structure of tasks (organizing), the placement of human beings in the structure (staffing), and the integration of the two functions into a human system of activities.

CLASSICAL THEORY OF ORGANIZATION

The classical theory of organization contributes provocative observations about the *design* of a formal structure of organization and the manner in which *specialization* can be applied in the organizing process. The foundation for this approach is in the proposition that planning of positions and departments should precede consideration of the particular individuals who might fill the positions. Although this proposition made it possible to state a group of principles about organization structure, there has been little empirical verification of the assumed human characteristics and the assumed manner in which human beings interact in social groups. The chief contributions of traditional theory include (1) a clear definition of types of formal organization, (2) certain generalizations that offer first approximations for planning an organization structure, and (3) limited models for organizing activities.

Types of Formal Organization

Traditionally, organization has been analyzed as a structure of authority relationships. **Authority** was defined as the right to act. In this legal sense, authority flows down in an organization. For example, an industrial chief executive delegates authority to lower levels in his organization and is viewed as receiving his authority from the Board of Directors, which receives authority from stockholders, from the government, and ultimately from the people (in a democracy).

Three types of organization are classified by the nature of authority: line, staff, and functional. **Line organization** is the simplest, most direct type, in which each position has general authority over lower positions in the hierarchy in the accomplishment of the main operations of the firm. **Staff organization** is purely advisory (either generalist or specialist) to the line structure, with no authority to place recommendations into action. Functional organization has developed from the increasing complexity of operations and the need for a great number of specialists for aiding line positions. **Functional organization** permits a specialist in a given area to enforce his directives within a limited and clearly defined scope of authority. Staff becomes desirable when the line needs advisory help; yet, in effect, it complicates the supervision problem faced by the line manager. Functional organization decreases the line manager's problem because it permits orders to flow directly to lower levels without attention to routine technical problems by the line positions.

Line organization is the backbone of hierarchy; staff and functional organization merely supplement the line. In an actual organization, a single position might serve as line, staff, and functional at the same time but for different phases of activities. For example, the chief accountant in a business firm might give tax and accounting advice (staff) to the chief line officer, supervise his own accounting department of one hundred people (line), and set specific accounting procedures for lower levels with his own specialist authority (functional). In fact, the value of the distinction among the three types of organization is in focusing attention on the different types of authority assigned to individual executives. The determination of the particular use of these types will depend upon the situation in which the manager finds himself (see Table 6-1).

Classical Principles of Organization

Traditional organization theorists developed certain generalizations which they considered to be principles of organization. These principles are useful first approximations, or guides for thought, in the organizing function. They provide a simple group of intuitive statements that provoke thought by both operating managers and researchers in an organization. The most important of these principles are (1) unity of command, (2) exception principle, (3) span of control, (4) scalar principle, (5) departmentation, and (6) decentralization.

Unity of Command

One of the traditional principles of organization, generally referred to as **unity of command**, states that no member of an organization should report to more than one superior on

Table 6-1
Comparison of Line, Staff,
and Functional Organization

Line Organization

Advantages
1. Maintains simplicity
2. Makes clear division of authority
3. Encourages speedy action

Disadvantages
1. Neglects specialists in planning
2. Overworks key people
3. Depends upon retention of a few key people

Staff Organization

Advantages
1. Enables specialists to give expert advice
2. Frees the line executive of detailed analysis
3. Affords young specialists a means of training

Disadvantages
1. Confuses organization if functions are not clear
2. Reduces power of experts to place recommendations into action
3. Tends toward centralization of organization

Functional Organization

Advantages
1. Relieves line executives of routine, specialized decisions
2. Provides framework for applying expert knowledge
3. Relieves pressure of need for large numbers of well-rounded executives

Disadvantages
1. Makes relationships more complex
2. Makes limits of authority of each specialist a difficult coordination problem
3. Tends toward centralization of organization

any single function. This principle appeals to common sense in a pure line organization, in which each superior has general authority; however, it becomes a complex problem in actual cases in which some form of staff and/or functional organization is used. In practice, instructions may be received from several sources without loss of productivity. The central problem is to avoid conflict in orders from different people relating to the same subject. One should recognize immediately that the actions of a subordinate may be *influenced* by many persons who are not recognized in the formal hierarchy of authority. The principle of unity of command may be useful in the planning of an organization if it is interpreted as a tendency toward the simplification of relationships between superior and subordinate; it is not realistic if it is interpreted as an immutable law that would eliminate useful relationships among executives.

Exception Principle   A second principle, called the **exception principle**, states that recurring decisions should be handled in a routine manner by lower-level managers, whereas problems involving unusual matters should be referred to higher levels. This principle emphasizes that executives at the top levels of an organization have limited time and capacity and should refrain from becoming bogged down in routine details that can be handled as well by subordinates. Thus, it is an important concept concerning the delegation of authority in an organization.

The exception principle can be very useful to an executive by focusing attention on those matters that should receive attention first. It is applicable at all levels and, if kept in mind, can help the inexperienced executive compensate for a human tendency to concentrate on the concrete, immediate, and detailed problems at the expense of the more fundamental, difficult, and abstract issues. At the same time, attention to the principle can help the lower-level managers understand exactly what they are expected to do.

The principle has remained important in modern theory because of the distinction it makes between programmed and nonprogrammed decisions. **Programmed decisions** are those that are repetitive and routine and that can be handled by a definite procedure. **Nonprogrammed decisions** involve new, one-shot, and unstructured elements that require tailored handling by superiors. Programmed decisions may be easily delegated; nonprogrammed decisions usually need the attention of the superior in handling "exceptions."

Span of Control   A third traditional principle involves the **span of control** of a manager and states that there is a limit to the number of subordinates that one superior should supervise. Often this principle is stated in terms of the exact number of subordinates that should report to a superior and thus has become highly controversial. The determination of the optimum number depends on many factors in a given organization and should always be tied directly to the question of the number of levels in the hierarchy. If it appears that a small span of control for each manager is desirable, then the number of necessary levels will be larger than would be the case with a larger span of control. The organization with more levels will be "tall," whereas the organization with a larger span of control will be "flat."

Span of control focuses attention on the basic fact that any human being has limitations. First, one has limited *time available* for one's activities. Second, one has limited *available energy* and must depend on others to supplement one's energy. Third, the number of subjects to which a manager can give *attention* is limited. These limitations not only support the concept of span of control but indicate that the optimum span of control varies among individuals. Also, the span of control under one set of physical conditions will differ from the span under another set. For example, the problems of a military commander fighting in the desert differ from the problems of a commander fighting in the jungle. Improving communication devices may make a larger span of control desirable. The dispersion of necessary information may change the optimum span.

Span of control refers to the number of people that one person can supervise directly. A related, but broader and possibly more useful, idea is the **span of managerial responsibility.** It refers to the number of people whom one superior can assist, teach, and help to reach the objectives of their own jobs—that is, the number who have *access* to the superior. The span of responsibility probably can be larger than the span of control.

The span of control principle does not resolve the conflict between the advantages of a "tall" organization versus those of the "flat." It is evident that as the number of levels increases, the number of channels through which orders must flow increases. Questions of span of control and number of levels must be handled concurrently in any decision about the structure of an organization.

Scalar Principle   A fourth traditional principle, called the **scalar principle**, states that authority and responsibility should flow in a clear unbroken line from the highest executive to the lowest. The military stresses this idea under the term *chain of command.* One writer describes this vertical relationship as a job-task pyramid. The principle simply states that an organization is a hierarchy. The importance and usefulness of the principle is evident whenever the line is severed. The splintering of one organization into two or more results from a permanent breach of this principle.

Departmentation   The manner in which activities should be divided and formed into specialized groups usually is referred to as **departmentation.** The purpose of departmentation is to specialize activities, simplify the tasks of managers, and maintain control. Three common types of departmentation are: geographical, commodity, and functional. Often, different types are used at different levels of the organization structure. For example, Figure 6-1 illustrates geographical departmentation at the top level, commodity at the second level, and functional at the third.

No single formula for departmentation applies to all situations. The following criteria may help the organization planner:

1. Similar activities may be grouped together, based upon likeness of personal qualifications or common purpose, for example, medical and dental personnel.

71

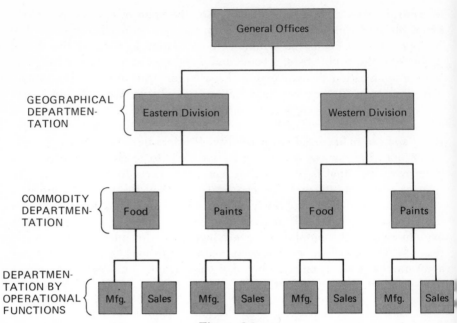

Figure 6-1
Types of Departmentation

2. An activity may be grouped with other activities with which it is used, for example, safety with production.

3. Functions may be assigned to that executive who is most interested in performing them well.

4. Activities may be grouped to encourage competition among departments or to avoid friction among departments.

5. If it is difficult to make definite distinctions between two activities, they may be grouped together.

6. Certain functions require close coordination and, if separated, would increase problems of higher-level managers; in this case, such functions should be grouped together.

Decentralization   The concept of decentralization has been an important organizing principle, especially in large corporations. However, the concept has been confused by the use of the term to describe different ideas. Often, it refers to operations at different geographical locations. In this sense, decentralization describes physical characteristics of a company but does not indicate the type of organization structure used.

Decentralization, as an organizing concept, refers to the process of pushing decision making to lower levels of the organization. It is closely related to the delegation of authority to the broader base of executives who are at the lower levels of the hierarchy. Decentralization is a matter of degree. Basic decisions and policies must receive attention at the top levels. Although delegation is generally recognized as an important art by most operating executives, in practice delegation involves significant costs and risks. Two important considerations determine the degree of decentralization desirable in a given situation. First, the amount of skills and competence possessed by subordinate executives influences the success of any program of decentralization. Executives must be developed who can adequately handle the decisions delegated to them. Second, the distribution of the necessary information to points of decision is critical to any delegation process. Unless an executive has sufficient information available for a decision, he will have little chance to make a good decision.

Decentralization is not universally good. It may be preferable for Firm A but disastrous for Firm B. If speed in making decisions is important, decentralization of decisions may be desirable. Divisionalization along product lines has proved to be desirable for many large multiproduct firms.

Bureaucracy

The traditional theory of organization has received systematic treatment by many thinkers in management (see Figure 2-1). Max Weber[1] stands out as developer of a model of formal organization structure. Weber, in his historical study of social behavior, noticed three influences on organizational behavior: (1) the traditional taboos of society, (2) personal leadership of the great men (which he called charisma), and (3) the concept of bureaucracy. The characteristic of the third influence has been the subject of study by social scientists and offers a model of a formal theory of organization.

Bureaucracy, as used by Weber, does not have the opprobrious meaning that it has in general usage. It has a technical meaning and identifies the following basic characteristics of a formal model:

1. Regular activities aimed at organization goals are distributed as fixed official duties.
2. Organization follows the principles of hierarchy.
3. Operations are governed by a consistent system of abstract rules that are applied to individual cases.
4. The ideal official operates as a formalistic impersonality without emotion.
5. Employment in the organization is based on technical qualifications and is not subject to arbitrary termination.

[1]Max Weber, *The Theory of Social and Economic Organization* (New York: Oxford University Press, 1947).

6. From a purely technical point of view, bureaucracy attains the highest degree of efficiency.

Bureaucracy concentrates on a rational structure with universal applications in social institutions. Although Weber has been criticized as being too autocratic, his concept of bureaucracy has had great impact on classical thinking about formal organization.

Assumptions of the Classical Theory of Organizing The classical theory of organizing remains important because it offers explicit guidelines for many present organizations. Yet it has been attacked by many writers because, in spite of its efficiency, it has led to social dissatisfaction. Douglas McGregor referred to it as Theory X and identified the assumptions about human nature implicitly made by the principles which he used as the foundation for his criticism:[2]

1. Members of an organization are unable to work out relations among their positions without thorough guidance and planning.
2. Some members are aggressive and will trespass on the domain of others unless clear boundaries are drawn.
3. Members are reluctant to assume responsibilities unless assigned a definite task.
4. Members generally prefer the security of a definite task to the freedom of a vaguely defined one.
5. Members are prone to conflict.
6. Justice is more certain if the enterprise is organized on an objective, impersonal basis.

HUMAN AND PARTICIPATIVE THEORIES OF ORGANIZING

The classical theory of organization has met increasing opposition starting with the human relations proponents in the 1950s and the behavioralists in the 1960s and 1970s. McGregor proposed an alternative theory based on different assumptions about human nature. The assumptions of his Theory Y are:

1. The expenditure of physical and mental effort in work is as natural as play or rest.
2. People will exercise self-direction and self-control toward objectives to which they are committed.

[2]Douglas McGregor, *The Human Side of Enterprise* (New York: McGraw Hill Book Co., 1960), pp. 33-35, 45-49.

3. The average individual learns not only to accept but to seek responsibility.
4. The human capacity of imagination, ingenuity, and creativity is widely distributed among individuals.
5. In modern industrial life the intellectual potentialities of the average human being are only partially utilized.

Although McGregor did not focus on organizational design, R. Likert and others have proposed structural recommendations that are consistent with the Theory Y assumptions.

Likert developed a theory of organizing which he called **System 4.**[3] His System 4 theory is built on three concepts:

1. *Principle of Supportive Relationships:* The process of organization must ensure a maximum probability that in all interactions and relationships each member will view the experience as supportive and one which builds and maintains a sense of personal worth and importance.
2. *Linking Pins:* The charting of hierarchical relationships should provide "linking pins" among groups (not individuals), and these relationships should be overlapping (not in a tight chain of command). Management should deliberately endeavor to build effective groups, linking them in an overall organization by means of people who hold overlapping group membership, i.e., a manager at each level participates in groups of higher-level managers and joins lower-level managers in participating as a group.
3. *Performance Goals:* Goals describe the interrelationships of the organization better than job descriptions and charts of flow of formal authority.

These assumptions and concepts of the participative theories of organizing yield propositions that conflict with those of classical theories. Both claim universality. The participative theories are less mechanistic, less impersonal, and less formal. They focus on human face-to-face relationships with allegedly greater satisfaction and productivity. Some participative theories propose an extreme view of "shared leadership." According to this view, no sharp distinction should be made between leadership and membership in a group. Diffusion of leadership should be encouraged. Members should share in setting goals. Groups should be continually in the process of self-examination, self-training, and the flexible reallocation of roles. Concepts of participative theories have been applied with remarkable success. With the clear lines drawn between the classical and participative theories, the manager needs guidance as to which theory to use.

[3]Rensis Likert, *The Human Organization* (New York: McGraw-Hill Book Co., 1967).

The manager's choice of organizing theories depends upon several factors:

1. One's assumptions about human nature.
2. The preference, personality, and educational background of the organizer.
3. The technology and environment faced by the specific organization.

For these reasons, modern organizing concepts have evolved into a group of contingency theories.

CONTINGENCY THEORIES OF ORGANIZING

Managerial practitioners and empirical researchers have developed new approaches to organizational design that help the manager make rational choices both in situations where classical concepts are relevant and in those where the participative theories are preferable. Thus the contingency approach to organizational structure emphasizes that the proper approach is to refrain from choosing one of the two universal theories on an all-or-nothing basis but to adapt certain ideas from both to the situation. The contingency approach has identified four groups of factors important in a manager's choice: (1) the nature of the people in the organization, (2) the type of task and technology, (3) the environment within which the organization operates, and (4) the degree of change and uncertainty faced by the organization. Most studies are directed to the latter three factors.

Task and Technology Determinants of Structure

Rapid changes in technology such as computer controls, machine-paced production, and increased use of indirect labor have increased the need for flexible structures. Structures compatible with dynamic technology differ from the structures that work in stable situations.

Results of research by Joan Woodward and her associates in Great Britain offer more specific elements indicating the relationship of technology and structure. Woodward classified production technology into three types: (1) small-batch, job-order production; (2) mass production using assembly lines; and (3) continuous process production, such as used in oil and chemical manufacture. She found that the more successful firms using each of these three technological processes had different structures. Span of control of both the chief executive and first-line supervisors varied with the type of technology, as did the ratio of direct to indirect workers and the ratio of line operators to staff workers. The flexibility gained by participative approaches indicated that for job-order production and for continuous-process production System 4 type organization was more successful; yet for assembly-line processes the more successful firms used classical and bureaucratic guidelines.

Based on Woodward's pioneering research and follow-up studies, the modern approach to organization design is to adapt the structure to the different technological processes. Using this approach, a single company may have different structures depending upon the processes of different parts of the company. The result is that the overall structure is more complex, using ideas from each of the pure, or universal, prescriptions.

Environment's Impact on Organization Design The industrial environment is a second determinant of organization structure. A firm in one industry may find one type of structure to be best, while a firm in a different industry may find a different type to be suitable. Early work by Paul Lawrence and Jay Lorsh led to the identification of different characteristics of the industrial environment that affect the suitable structure for a firm operating within that environment. They identified three classes of environments related to the sales, production, and R & D functions: market, technical-economic, and scientific. Each of these environments may vary as to (1) the rate of change experienced in the industry, (2) the degree of uncertainty of information about the situation, and (3) the length of the feedback time in which results become known.

Lawrence and Lorsch studied three industries: plastics, food, and containers. Initial focus was on the plastics industry, with its diverse and dynamic environment. The food and container industries were then added to provide comparison with more stable industries. Using three concepts—*differentiation* (differing orientations of functional departments), *integration* (the unity of efforts among subsystems), and *environment* (all factors outside the boundaries of the entity under consideration)—Lawrence and Lorsch found that the best structures of organization differed among different departments and industries, since each structure made accommodations to the demands for differentiation and integration in the light of the environment. For example, different structures were successful in each of the plastics, food, and container industries. Furthermore, within the plastics industry, the companies used different structural approaches for different departments. The production departments were more formalized along the lines of classical theories; the sales departments used some participative concepts and were less formally organized; the

77

research and development departments focused primarily on the flexibility of participative approaches.

Most recently, comparative research across national boundaries has indicated that organization structures differ as they are affected by moral values, political systems, stages of economic development, educational systems, and culture. In adjusting to the multiple environments, multinational firms have developed complex overall structures that permit variations for subsidiaries operating in different external environments.

Although some contingency theories have yet to identify and measure the effect of other specific variables on organization design, the current approach is to recognize that many environmental factors have a significant impact. Thus, the earlier trend to search for a single universal theory has given way to a search for the individual environmental variables that must be considered.

Effect of Change and Uncertainty on Organization Design

No organization design remains unchanged. People change, technology changes, environment changes, and the organization itself matures. Thus, even a manager who has discovered an optimum structure for a given technology and environmental setting must continually modify the structure to fit new stages in the organization's growth. Case studies have always indicated that an entrepreneur of a small firm tends to minimize formal organization structure and to operate in a manner consistent with participative theories. Upon developing a larger and more complex organization, this entrepreneur reaches a stage that requires hiring professional managers and formalizing their relationships on the basis of classical concepts. Later, upon diversification into varied industries, concepts of System 4 become more relevant.

Organization design tends to change as the characteristics of the economy and society change. In less developed societies, the supply of educated managers is scarce, reducing the possibilities of delegating authority to trained supervisors and developing skilled staffs of specialists. The classical approaches serve as the basis for structural decisions. As the workforce becomes more specialized and educated and subordinates develop aspirations for more involvement, demands for participative approaches increase. Thus structural guidelines must change to accommodate these aspirations. Transfers of structural concepts from one environmental setting to another therefore depend upon a careful study of the characteristics of both environments.

Contingency approaches to organization design are rapidly expanding. Empirical research is providing additional factors to be considered in adapting structure to the needs of the organization. Practitioners with little sophistication in design have experimented with unique approaches that have been successful. The result is that the subject of design has moved from a routine application of simple concepts to a challenging matching of designs to new technologies and environments.

CONCEPTS FUNDAMENTAL TO ORGANIZING

Certain basic concepts for organizing are important to all of the preceding theories. Authority, influence, power, identification, loyalties, and responsibility are six terms that have special meanings in the thinking of organizing. Furthermore, economists' assumptions used by economists about the economic man have evolved into a behavioral assumption commonly referred to as **administrative man**. These concepts provide additional foundations for organizational design.

Probably one of the most important and controversial contributions of modern theory involves the concept of authority. Barnard and Simon proposed an **acceptance theory of authority**, which states the view that a communication carries authority only if the receiver accepts it. This theory upset the traditional assumption that authority invariably flows from the top of a hierarchy. The apparent conflict in concepts of authority has resulted in two schools of thought on the subject. The conflict is not necessarily great, however, if one recognizes that the acceptance theory contributes a new perspective to the subject. One approach to reconciling the two theories would be to consider that a right to act which is delegated from the top must be met with the willingness and capacity to act which flows from below.

Several concepts related to authority are often confused with it. Persons with little or no authority may influence others through comments, advice, or suggestions, or by expediting, or blocking, the flow of information. For example, the secretary of a chief executive may have no authority over subordinates in the organization but may have great influence. **Influence** implies a voluntary, and even unconscious, manner of affecting the actions of others through persuasion, suggestion, and other methods. Organization can be described by determining the flow of influences in the decision-making process.

While the concept of authority remained important from its emphasis in classical theory and influence received special attention in participative approaches, the concept of power has only recently been emphasized. **Authority** is the right to act as indicated in the organizational hierarchy; **influence** is the effect of one person on the behavior of others. **Power** is the potential force that others perceive a person to possess that gives the capacity to influence actions of others. Power, then, is a psychological force that identifies the potential of a person as perceived by others. The design of structure helps to identify one's authority and the interrelationship for influencing others, but power is a more general term that includes other sources of potential force in the organization. For example, a person may be low in the hierarchy of authority and yet have significant power as a result of personal characteristics, associations with family or political connections, expert knowledge or strategic duties, or physical location at a particular time. Thus recognition of power centers is essential to effective organization design.

Still another concept useful in understanding organizations relates to the manner in which individuals decide to participate in an organization by accepting its goals as theirs. This concept is referred to as **identification** with the organization. The idea is that *self-involvement* of an individual is most important in organizational activities. At the time of a decision, this identification of the individual with the group enables the individual to accept the premises provided by the organization without the necessity of continually reappraising all the value judgments important in the situation.

Loyalties to an organization strengthen the tie of relationships between the individual and the organization. Loyalties help coordinate decisions by assuring that the members of an organization will act in a predictable pattern. Problems involving loyalties develop when the individual feels torn among the goals of different groups. At times the loyalty toward a narrow group—say, a particular department of a company—may conflict with the loyalty toward the broader group, the company.

Responsibility has always been an important concept in organization and usually refers to the obligation or duty of a person to act. Barnard, however, stressed the importance of **responsibility**, in broader terms, as the power of a personal code of morals to control the conduct of an individual. Organization behavior is affected by the entire moral framework of those within the organization. Effective organizational activities depend upon some common moral foundation.

The approach to organization (established in Chapter 4) depends upon the assumptions that one makes concerning the type of people who operate in an organization. Are they primarily rational beings? Do they try to maximize absolutely? Do they, by nature, like to fit into organizations, or do they naturally have conflicts with organizations?

The economist makes the assumption that people are economic, that they strive to maximize profits, and that they act rationally and intelligently toward their goals. The psychologist points out that people have emotions and often respond in non-rational ways. Organization theorists assume that the administrative man tries to be rational and that he attempts to find a satisfactory solution that may not necessarily be the optimum. Administrative man thus tries to act rationally, although conscious of limitations and tendencies to act in a non-rational manner.

**EVOLVING
ORGANIZATION DESIGNS** At the beginning of this chapter we outlined three classical types of organization: line, staff, and functional. Later, we have seen that decisions on structure depend upon many factors, including one's assumptions of the nature of man, differing technology, and varieties of environments. The result is that new designs have evolved: designs using a matrix approach, project organization, and grid organizations. This section will summarize these developments to indicate current responses to the theories and concepts discussed earlier.

The **matrix approach to organization** concentrates on three crucial variables: (1) the intrinsic properties of the task along a continuum from repetitive to unique, (2) the personality (norms and aspirations) and the competence (expertise) of the personnel within a unit, and (3) the institutional and/or historical circumstances associated with the unit. This approach identifies subsystems of a complex organization, each with its appropriate strategy of planning, control, rewards, and boundary negotiations. These subsystems are viewed along a continuum from dependence on hierarchical concepts to autonomous units or projects.

Based upon five observable characteristics of an organization—group structure, group roles, group processes, group style, and group norms—one recommendation of organizational design strategies provides the following guidelines: (1) a routine situation that deals with a task requiring similar or repetitive solutions, calling for Taylor's functional specialists in the design; (2) the engineering situation that deals with nonrepetitive solutions by personnel who are professionally educated, calling for professional staffs in the structure to advise line managers; (3) the craft situation that deals with uniquely different but repetitively processed outputs, calling for a flexible and person-oriented structure; (4) the heuristic situation that deals with unique and nonrepetitive tasks with output ill-defined, calling for a flexible and group design with considerable participation.

Project organization is one that can be tailored to a particular mission or project, to coordinate actions toward the completion of the project while retaining the advantages of functional specialists. Whereas the classical approach is built around authority centers and the participative approach is built around people, project organization is designed to meet the demands of a particular job. A functional specialist can be lent for a particular project and answer to the project manager as in a line organization. When the project is finished, however, the specialist returns to the functional department, thus retaining relationships with others in the specialty.

Project organization has been adopted to fit a number of widely differing situations, from building contractors and advertising agencies to accounting and consulting firms. Its suitability to modern complex projects makes it particularly valuable in meeting modern needs while retaining the stability of functional specialists. The structure accommodates the formal ideas of classical thinking, together with the team and participative ideas.

With the rapid development of multinational firms, a third design has evolved that uses the matrix approach. Multinational firms typically have used one of three bases for developing their design: grouping functional specialists such as production, marketing, and finance together; geographical groupings by continents or regions; product groupings with similar products in distinct divisions which operate globally. The problem in using any one of these is that there are rational advantages for each and yet each has definite shortcomings. For example, if geographical divisions are used as the primary basis for top-level organization, each division must have duplicate product specialists and functional specialists. Coordination suffers, and duplication of specialists raises costs. Several multinational firms, including General Electric, have experimented with **grid organization.** This design attempts to assign responsibilities on one of the above three bases, such as product divisions, while retaining geographical responsibilities under a collateral group of departments and attempting to provide functional specialization in a third set of departments. The result is, of course, a complex and overlapping flow of authority down in the organization, with resultant coordinating problems. However, the grid organization recognizes that multinational firms must attempt to maintain a consistent global approach while at the same time encouraging adaptability to differing national environmental situations.

STAFFING— HUMAN RESOURCE ADMINISTRATION

Any organizational structure requires a variety of people, and the supply of people consists of differing types. The **staffing function** includes the process by which the right person is placed in the right organizational position. **Human resource administration** involves matching the jobs and people through preparation of specifications necessary for positions, appraising the performance of personnel, training and retraining of people to fit the needs of the organizational positions, and developing methods by which people will respond with maximum effort and increased satisfaction. Often the organization structure includes a special functional department to administer the program. This often is called the personnel or industrial relations department.

The functional aspects of **personnel management** include recruitment of personnel, placement of personnel in the proper positions in the structure, training and development of personnel to suit the needs of the organization, and service activities directly related to the welfare of personnel.

Formal routines and techniques have been developed for the rationalization of the personnel functions. Interviewing techniques have received considerable attention. The development and standardization of tests to measure aptitude, achievement, and personality have provided management with additional tools for providing objectivity in the process. **Job evaluation** has remained an important process in its use of job descriptions, job specifications, and job analysis. **Merit rating** systems have formalized procedures of evaluation of performance in a specific job for purposes of pay increases and promotions.

After the needs of the organization are determined through establishing a rational job structure by means of detailed job descriptions and analysis of facts about the jobs, staffing involves locating suitable people to fit the jobs. Recruitment of personnel involves the use of several general techniques, including (1) personal data sheets or resumes; (2) batteries of tests measuring achievement, aptitude, proficiency, personality, and interests; and (3) interviews with the screened prospective candidates. These techniques are described in specialized literature on personnel management.[4]

After the personnel are hired, the staffing function shifts to administering the human assets of the organization by planning and implementing a system of performance appraisal. Concurrent with this appraisal is the development of a compensation system which will reward the personnel in an equitable and feasible manner.

As a result of demands of the organization for continual improvement of qualifications, the staffing function devotes a large portion of its efforts to special programs of training and development. These efforts include use of orientation sessions, apprentice training, programed instruction, formal short courses administered by the organization, and support of continuing education offered by educational institutions.

Human resource administration, furthermore, deals with handling grievances and the resolution of conflicts of personnel in their performance of duties. Suggestions systems, grievance procedures in conjunction with union representatives in organized plants, and improved participation of employees are techniques available for this part of the function.

Manpower planning and forecasting future needs of the organization have received increased attention. Systems by which replacements are trained for each position are often elaborate. For example, many firms use a threefold approach to planning for each position: development of the present occupant of the position, a trained replacement who can take over

---

[4]For a concise summary of these techniques, see Joseph L. Massie and John Douglas, *Managing: A Contemporary Introduction* (Englewood Cliffs, N.J.: Prentice-Hall, Inc., 1977).

immediately if needed, and a third person who is being trained for the position and who can be available within a specified period of time.

The details of the above administrative systems of human resource administration are beyond the scope of this book. However, many of the fundamental behavioral topics will be covered in Chapter 11.

REFERENCES

BARNARD, CHESTER I., *The Functions of the Executive.* Cambridge, Mass.: Harvard University Press, 1938.

CHANDLER, A., *Strategy and Structure.* Cambridge, Mass.: The M.I.T. Press, 1962.

DALE, ERNEST, *Planning and Developing the Company Organization Structure.* New York: American Management Association, 1952.

LAWRENCE, P. and J. LORSCH, *Organization and Environment.* Boston: Division of Research, Graduate School of Business, Harvard University, 1967.

LIKERT, RENSIS, *New Patterns of Management.* New York: McGraw-Hill Book Company, 1961.

MARCH, JAMES G., *Handbook of Organizations.* Chicago: Rand McNally & Company, 1965.

―――― and HERBERT A. SIMON, *Organizations.* New York: John Wiley & Sons, 1958.

PERROW, C., *Organization Analysis: A Sociological View.* Belmont, Calif.: Wadsworth Publishing Co. 1970.

SIMON, HERBERT A., *Administrative Behavior* (2nd ed.). New York: The Macmillan Company, 1957.

THOMPSON, J. D., ed., *Approaches to Organizational Design.* Pittsburgh: University of Pittsburgh Press, 1966.

WOODWARD, JOAN, *Industrial Organization: Theory and Practice.* London: Oxford University Press, 1965.

7

PLANNING
AND
CONTROLLING

⟸ **IDEAS TO BE FOUND** ⟹
IN THIS CHAPTER

- Meaning and importance of planning
- Planning principles
- Essential elements of any control system
- Principles of control

Two closely related functions of management will be discussed together in this chapter. Planning looks to the future; controlling checks the past. The two, thus, jointly serve as perspectives for the manager who makes decisions in the present. Both have been the subjects of considerable research and both have developed separate theories.

PLANNING   **Planning** is the process by which a manager looks to the future and discovers alternative courses of action. This chapter outlines those essentials of planning that serve as common threads of thought throughout any discussion of management. Some techniques and applications will be discussed in later chapters.

Importance and   The planning function has received
Nature of Planning   increased attention as organizations have grown and management theory has developed. The need for planning becomes more obvious as persons and organizations develop an awareness of the precise nature of their objectives. Therefore, the first

stage of any type of planning is the conscious and explicit statement of the ultimate objectives.

Planning pervades management. Plans from the view of the top levels of an organization may be overall and broad or they may be the detailed day-to-day type, important to the individual employee. Planning at all levels of an organization is desirable.

Planning is that function of management in which a conscious choice of patterns of influence is determined for decision makers so that the many decisions will be coordinated for some period of time and will be directed toward the chosen broad goals. The process of planning may begin with a vague hunch or an element of intuition on the part of an individual or a group; yet, good managers will visualize quickly a clear pattern for handling current thought about future actions. In planning for group action, this pattern must provide a reference for all members of the group. Each member need not understand all the details of all related plans, but must comprehend how that member's own detailed plans fit into the general overall plan.

A **plan** is a predetermined course of action. Plans may be tailored to a specific project, or they may be established as standing plans for any future actions. If prospective actions appear to be routine, standard operating procedures have the advantages of economizing on thought processes and making control more uniform. Checklists, developed after considerable detailed study of a routine set of actions, can serve as a predetermined pattern, which will insure correct future action with a minimum of rethinking on the part of the operator. Emergency fire plans and the detailed countdown program in missile firing are illustrations of standard procedures.

Planning not only involves predetermining a course of action to be taken, relative to a known event, but includes mentally searching for possibilities of future problems that might appear. Techniques of handling uncertainty are extremely valuable. If the probability of the occurrence of several events is great enough, alternative plans might be developed. The economics of alternative uses of the managers' time governs the extent to which alternative plans are desirable. A small business, with limited resources, may devote less time to detailed planning than will a large firm, with its planning staff.

Plans become premises for decisions to be made in the future. Planning provides frames of reference for decisions of individuals in an organization. Policies, as guides to decisions and actions, depend upon the deliberate planning of future possibilities.

The increased importance of planning in a business enterprise is the direct result of the changing environment in which the enterprise operates. The modern manager must continually anticipate changes which will require discarding old ways and adopting new ones. Thus, the need for planning results from various changes in the environment. The aspects of this changing environment are:

1. Changes in technology.
2. Changes in government policy.
3. Changes in overall economic activity, including prices, employment of labor, raw materials, etc.
4. Changes in the nature of competition.
5. Changes in social norms and attitudes.

A Model
for Planning

Scientific managers, starting with Taylor, have advocated that the planning function be separated from actual performance. Because line executives have limited time available, the function tends to be delegated to specialists. This delegation helps to set aside time for planning and avoids continual "fighting of fires," caused by the failure to think in advance. However, the use of planning specialists increases the need for means by which a set of plans by one group of specialists can be coordinated with plans set by another group of specialists.

The planning process can be viewed systematically as composed of five elements. Each of these elements may be handled by different groups of people, as indicated in the following outline of the model:[1]

I. *Setting Primary and Intermediate Goals.* The primary goals are affected by the personal values of the top management. The principal goal setters in a business firm are the board of directors, president, executive committees, and stockholders. The intermediate goals help to clarify the primary goals and are usually set by vice-presidents, general managers and functional specialists. Examples of intermediate goals are diversification of a product line, concentration on production of a limited line of products, reasonable prices, volume production, and so on.

II. *Search for Opportunities.* The search or scanning element is primarily a data-collecting function in which a group of specialists directs its attention toward discovering in the environment opportunities for the firm's activities. This element includes forecasting events in the future and identifying changes in demand, competition, technology, finances, and industrial structure. The principal searchers are market researchers, economic forecasters, research

[1]For further details, see W. Warren Haynes, Joseph L. Massie, and Marc Wallace, *Management: Analysis, Concepts, and Cases,* 3rd ed. (Englewood Cliffs, N.J.: Prentice-Hall, Inc., 1975), Chapter 11.

and development scientists, and other technical specialists who influence planning.

III. *Formulators of Plans.* The formulators of plans usually are grouped together and consider themselves as *the* planners, since it is they who translate or convert the opportunities discovered through search into strategies and policies which are directed toward the primary and intermediate goals. Formulators in a firm are generally called planners, program developers, or assistants to the line manager.

IV. *Target Setters.* In the implementation of plans there is the indispensible group of people who influence the carrying out of the plans and thus are in a position subtly to change elements of the plan or to ignore certain parts. The target setters are usually the line or operational managers who translate the broader plans into specific and detailed quantities and times for the many decision makers and workers. This stage of planning involves all levels of management and ultimately has an impact on the workers in planning their own activities.

V. *Followup of Plan.* Unless there is a mechanism in a planning model to check whether the actual performance is related to the estimated activities, planning can result in considerable thought without any direct results. Operating the plan involves continual checks to determine whether the plan actually results in performance consistent with the original previous thinking.

The element of *time* must be considered in planning. First, it takes time to prepare plans. The complexity of the subject planned and the techniques used affect this time. Broad plans, involving a number of specialists and departments, need extra time for coordination. Second, the length of time between the preparation of plans and the beginning of implementation, often called lead time, may be significant. For example, in the automobile industry, the lead time for designing a new model is determined by other departments' need for completed designs before starting to plan for the raw material supply, purchase of new tools, and so on. Third, the time needed to place the plan into full effect is important, because the speed of implementation may affect the degree of details covered in the original preparation. Fourth, the length of the time period a manager attempts to plan for is a big question. Long-range plans may cover ten to twenty years; short-range plans may be for the next month or year.

The *cost* of planning necessarily affects the degree of specific details to be covered, the completeness of factors to be considered, the formality of necessary approval, and the amount of data to be studied. If there is little information available upon which to base plans, it may be economical to postpone planning until immediately before action is necessary. In other words, a master plan sets a pattern by which other plans can be developed quickly at a later date.

Programming is a recent development that increases precision in planning. A **program** is an explicit statement of steps to be taken in order to achieve an objective. The development of a program requires that the programmer anticipate the what, who, how, and when of action. The existence of a program enables the planner to test its workability prior to its actual use. With existing computers, a program can be checked out and operating conditions can be *simulated*. In this way, difficulties that may develop can be carefully considered in advance of actual implementation of the program.

Because planning is assumed to be a rational process of human beings, it is important to be aware of some of the psychological hazards that might be encountered. Several hazards are: (1) The imagination of a human being is conditioned by past experiences. Plans are usually confined to assumptions based upon past experiences of the planner. (2) Often, assumptions used in a plan are mistaken for "facts." If there is not enough time available to validate facts, assumptions can be made, but the planner should not confuse assumptions with facts. (3) Human beings are often reluctant to accept the unpleasant. If planning uncovers disagreeable factors, the planner should concentrate on accepting them and adjusting the planning accordingly. (4) The popularity of the humorous statement of **Murphy's Law**—i.e., if anything *can* go wrong, it *will* go wrong—has an interesting impact on planning processes, for it is possible to build into the plans adjustments for the probability that things will not work out as planned.

Useful Generalizations of Planning	Certain generalizations of planning may be useful guides for the manager:

1. A plan should be directed toward well-defined *objectives*. Unless plans help lead toward well-understood goals, performance in the future cannot result in purposive effort.

2. Plans made by different specialists should be *coordinated* through adequate communications among specialists. For example, a sales planning specialist must transmit to the production planners estimates of the amount of products that can be sold in order to balance production with sales.

3. Planning is a *prerequisite* to other functions of management. We shall see, in the next section, that the concept of control is meaningless without planning. Moreover, each of the other functions depends upon thinking in advance of execution.

4. Adaptation of plans to current actions demands continual *redrafting* of plans. If a firm makes a long-range plan covering ten years in the future, it should reconsider periodically—say, yearly—making changes warranted by new developments and extending the plan to cover the new ten-year period. This has been called the principle of navigational change, in which the analogy of tacking a sailing vessel is used. The firm continually "tacks" (shifts back and forth) to take advantage of immediate opportunities, yet gradually gets closer to its ultimate destination.

5. Planning pervades the hierarchy of an organization. Planning at lower levels tends to be detailed and for short periods in the future; planning at higher levels tends to be general and for long periods of time.

6. A manager should relate the degree of *commitment* of his resources to the need for definite plans. If a firm plans to construct a new building, which will tie up funds for an extended period of time, it should make its plans in some detail and for the time period in which the funds will be tied up. The "firmness" of a contract might indicate the degree of commitment. Options in a contract, short-term leasing, and buying rather than making one's products are some of the techniques that may be used to decrease the degree of commitment of resources and thus to decrease the need for detailed plans.

7. Plans should retain *flexibility*. Planning tends to preset a rigid course of action unless change is incorporated in plans. Alternative courses of action will help provide flexibility, though often only at extra cost.

With this understanding of the nature of the planning function and some of its useful generalizations, we now turn to a closely related function of management.

CONTROLLING   Many advancements in management are essentially improvements in the individual techniques of control. In this chapter, we collect and state the factors common to any type of control.

Control is the process that measures current performance and guides it toward some predetermined goal. The essence of control lies in checking existing actions against some desired results determined in the planning process.

Essential Elements
of Any
Control System

The essential elements of any control system are:

1. A *predetermined* goal, plan, policy, standard, norm, decision rule, criterion, or yardstick.
2. A means for *measuring* current activity (quantitatively, if possible).
3. A means of *comparing* current activity with a criterion.
4. Some means of *correcting* the current activity so as to achieve the desired result.

The first element of a control system involves the answer to the question: What *should* be the results? This element forces attention on the future and what is desired or expected. The attempt to predict future events provides the basis for interpreting the meaning of events when they actually occur. Even poor prediction provides a framework for better understanding of current experience. The predetermined criterion may even be set arbitrarily. The goal may be judged by others to be bad. A useful control system does not evaluate the goodness of the goal; it merely provides a means by which activity can be directed toward an actual goal.

The predetermined criterion should be stated explicitly. For this reason, quantitative statements are usually preferable. In production management, physical units, such as ton-miles of freight, units per machine-hour, or pounds of scrappage per unit of output, may provide a simple and direct yardstick for operations. In financial management, dollar values serve as explicit statements of norms. Often, financial managers use past achievements of the firm as crude yardsticks for controlling current operations, for example, the record of the past twelve months. The assumption is that past performance was not too bad and that if it can be equalled or surpassed, the firm will not decline. Marketing managers often use such industry data as benchmarks against which the company can compare its own sales efforts. They also develop quotas based on market potential to serve as predetermined goals.

The second element in any control system is the measurement of actual performance. This step usually requires the greatest attention and expense, because records and reports must be devised to present information in a form that will fit the control system. Measurements of actual performance must be in units similar to those of the predetermined criterion. Prompt reporting of actual performance increases the value of a control system. Recent improvements in data processing increase the speed of reporting this data.

The degree of accuracy to which measurement is carried will depend upon the needs of the specific application. All measurement is accurate only to some limited degree. There are many instances in management when it is desirable to round a number to emphasize important magnitudes. Concern over small errors might overshadow major factors and confuse the interpreter. The ability of a good manager to strike quickly at the heart of the meaning of past performance is a most important factor in successful management.

Comparison of a criterion with actual performance indicates variations in activity. This key step adds meaning to the data provided by the control process. Because some variation can be expected in all activity, a critical question facing a manager is the determination of what amount of variation is large enough to be significant and worth attention. If limits of variation are not clear, the manager may waste time studying unimportant problems while failing to give sufficient time to pertinent issues.

The method of presenting comparisons of performance with the predetermined goal is an important question. The simplest and most direct method is usually the best. Graphical techniques provide means of visualizing important relationships, uncluttered by insignificant details. Anyone who has attempted to interpret large volumes of quantitative data will recognize the sense of futility that develops unless some simplified approach can be devised.

This third element of a control system involves the study of relationships. Such techniques as ratios, trends, mathematical equations, and charts help add meaning to the measurements of actual performance by showing the relation of actual experience to the predetermined criterion.

The purpose of comparing past performance with planned performance is not only to determine when a mistake has been made but to enable the manager to *predict* future problems. A good control system will provide information quickly so that trouble can be prevented. A good manager will not be lulled into inactivity by success, but will remain alert to controls that indicate the need for some present action that will eliminate future potential problems before they develop.

The fourth element of a control system is the action phase of making corrections. This fourth element may involve a decision not to take any action—if the performance is "under control."

Two basic types of error face the manager taking corrective action: (1) taking action when no action is needed and (2) failing to take action when some corrective action is needed. A good control system should provide some basis for helping the manager estimate the risks of making either of these types of error. Of course, the final test of a control system is whether correct action is taken at the correct time.

Principles
of
Control

Certain basic ideas are useful in the development of a control system. Applications of these principles will appear in Chapter 14.

1. *Strategic Point Control.* Optimum control can be achieved only if critical, key, or limiting points can be identified and close attention directed to adjustments at those points. An attempt to control all points tends to increase unnecessary efforts and to decrease attention to important problems. This principle of control is closely related to the exception principle of organization. Both emphasize the discrimination between important and unimportant factors. Good control does not mean maximum control, for control is expensive. For example, the development of a good fire-control program in a forest depends upon the strategic placement of towers on hills. The haphazard addition of a large number of devices and people in the forest cannot yield an equal degree of control.

2. *Feedback.* The process of adjusting future actions on the basis of information about past performance is known as **feedback.** Although applications of the idea date back to controls on windmills, the fly-ball governor of Watt's steam engine, and the steering of steamships, recent developments in electronic hardware of automatic control have reenforced the importance of this principle. The electrical engineer refers to a **closed-loop system of feedback** when the information of actual performance is fed back to the source of energy by electrical or mechanical means in an endless chain. An **open-loop system of feedback** involves human intervention at some point in the flow. Management has many uses of the feedback principle in areas that, at first, appear to be unrelated.

3. *Flexible Control.* Any system of control must be responsive to changing conditions. Often, the importance of a control system demands that it be adaptable to new developments, including the failure of the control system itself. Plans may call for an automatic system to be backed up by a human system that would operate in an emergency; likewise, an automatic system may back up a human system.

4. *Organizational Suitability.* Controls should be tailored to fit the organization. The flow of information concerning current performance should correspond with the organizational structure employed. To be able to control overall operations, a superior must find a pattern that will provide control for individual parts. Budgets,

quotas, and other techniques may be useful in controlling separate departments.

5. *Self-control.* Units may be planned to control themselves. If a department can have its own goals and control system, much of the detailed controls can be handled within the department. These subsystems of self-control can then be tied together by the overall control system.

6. *Direct Control.* Any control system should be designed to maintain direct contact between the controller and the controlled. Even when there are a number of control systems provided by staff specialists, the supervisor at the first level is still important because of having direct knowledge of performance.

7. *Human Factor.* Any control system involving people is affected by the psychological manner in which human beings view the system. A technically well-designed control system may fail because the human being reacts unfavorably to the system. For example, a dynamic and imaginative leader tends to resist control. Controls for such a person demand special attention to the human factor.

The essentials of any control system and the principles of control provide a sound basis for a manager; planning is a prerequisite for this important managerial function. Control is closely related to the communication function, which is discussed in the next chapter.

REFERENCES

HAYNES, W. W., J. L. MASSIE and MARC WALLACE, *Management: Analysis, Concepts and Cases* (3rd ed.). Englewood Cliffs, N.J.: Prentice-Hall, Inc., 1975.

JEROME, W. T., *Executive Control.* New York: John Wiley & Sons, Inc., 1961.

LE BRETON, PRESTON P. and DALE A. HENNING, *Planning Theory.* Englewood Cliffs, N.J.: Prentice-Hall, Inc., 1961.

NEWMAN, W. H., C. E. SUMMER and E. KIRBY WARREN, *The Process of Management* (4th Ed.). Englewood Cliffs, N.J.: Prentice-Hall, Inc., 1977.

STEINER, GEORGE, *Top Management Planning.* New York: The Macmillan Company, 1969.

8

COMMUNICATING AND DIRECTING

<== IDEAS TO BE FOUND ==>
IN THIS CHAPTER

- Communication problems
- Communication networks
- Nature and meaning of directing
- Types of leadership
- Supervision

In this chapter, we complete the discussion of the seven functions of the managerial process by focusing attention on communicating and directing. Communicating provides a link among all the other functions; directing (or supervision) initiates actual performance and depends upon different leadership styles.

COMMUNICATING   Managers spend a major percentage of their time transmitting their ideas to others, orally and in writing. They most often use the symbols of their language but also employ mathematical symbols, codes, graphical devices, electronic impulses, and other media for expressing their ideas. Other managerial functions, especially controlling and organizing, involve communication problems. Communication serves as a linking process by which parts of a system are tied together. The subject has received the attention of many specialists, including the technical communications engineer, the linguist, the psychologist, the sociologist, and the organization theorists.

Types of Communication Problems

All communication problems can be treated in three basic groups:

1. The technical problem of how accurately the symbols can be transmitted.
2. The semantic problem of how the symbols convey the desired meaning.
3. The effectiveness problem of how meaning effects the desired results.

Cybernetics has contributed new insights into answers to the first group of problems. The terms in this new discipline have precise meaning to the communications engineer but may be confusing to a manager. Several important distinctions made by the communications engineer will provide an introduction to this interesting subject and will hint at some fundamental ideas of use to a manager in transmitting messages.

In cybernetics, information has nothing to do with meaning (the subject of the second group of problems). It is a quantitative measure of the amount of order in a system and is related not to what you *do* say but what you *can* say about a matter. If a system is highly disorganized, a message can say a great deal. **Information** is a measure of one's freedom of choice when one selects a message. If there is no freedom of choice, there is no information. If "Q" is always followed by a "U" in a language, "U" is perfectly predictable and, therefore, no information is added. The more probable a message is, the less information it gives. If a subordinate always sends his superior the message "Things are fine," the superior can predict the message before he receives it and thus receives no information. The more disordered a situation is, the more information is required to describe it completely.

The idea of **noise** in information theory includes the undesirable uncertainties in the transmission process. "Snow" on television, "static" on the radio, or any interference in the receipt of a message increases uncertainty. Redundancy is used to help combat noise and insure against mistakes. **Redundancy** is anything that makes the transmission more predictable. Redundancy provides some structure (the opposite of randomness) that will increase the probability that the message will be received. Because all transmission of messages is subject to the "loss of information" through noise, the sender of a message should always be conscious of the need for redundancy and the minimization of the number of times that the message is to be retransmitted.

The second group of communication problems involves the meaning that a message has to the receiver. A person may *say* one thing but the receiver may *hear* something different, even if the word sent and the word received are exactly the same. This is a matter of semantics. Securing understanding of a message is affected by a number of factors: (1) the similarity of past experiences of the sender and the receiver; (2) the environment in which the communication takes place; (3) the distinction between facts and opinions; (4) the degree of abstractness of the symbols used; and (5) the complexity of the phrases used. A manager must constantly check whether the *meaning* of his communications has been understood.

The third group of communication problems involves the effectiveness of the communication. Usually the more direct the communication, the more effective it will be. In organization, the number of levels through which a communication travels affects the action that is finally taken. Thus, the communication problem increases as the size of the firm increases. Of course, effectiveness of communications depends upon both efficient transmission of messages and the understanding of their meaning. In the final analysis, the acceptance of the communication is the key to effectiveness.

Acceptance of a communication by the receiver is a psychological phenomenon depending on the needs and past experience of the receiver and the environment in which the communication takes place. We all tend to hear what we want to hear and to reject what we do not want to hear. A communication will be accepted if it does not seriously conflict with the receiver's own goals. Usually a person has a broad "zone of acceptance" and will accept communications even without agreeing with the entire message. A person who feels a part of a well-developed working team will tend to accept many communications without consciously questioning them.

Flow
of
Communications

Three types of communications in an organization can be classified by their flow: vertical, horizontal, and informal. In directing activities of subordinates, the manager issues orders to others further down in the hierarchy. Organization charts show the flow of authority and the channels through which this downward, vertical communication flows. Authority lines are important channels of communication, but they comprise only one type of channel. Control reports and memoranda flow back up through the levels of the hierarchy as subordinates are made accountable for their actions. This upward vertical flow of communications is the heart of a control system.

Horizontal channels provide means by which managers on the same level of an organization coordinate their activities without referring all matters to their superior. One writer has called this a "gang plank." His idea was that many matters can be handled on the same level of an organization, thereby speeding action while at the same time relieving superiors of unnecessary problems. Multiple copies of memoranda that flow to all positions needing the information increase coordination of effort.

Formal communications are planned to meet the specific needs of the organization; however, many communications are informal. The "grapevine" may be helpful for the attainment of organizational goals, but it also serves the social needs of the individuals in the organization. A manager can utilize the grapevine as a positive aid, but may also face problems of rumors, gossip, and other negative outlets of expressions by people in the organization. The grapevine cannot be destroyed; therefore, it should receive conscious attention. Informal channels may be superior for some organizational purposes. A "word" can be dropped at the proper time and may remedy a disciplinary problem without resort to a formal reprimand. Because the speed at which information flows through a grapevine is often astounding, management must seriously consider this third type of communication.

Communication may be viewed as a pattern of interconnecting lines, referred to as **networks**. We have already seen an example of one type of network in the illustration of feedback. Researchers have experimented with various structural patterns of communications in small groups. Figure 8-1 illustrates some possibilities. The simple, direct, one-direction network in Figure 8-1a tends to be speedier and less disorderly. The star, or circular, network in Figure 8-1b provides the individual with more choice of channels and offers more satisfaction; yet it tends to be slower, noisier, and, on first observation, more disorganized. The serial and radial network of Figure 8-1c insulates the chief from overt criticism by the lowest level and places the intermediate superior in a position of considerable power. Of course, there are many other networks that may be used. Analysis of communications networks offers a means by which a manager can study the flow of communication and choose the type best adapted to a given situation.

Communication Problems of communication directly
Barriers retard the success of managers in the performance of their functions. If messages are poorly transmitted, or if the action is not effected, management cannot plan or control activities properly. The barriers to good communication require constant attention. Some of these barriers and remedies will now be considered.

Distortion may be a matter of noise in transmission or it may result from inadequacy of the words in carrying the precise ideas of the sender. If an accountant submits a report on "costs" to an economist, distortion may result because of differences in meanings of the word "costs." If the

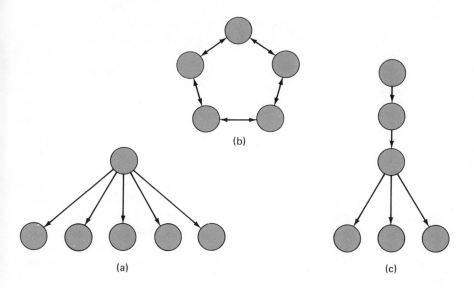

Figure 8-1
Types of Communication Networks

industrial engineer receives the report, he may get ideas entirely different from those of the accountant or economist. The financial manager will view "costs" as outgo of funds; the production manager may think of unit costs of the manufactured product; the marketing manager will think of costs as part of the total selling price; the industrial relations manager may view "costs" as a social factor of employment. Each of these specialists will tend to have different frames of reference within which to interpret a report.

An important means of overcoming the distortion barrier is to expand the horizons of each member of the management team so that each can understand the meaning in the minds of other members. Another means is to use what the psychologist calls **empathy**—attempt to project oneself into the viewpoint of the other person. A major step in handling distortion is the development of an awareness that some degree of distortion always exists.

Filtering is a barrier to communication that takes the form of intentionally sifting the information so that the receiver will look favorably on the message. No one likes to admit mistakes to some one else, especially to the boss. The boss, on the other hand, wants to secure information about what is actually going on, especially those actions that need attention. If management is not careful, it may encourage a free flow of just those messages that provide little information. The remedies for filtering are a well-designed control system, the development of rapport with subordinates, listening to subordinates with an understanding attitude, reducing the fear of failure, and increasing the awareness of management to problems of subordinates.

Overloading of communication channels can cause the network to be jammed with irrelevant messages. Newer methods of processing and transmitting data have increased the number of communications which flow to executives. Managers can literally be buried in memoranda and reports with no hope of digging themselves out. The answer to this problem lies in monitoring the channels to clear messages in order of priority and importance. More messages do not necessarily mean more information. The communication system should provide for editing devices, or persons, to regulate the quality and quantity of communications with regard to sufficiency of information for decision centers.

Timing of communications can result in problems for management. Some types of messages need to be released so that everyone will receive them simultaneously. Other types of messages being transmitted should be timed sequentially so that receivers will not be confused by issues that are not important to them at the moment.

Routing of communications should provide sufficient information for a decision to be made by the proper persons. The route may determine the content of the message and the language in which it is stated. If official information is first received by the grapevine, or from persons outside the organization, the employee may be placed in an insecure position. If a supervisor receives information from subordinates, it signifies a short circuit in the line of communication from top management, and thus threatens the supervisor's status and authority. The answers to the problem are in the proper planning of a communication system and in the recognition of its human elements.

Determination of the flow of communications and recognition of the many barriers to good communication are basic to the communicating function. Communication networks, communication channels, and barriers to communication must continually receive attention.

DIRECTING   Directing, the last of the seven functions of management discussed in this part, is the heart of the managerial process, because it is involved with initiating action. Other terms identifying the same idea are leading, executing, supervising, ordering, and guiding. Whatever term is used, the idea is to put into effect the decisions, plans, and programs that have previously been worked out for achieving the goals of the group.

Directing concerns the total manner in which a manager influences actions of subordinates. First, it includes the issuing of orders that are clear, complete, and within the capabilities of subordinates to accomplish. Second, it implies a continual training activity in which subordinates are given instructions to enable them to carry out the particular assignment in the existing situation. Third, it necessarily involves the motivation of workers to try to meet the expectations of the manager. Fourth, it consists of maintaining discipline and rewarding those who perform properly. In short, directing is the final action of a manager in getting others to act after all preparations have been completed.

The manner in which activities are directed depends upon the manager's own personal *traits* and the *situation* involved. In direction, more than any other function, the manager must determine an approach alone, after surveying the possibilities that are open. Each manager will do well to act as an individual and not to try to act as others act or to proceed according to the textbook. Moreover, a manager will be involved in various situations calling for different approaches in directing. If subordinates are unskilled and need detailed instructions, the manager may find the direct, simple order advisable. If the subordinates are highly educated persons in a research activity, a permissive and consultative approach may be advisable. In cases of emergency, the manager may assume a "take charge" role and give short, clear authoritative commands, whereas if action is not pressing, a deliberate and analytical attitude may be appropriate.

A large amount of research has been directed toward finding the characteristic types of leaders that are most effective. Much of this research has been carried out in the behavioral sciences and will be discussed in Chapter 11. Different leadership types have been identified and provide a framework for a manager in selecting an approach to directing. For some time the types of leadership were grouped under four headings: (1) the dictatorial leader, (2) the benevolent-autocratic leader, (3) the democratic leader, and (4) the laissez-faire leader.

The dictatorial leader accomplishes tasks through fear of penalties, and maintains a highly critical and negative attitude in relations with subordinates. As boss, such a person expects subordinates to perform well or be subject to punishment or replacement. At times, this approach apparently is effective in the short run, but it does not provide a solid foundation for continued performance, because it does not provide lasting satisfaction for those being led.

The benevolent-autocratic leader assumes a paternalistic role which forces subordinates to rely on the leader for their satisfactions. If this type of leadership is to be successful, the leader must be an exceptionally strong and wise individual who, by force of personality, generates respect and allegiance. The satisfactions of the subordinates of this type of leader depend solely on the good will of their superior. Because this leader makes decisions without the participation of others, subordinates have little chance to develop leadership qualities. This type results in dependency on the continued presence of the leader, and work deteriorates when that person is absent.

Democratic leaders depend not only on their own capabilities but encourage consultation with subordinates. Subordinates are invited to participate in planning, decision making, and organizing. They tend to venture on their own initiative and to communicate freely with their fellow subordinates. This type of leadership results in a cooperative spirit and the development of managerial abilities on the part of subordinates. Satisfaction is gained through a feeling of group accomplishment.

The laissez-faire leader depends completely on subordinates to establish their own goals and to make their own decisions. This leader assumes the role of just another member of the group. Under these conditions members of the group are permitted to act individually and, therefore, may easily head in different directions.

The manager, in developing an individual style of leadership, need not be limited to choices from among the above four classes. Tannenbaum has argued that the style a manager chooses depends upon three groups of forces: (1) forces in the manager, e.g., the manager's value system, confidence in subordinates, inclinations, and feeling of security in an uncertain situation: (2) forces in the subordinate, e.g., subordinates expectations; and (3) forces in the situation, e.g., type of organization, the nature of the problems, and the pressure of time. Given these forces, leadership behavior can be viewed along a continuum from "boss-centered" to "subordinate-centered" leadership. Moving from the boss-centered to subordinate-centered, one can observe the following styles:

1. The manager makes the decision and announces it.
2. The manager "sells" the decision.
3. The manager presents ideas, invites questions.
4. The manager presents a tentative decision subject to change.
5. The manager presents the problem.
6. The manager defines the limits and requests the group to make a decision.

7. The manager permits the group to make decisions within pre-scribed limits.

Leadership styles depend upon which set of assumptions about human behavior the manager uses. In Chapter 6 we have seen that Douglas McGregor summarizes two sets which he calls Theory X and Y assumptions.[1] Blake and Mouton[2] have developed **a managerial grid** which cross-classifies managerial styles according to the degree to which the manager exhibits concern for subordinates (which they call consideration) and concern for production (which they call initiating structure). For example, on this grid a 9,9 style indicates high concern for employees and high emphasis on production.

The current approach to leadership styles is to emphasize the contingency approach, that is, to attempt to adapt a particular style to the situation faced by the leader. Most current works view leadership styles along a continuum from extreme employee orientation to extreme task orientation. Fred Fiedler,[3] probably the most influential theorist and researcher, recognizes that leadership effectiveness is multidimensional and that the style used in practice depends upon the situation. He identifies three situational factors as important determinants: (1) leader-member relations (the degree of confidence and loyalty of members in regard to the leader), (2) task structure (the degree to which tasks are routinized), and (3) position power (the amount of formal authority and support by upper management held by the leader).

Practicing managers can be helped by analyzing the above approaches to leadership styles; however, they must develop their own viewpoint after considering their own assumptions and inclinations and adapting them to each situation.

The traits, skills, and approaches of leadership are essential considerations in the directing function. No amount of analyzing, talking, thinking, and preparing will substitute for executive action.

Supervision The directing function includes all processes for initiating action. A part of this function is called **supervision** when the manager is in direct physical contact with nonmanagers. Supervision literally means overseeing and thus implies that there is face-to-face contact. All levels of management usually are engaged in some face-to-face contact with subordinates,

[1] For further information see Douglas McGregor, *The Human Side of Enterprise* (New York: McGraw-Hill Book Company, Inc., 1960), pp. 33-35, 45-49.

[2] Robert R. Blake and Jane S. Mouton, *The Managerial Grid* (Houston: Gulf Publishing Company, 1964).

[3] Fred Fiedler, *A Theory of Leadership Effectiveness* (New York: McGraw-Hill Book Co. 1967).

even if only with a private secretary, but the lowest managers have as their primary duty the supervision of workers in basic operations. This level is composed of supervisors, foremen, and section bosses.

In simple line organizations, the supervisor must perform all the functions of management. Even in highly functional organizations in which planning, controlling, organizing, communicating, staffing, and decision making are handled by specialists, the supervisor will contribute to these functions, even if only in a small way. For example, in a highly developed control system, using mechanical and electronic devices as well as inspectors and other specialists, the supervisor retains the residual control function of personally seeing that performance is accomplished in line with predetermined criteria. Moreover, the supervisor is the key person on the spot when corrective action must be taken.

It is often said that the most critical element in the management of a firm is the supervisor. This remains true even in cases where many staff departments are available for help. Therefore, the training of supervisors continues to be a most important problem for management. Numerous approaches have been used successfully in training programs for supervisors, including special schools, experience on the job, and individual reading plans. In terms of numbers of persons, supervisor training is the biggest challenge to management education.

The importance of the supervisor's position is increased by the uniqueness of this position in the management hierarchy. It is the major link between management and actual operations. The supervisor's task is made more difficult by the fact that to the individual worker the supervisor *is* the management. Having daily contact with the workers and interpreting company policies place the supervisor in a strategic position, as an important medium through which the workers can communicate with top management. Any failure on the part of a supervisor to represent workers to management may cause the workers to seek supplemental channels.

This overview of the functions of management provides a framework for looking to the many disciplines that can help improve the management process. The basic concepts and the results of continuing research in these disciplines will be summarized in the next part of this book.

REFERENCES

BLAKE, ROBERT R. and JANE S. MOUTON, *The Managerial Grid.* Houston, Texas: Gulf Publishing, 1964.

FIEDLER, FRED, *A Theory of Leadership Effectiveness.* New York: McGraw-Hill Book Company, Inc., 1967.

JOHNSON, RICHARD A., FREEMONT E. KAST and JAMES E. ROSENZWEIG, *The Theory and Management of Systems* (3rd ed.). New York: McGraw-Hill Book Company, Inc. 1973.

KOONTZ, HAROLD and C. O'DONNELL, *Essentials of Management*. New York: McGraw-Hill Book Company, Inc., 1974.

MCGREGOR, DOUGLAS, *The Human Side of Enterprise*. New York: McGraw-Hill Book Company, Inc., 1960.

NEWMAN, WILLIAM H., *Administrative Action* (2nd ed.). Englewood Cliffs, N.J.: Prentice-Hall, Inc., 1963.

————, C. E. SUMMER and E. KIRBY WARREN, *The Process of Management* (4th ed.). Englewood Cliffs, N.J.: Prentice-Hall, Inc., 1977.

TANNENBAUM, ROBERT and W. H. SCHMIDT, "How to Choose a Leadership Pattern," *Harvard Business Review*, 36, No. 2 (March-April 1958), 95-101.

WIENER, NORBERT, *The Human Use of Human Beings: Cybernetics and Society* (2nd ed.). Garden City, N.Y.: Doubleday Anchor Books, 1954.

PART

3

DISCIPLINARY FOUNDATIONS FOR MANAGERS

Although management is a separate field of study, it has benefited greatly from research in a number of other disciplines. This interdisciplinary relationship has been encouraged in several ways. On one hand, a number of students in other fields have concentrated on management problems while remaining in their respective fields. On the other hand, some students trained in other disciplines have transferred to the management field, bringing with them new viewpoints and techniques. Both trends promise that management in the future will be built on a broad foundation of disciplines.

Many disciplines have interests in common with those of management. The history of business enterprises has received considerable attention from historians as well as management specialists. Theologians have shown new interests in the moral and ethical problems of managers. The legal profession has attempted research on decision making (by juries) and other subjects having implications for management. Other disciplines also have interests related to management, but the contributions of the five most important will be summarized in Part 3: managerial economics, managerial accounting, the quantitative disciplines of mathematics and statistics, the behavioral sciences especially psychology and sociology, and computer science. Accounting has always been related to management, but in the last two decades accounting has come closer to helping management perform its functions. A sizable section of economics today concentrates on those economic principles of particular importance to managers. Two groups of disciplines which recently have concentrated on improvements in management are the quantitative fields (for example, mathematics and statistics) and the behavioral sciences. The last discipline discussed in Part 3, systems and computer science, has emerged only in the last three decades. The roots of management, therefore, are in these five fields of study. Any treatment of the essentials of management necessarily must discuss these subjects, often considered to be parts of other disciplines but more recently recognized as integral parts of the field of management.

9

MANAGERIAL ECONOMICS

Economics and business management have always been closely related; in fact, most schools of business have their origins in departments of economics. Yet the viewpoints of the economist and the manager have, until recently, been different. The economist has been concerned chiefly with the functioning of the economy as a whole and social issues such as monopoly and competition, tax policy, the pricing system, and the distribution of income. The manager has been concerned primarily with maximization of profits, from the viewpoint of the individual firm, and with such company policies as pricing, wage payments, market share, and employment of resources. Both the economist and the manager, nevertheless, face similar problems of using scarce resources in the satisfaction of human wants. Both concentrate on the analysis of demand characteristics and supply factors, but the manager must orient his thoughts to making decisions in business operations. **Managerial economics**, therefore, may be defined as the management's application of economic principles in the decision-making process.

This chapter will deal with those economic questions in which a manager's discretion is of greatest importance. It will not deal with those economic questions over which the manager has little control. Of course, all managers should have a knowledge of the economic system in which they operate and should understand the institutional setting and the environment of the industry to which they must adjust. This broader subject, however, is not within the scope of this book.

The simplest meaning of **profit** is the revenue that is left over after all costs are subtracted. Even this definition becomes complicated when we attempt to define the two important terms: revenue and costs. The analysis relating to these terms will provide the heart of this chapter: Revenue is determined by the demand factors affecting the quantity of items that can be sold at various prices; cost is a component of the supply function over which the managers have control. The simplest approach for showing the relationship of revenue to cost is the breakeven chart.

BREAKEVEN ANALYSIS

Revenue and cost can be studied by directing attention to: (1) total revenue and total cost, (2) average revenue and average cost per unit of output, and (3) changes in revenue and cost. Breakeven analysis directs attention to the first of these. Breakeven analysis implies that at some point in the operations total revenue equals total cost—the breakeven point. This analysis can be handled algebraically or graphically; however, in all cases, the first step is to classify costs into at least two types—fixed and variable.

Distinction Between Fixed and Variable Costs

The manager has long recognized that, during a given period of time, some costs are subject to change as the rate of production changes and other costs will continue unchanged. If the time period is extremely short—say, one minute—all costs will remain unchanged or fixed. If the time period is very long—say, ten years—all costs will be subject to change. Generally, it is useful to use a time period, which economists call the **short run**, in which it is possible to vary the rate of production but which is so short that the capacity or scale of operations cannot be changed. In this period, some costs will be **variable** as a result of a change in rate of operations (for example, materials and direct labor) but other costs will be **fixed** (that is, will remain constant regardless of the quantity of output). The manager continually is faced with decisions in which the classification of total costs into variable and fixed costs will help focus attention to the correct costs.

The distinction between total fixed and total variable costs stresses that only variable costs will increase with an increase in the production rate of output. However, it should be clear that when average cost *per unit* is considered, fixed cost per unit of output will *decline* as volume increases—the constant fixed costs are spread over more units of output. Variable costs per unit of output may increase proportionally with an increase in output (which will be the assumption in the breakeven charts in this chapter), or they may decrease per unit of output (for example, if quantity discounts are significant), or they may increase per unit of output (if the quantity of materials is very short and thus price increases as output increases). In most industries, variable costs per unit can reasonably be assumed to be constant, and thus total variable costs will appear as a straight line (linear) when plotted against various quantities of output.

The process of classifying costs into fixed and variable costs is a necessary first step in breakeven analysis. At times, this process is complicated by the fact that the types of costs being classified may be partly fixed and partly variable (semi-fixed costs). For example, electrical current may be used partly for lighting the plant (fixed) and also for running machines that may be turned off if output declines (variable). In such cases, additional breakdowns of costs may be necessary in order to segregate fixed from variable. If there is no basis for additional breakdowns, the manager may resort to using judgment (or analysis of past experience) and to considering some fraction of the type of costs as fixed and the other fraction as variable. For example, if it appears that maintenance costs are partly fixed and partly variable, the manager may take some percentage of maintenance costs as fixed and some percentage as variable. In any case, a clear distinction between fixed and variable costs must be made in order to secure the value of breakeven analysis.

Construction of a Breakeven Chart

The cost-volume-profit relationship can best be visualized by charting the variables. A **breakeven chart** is a graphical representation of the relationship between costs and revenue *at a given time*. Figure 9-1 is one form in which the chart typically appears. Fixed costs also may be drawn below variable costs, in which case the fixed-cost line will be horizontal with the X axis.

The simplest breakeven chart makes use of straight lines that represent revenue, variable costs, and total costs. The construction of this chart requires only that the costs and revenue be known at two points (volumes of output), because only two points are required to draw a straight line. The points at the Y intercept (left-hand side of chart) are given by definition: Revenue line will start at zero at zero volume; variable costs also will start at zero at zero volume; fixed costs will be a given level on the Y axis because, by definition, they would continue even if there were no production. Cost and revenue data at an actual volume level provide the basis for the necessary second point. All other points on the lines are the result of the assumption of linear relationships for both revenue and costs.

This simple analytical device is very useful if interpreted properly but can cause trouble if certain assumptions, upon which it is based, are forgotten. These assumptions are:

1. The linear revenue line indicates an assumption that the price at which any quantity of the output can be sold is fixed and does not change with output. (For example, points along the line merely indicate that Price P [$6.00 per unit] is multiplied by the number of items sold Q [100 units] to obtain Revenue R [$600].)
2. Variable costs vary proportionally with output.
3. The product mix (the percentage of each of the several types of products produced) remains constant.
4. The relationship is for a given point in time (and thus volumes, other than the ones used in the construction of the chart, are merely assumed values).
5. Fixed costs and variable costs are clearly distinguishable.

Interpretations of a Breakeven Chart The value of the breakeven chart is in the simple and straightforward manner in which it illustrates some important economic concepts. One obvious observation is that profits do not appear, if any costs are fixed, until a given volume of output is reached. Once the breakeven point is reached, profits appear and increase at a faster rate than do total costs.

The idea of **contribution toward fixed costs and profit** is clearly indicated in Figure 9-1. We can simply state that a decision to produce extra volume first depends upon whether the revenue will at least cover *variable costs*, provide extra funds to help cover fixed costs, and add to profits. This point appears so simple, in the interpretation of this break-even chart, that the reader may feel that there is nothing profound about the idea. Further deliberation on the question will indicate that this idea can be one of the most useful concepts for a manager to understand thoroughly.

Numerous applications of breakeven charts superimpose different charts (one useful way is by drawing with a grease pencil on acetate) over the basic chart. Each chart that is superimposed can graphically represent the effect of changing a single assumption. For example, if the problem is to determine the effect of an increase in price on profits per unit, a new revenue line (dashed line) will be drawn with a greater slope. If costs remain unchanged, the breakeven point will be at a lower volume and profits will increase (see Figure 9-2a). In a similar manner, a new chart that assumes an increase in fixed costs (possibly from the purchase of a

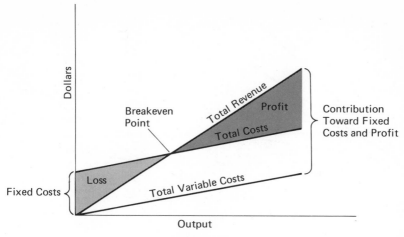

Figure 9-1
A Simple Breakeven Chart

new machine) will indicate the effect on the breakeven point and profits (see Figure 9-2b). In Figure 9-2c, the dashed lines indicate a prospective increase in variable cost (because a basic raw material has increased in price). In Figure 9-2d, the "stairstep" is caused by an increase in fixed cost at some volume of output because it is necessary to add a second shift with extra supervision or because there is an increase in light and heat. The manager will be able to visualize the effect of many possible decisions before actually making them, by using a breakeven chart.

Several formulas for computing the breakeven point make it possible to compute the exact value without making a chart. The formulas also aid in understanding the relationships of fixed and variable costs and revenue, because the formulas are merely common-sense expressions, in symbols, of assumed relationships. The formulas are:

$$\text{Breakeven Point} = \frac{\text{Total Fixed Cost}}{1 - \dfrac{\text{Variable Cost}}{\text{Sales}}} \quad \text{or} \quad \frac{\text{Total Fixed Cost}}{\text{Profit Margin as \%}}$$

$$\text{Sales} = \text{Fixed Costs} + (\text{Variable Costs as a \% of Sales}) \text{ Sales}$$

COST PRINCIPLES

Computation of profit is directly affected by the determination of what costs should be subtracted from total revenue. Because the conditions under which one decision is made may differ from the conditions under which another decision is made, it should be clear that costs should be tailored to a given decision. To an econo-

113

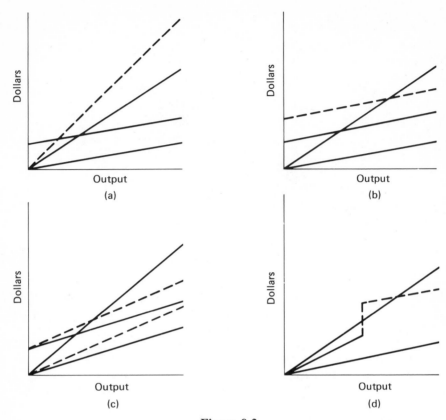

Figure 9-2
Interpretation Using Breakeven Charts

mist, the basic idea of **cost** is that it is a *sacrifice*. Measurement of cost involves an attempt to determine the amount of sacrifice that will be made in a particular decision. Because a decision is made in the present about consequences that will occur in the future, the manager's judgment may be important in estimating the total costs or sacrifices involved in the decision. This judgment can be improved by good analysis. Several cost principles are basic to this analysis.

<table>
<tr><td align="right">***Future Costs***
Are the
Important Costs</td><td>*Only those costs not yet incurred are important in a manager's decision.* A manager makes decisions for future actions. The manager's viewpoint,</td></tr>
</table>

like that of the managerial economist, requires concern with *future* rather than with *past* costs. It is true that the manager will know more about past costs, which concern actions already taken place, because they have been recorded; yet, historical costs (those usually provided by the financial accountant) have limited value for the manager. They are important because they help the manager learn to make better future decisions. Also, certain computations, such as income for tax reporting, must be based on past costs. However, the basic criteria for current decisions are the *expected benefits* to be realized as a result of the decision compared with *expected sacrifices* that will need to be made. If you had paid $1,000 for a useless item last year, it would be proper to forget the poor expenditure—it is a cost of a past decision. Any use (for example, scrapping) of the item in the future will involve only future sacrifices (certainly not the $1,000, which is a past sacrifice). On the other hand, if an item which cost $1,000 last year has become extremely valuable today, the use of this item will involve a greater sacrifice than its use last year involved. It should be clear, at this stage, that there are a number of cost classifications that are important under different conditions. Some of these cost concepts are summarized in Table 9-1.

Table 9-1
Comparative Cost Concepts Important
in Business Decisions

Concept	Antithesis	Distinction	Example of Use
Variable costs	Fixed costs	The costs that vary with changes in the rate of production vs. those that remain constant.	Breakeven charts; shutdown plant?
Implicit costs	Explicit costs	The sacrificed alternatives resulting from the use of facilities for a particular purpose vs. the actual expenses recorded.	Total costs including those found and not found in accounting records.
Out-of-pocket costs	Book costs	Costs that involve actual payments of cash vs. those that are recorded but do not involve cash outgo (e.g., depreciation).	Estimate of cash flows.
Incremental costs	Sunk costs	Those costs that are affected by the decision vs. those that have been incurred in the past and will continue regardless of the decision.	All decision making.
Controllable costs	Noncontrollable costs	Those costs that can be affected by the decisions of a given executive vs. those that are out of the power of the given executive.	Organizational control of costs.

Opportunity
Costs

Being interested in selecting the best alternative available, the manager must concentrate on the various opportunities that are open. A basic principle of economics is known as the **principle of opportunity** (*alternative*) **costs**, which is stated simply: The cost of any kind of action or decision consists of the opportunities that are sacrificed in taking that action. In deciding to use an hour of your time to file correspondence, you are sacrificing the chance of doing anything else with that hour. What is the cost of your filing correspondence for one hour? It depends. On what? If you otherwise would be waiting for someone and thus would have been idle, the cost is zero. If you are a doctor and could have performed an operation for which you would have been paid $200, the cost of filing would have been $200 (the sacrifice). If you could secure clerical help at the rate of $3.00 an hour so that you could perform the operation and have the correspondence filed, you would be able to allocate your time resources better (to the extent of $197, i.e., $200 less $3.00. Of course, it is often difficult to comprehend all the alternatives available and thus it is difficult to *know* all opportunity costs; yet the basic idea of opportunity cost is invaluable in helping to allocate resources properly.

Incremental
Cost

We saw earlier that total costs, as shown on a breakeven chart, are useful to an analysis of operations. We indicated then that two other computations are possible: average cost per unit and changes in costs. The idea of average cost per unit is generally understood as dividing total cost by the number of units. Average cost is most useful when analyzing past costs; in fact, it can be misleading if used improperly in considering decisions for the future.

A most valuable concept in decision making is known as **incremental cost**—defined as the *additional* (change in) total cost that results from a particular decision. Incremental analysis involves a comparison of changes in revenue and the associated changes in costs. The idea is simple—you will want to do something if, and only if, you can expect to be better off than you were before. In a business firm, the manager would want to make sure that the additional total revenue would be greater than the additional total costs.

We have already employed the idea of incremental cost in Figure 9-1—by increasing volume, the extra revenue (change in total revenue) was greater than the extra cost (in this case, variable cost). We said that the difference was a contribution to fixed cost and profit—in other words, the incremental gain by deciding to increase volume. In many cases, therefore, the change in variable cost will give us incremental cost.

Incremental costs are valuable considerations in many other cases. For example, consider the problem of whether or not to accept a single order at a special price. The analysis would involve a comparison between the estimated profit based on accepting the order. In these estimates, we would have to consider the net effect on prices of other orders and all opportunity costs. Because opportunity costs are not recorded in accounting records, it is clear that we would have to tailor our costs to the particular decision. If we can offer a lower price on this one order without affecting prices on other orders and if we can cover all extra costs (including a possible loss of goodwill), it would be more profitable to accept the order even though all costs are not covered.

The logic of incremental reasoning is clearly sound. The greatest problem in the use of this reasoning is in the search for all variables that should be considered and the actual measurement of all costs. In the next chapter, we shall see that the accounting records provide a fruitful source of information but that this information must be adapted to the specific needs of the decision.

DEMAND ANALYSIS

Because the important determinants of profit are costs and revenue, we now proceed to an analysis of revenue. Revenue flows in from payments for sales or services. The manager must study markets in an attempt to estimate the forces that determine these payments. This section will provide the economic framework within which this analysis takes place.

The economist views demand as a basic price-quantity relationship. This approach rests upon a clear and rigorous definition of **demand**: a schedule that shows the amounts that would be sold at various prices, in a given place, and on a given date. In this sense, demand is *not* just the quantity that would be taken at a given price—it represents the total conditions of the market that describe the relationship between prices and quantities. Forces that determine the demand for a firm's product include the desires of the customers, the income of the customers, the prices of substitutes, and the characteristics of the market. A manager must recognize that the individual demand for a product is a component of aggregate demand of the economy and the total demand for the particular industry. Any estimate of demand for a given product must be based upon estimates of expected national and international activity and estimates of the factors that affect the demand of the industry. The manager is interested in demand because of the need to understand the external factors that affect decisions and policies. Specifically, three subjects are important as background for price decisions: the nature of a given demand schedule, factors that cause changes in demand, and techniques of forecasting demand.

Elasticity
of
Demand

Keeping in mind that demand is a schedule of price-quantities, the most important concept in demand analysis is elasticity. In general, **elasticity** may be defined as the percentage change in a dependent variable determined by a given percentage change in an independent variable. **Price elasticity** of demand is the most common application of this concept: It describes the effect of a given percentage change in price (P) on the percentage change in quantities (Q) that would be purchased. The simplest formula for price elasticity (E) is:

$$E = \frac{\dfrac{Q_2 - Q_1}{Q_2 + Q_1}}{\dfrac{P_2 - P_1}{P_2 + P_1}}$$

where Q_1 and Q_2 are quantities that would be taken before and after a price change, and P_1 and P_2 are the corresponding prices. The demand schedule normally is shown graphically as a demand curve; elasticity describes the nature of the curve. If the slope is steep so that the total revenue $(P \times Q)$ decreases if price is decreased (that is, E is less than 1.0), the demand is said to be **inelastic**. If total revenue increases as the price is decreased (that is, E is greater than 1.0), the demand is said to be **elastic**. In other words, price elasticity indicates the *responsiveness* of a change in quantity to change in price.

Elasticity of demand is an important concept in the determination of price policies. However, the measurement of the actual effect of changes in price on the changes in quantities is difficult in actual practice. The difficulty arises from the fact that elasticity is a concept relating to a given point in time, and price elasticity describes the effect of price on quantity, assuming all other determinants to be constant. Two statistical approaches attempt to estimate the nature of the demand curve: (1) study of past time series of prices and quantities and (2) controlled experiments. However, even if a manager does not want to go to the trouble of using these methods, the concept is valuable as an aid to judgment.

The nature of a demand curve, faced by a manager, obviously is important in pricing decisions. It should be clear that the simple approach of totaling costs of production and adding a margin tends to ignore the demand aspects of the problem. Some argue that it might be best to concentrate on demand as the most important factor in pricing.

Determinants
of
Changes in Demand

Elasticity describes the nature of demand at a given time; changes in demand refer to shifts during a period of time. Managers should be aware of those factors that are out of their control so that they can adjust to them; those within their control, of course, require their deliberate attention because their actions can affect them.

A primary means by which a manager can attempt to increase demand is through *advertising* and sales promotion. Advertising aims at shifting the demand curve to the right. This shift is clearly different from an attempt to sell more items by decreasing price—a lowering of price might merely be to operate on the same demand curve; an increase in demand would permit the seller to sell more items at the same price or even at a higher price. Advertising policies should be based on incremental reasoning, that is, a comparison of the extra revenue generated by additional advertising with the cost of the advertising. Small expenditures on advertising may yield net increases in profit; however, as expenditures on advertising increase, there is a tendency for the extra net increase to decrease because of the law of diminishing returns.

Forecasting

The manager must make decisions for future actions and thus must forecast future demand. Forecasting may be oriented to estimating economic conditions in the near future, or it may be directed toward estimation of specific quantities that will be purchased in various markets. This section summarizes the first of these problems; the latter problem will receive attention in Chapter 14.

We have seen that the individual demand for a given firm depends upon the health of the total demand in the economy; therefore, a first step is to forecast the conditions of the economic environment.

A second step in forecasting the demand for a given product usually concentrates on the total demand for the industry. Large firms keep close contact with all factors affecting the industry because they have a large stake in the problem. Smaller firms may accept the opinions of business economists of these large firms. The demand for the industry can be analyzed by individual components such as: (1) sales of products to new customers (for example, the sale of autos or television sets to people who do not own the product); (2) sales of additional products to old customers (for example, a second auto or television set); (3) replacement sales for products that have worn out; and (4) sales affected by recent technological developments. Each company may wish to concentrate on a particular segment of the industry and forecast sales in these segments more carefully, for example, sales to farmers, the retired workers, teenagers, and so on.

A third step in forecasting the demand for a given company is the estimate of the market share of the particular company. Past share of the market may serve as the base for this step. Adjustments, however, should be made by forecasting the effect of new programs planned by the company, expected reactions of competitors to the company's actions and to industry conditions, and detailed reports by salesmen in different localities.

SUMMARY   Although it is presumptuous to attempt to summarize all economic concepts in a single chapter, it is possible to emphasize four economic principles that managers should keep in mind daily:

THE INCREMENTAL PRINCIPLE: A decision is sound if it increases revenue more than costs, or if it reduces costs more than revenue.

THE PRINCIPLE OF TIME PERSPECTIVE: A decision should take into account both the short-run and long-run effects on revenue and costs, giving appropriate weight to the most relevant time period in each individual decision.

THE OPPORTUNITY COST PRINCIPLE: Decision making involves a careful measurement of the sacrifices required by the various alternatives.

THE DISCOUNTING PRINCIPLE: If a decision affects costs and revenues at future dates, it is necessary to discount these costs and revenues to present values before a valid comparison of alternatives is possible.

REFERENCES

BOULDING, KENNETH, *Beyond Economics: Essays on Society, Religion, and Ethics*. Ann Arbor: University of Michigan Press, 1968.

BRIGHAM, E. F. and J. L. PAPPAS, *Managerial Economics* (2nd ed.). Hinsdale, Ill.: The Dryden Press, 1976.

DEAN, JOE, *Managerial Economics*. Englewood Cliffs, N.J.: Prentice-Hall, Inc., 1951.

FARRAR, D. E. and J. R. MEYER, *Managerial Economics*. Englewood Cliffs, N.J.: Prentice-Hall, Inc., 1970.

HAYNES, W. WARREN and WILLIAM HENRY, *Managerial Economics* (3rd ed.). Dallas, Texas: Business Publications, Inc., 1974.

McKENZIE, R. B. and GORDON TULLOCK, *The New World of Economics*. Homewood, Ill.: Richard D. Irwin, Inc., 1975.

NORTH, DOUGLASS C. and ROGER LEROY MILLER, *The Economics of Public Issues* (2nd ed.). New York: Harper and Row, 1973.

SPENCER, M. H., K. K. SEO and MARK SIMKIN, *Managerial Economics* (4th ed.). Homewood, Ill.: Richard D. Irwin, Inc., 1975.

MANAGERIAL ACCOUNTING

by James L. Gibson, University of Kentucky

<== **IDEAS TO BE FOUND** ==>
IN THIS CHAPTER

- Budgeting
- Standard costs
- Responsibility accounting
- Direct costing
- Cash flow
- Trends in management accounting

Management and accounting have been closely associated for a long time. Historically, the functions of accounting have been to record, analyze, and report the results of business operations in various units of measurement, such as dollars, units of production, standard hours, and kilowatts. With such information, management can *plan* future operations, *control* key variables, *decide* among alternative courses of action, and *analyze* past performance.

The point of view of managerial accounting is different from that of financial accounting. The managerial accountant's purpose is to provide information for one user—the firm's management; the financial accountant's purpose is to provide information for a variety of users. This chapter provides a survey of the fundamentals of accounting that are needed for an intelligent use of accounting documents in the performance of management functions (but does not introduce even the words debits and credits). The chapter concentrates on managerial accounting and the functions of planning, controlling, decision making, and analyzing with the use of accounting data.

FINANCIAL ACCOUNTING AND MANAGERIAL ACCOUNTING All financial accounting information results from a recording and classifying process that is based on the fundamental law that the assets of a business entity are subject to the claims of two parties: owners and creditors. The law is:

$$Assets = Liabilities + Equity$$

To illustrate this relationship, consider a business transaction involving the investment of $10,000 cash in a new business. The balance sheet prepared immediately after the event would show:

$$Assets = Liabilities + Equity$$
$$Cash\ \$10,000 = 0 + \$10,000$$

Immediately thereafter, the firm owner borrows $8,000 from the local bank and purchases a truck for $5,000 cash. A new balance would reveal:

Assets		= Liabilities	+ Equity
Cash	$13,000		
Truck	5,000	Note payable $8,000	+ $10,000
	$18,000		

The balance sheet indicates that the firm has total assets of $18,000; of this total, creditors have a claim for $8,000 and the equity of the owner is $10,000. The **balance sheet** shows the financial position of a business firm with respect to asset values and the corresponding claims of creditors and owners on the assets of *a given point in time.*

The **income statement** is closely related to the balance sheet in that it reveals the changes in assets, liabilities, and equity that result from doing business. To illustrate, assume that all revenues are in the form of cash and that all expenses are paid in cash for a period of time subsequent to the last balance sheet shown above. The income statement might show:

Revenue	$10,000
Expenses	4,000
Net income	$ 6,000

The income statement indicates that the cash account has been increased by $6,000 and, assuming no change in creditor claims, equity will be increased by $6,000. The effect on the balance sheet would be:

Assets		= Liabilities	+ Equity
Cash	$19,000		
Truck	5,000	Note payable $8,000	+ $16,000
	$24,000		

The basic equation, Assets = Liabilities + Equity, holds true regardless of what transaction takes place, simply because the method of recording the transactions is designed to do just that! However, our illustration is a gross oversimplification. Accountants cannot prepare balance sheets and income statements immediately after each transaction. The volume of transactions consummated by a firm prohibits such a practice, but through the orderly process of recording and classifying, a whole series of transactions can be summarized and the net effects shown.

There are certain assumptions and practices that are basic to accounting and that must be understood by any party using financial accounting information. The understanding of these assumptions and practices is particularly critical for managers who desire to read financial statements.

1. *Going-concern Assumption.* Accounting measurements of value are based on the assumption that the firm has a continuity of existence. Thus the balance sheet shows assets valued at *original cost* rather than at realizable values. (Recently, as a result of inflation, some statements include modification to show market values.)
2. *Stable Monetary-unit Assumption.* All values in financial statements are based on dollars associated with the original transaction. The assumption is that the dollar represents a stable unit of value.
3. *Conservatism Assumption.* Accountants assume that they can best serve the users of financial statements by following a conservative approach in measuring changes in assets, liabilities, and equity. For example, marketable securities and inventories are valued at cost or market, whichever is *lower.*
4. *Consistency Assumption.* Accountants assume that the users of financial information are best served if valuations are made on a consistent basis.
5. *The Matching-process Assumption.* Allied to the assumption of a going concern is the assumption that business income is determinable by matching the revenue *earned* in a period of time with the

expenses *incurred* in that same period of time. This concept of net income is not the same as the economist's "profit," because the accountant does not record certain "economic costs." For example, interest on owners' capital is an economic cost because it involves a sacrifice of investing the funds in some other endeavor; yet, the accountant explains that such a cost was not incurred by the firm— that is, the assets of the firm were not decreased.

Financial accounting involves an orderly process by which the business transactions of a firm are recorded, classified, and summarized in a manner prescribed by a body of principles. The ultimate objective is to present the financial condition of a firm so that a variety of interested parties can make evaluations about the firm.

Managerial accounting, on the other hand, is not concerned with a variety of parties; rather, attention is focused on the operating manager. The principles and assumptions that underlie financial information limit the usefulness of this type of information for management purposes. Managerial accounting techniques must be flexible and "tailor made" to the individual firm. The remainder of the chapter is devoted to special accounting techniques designed to aid management.

PLANNING

Business budgets are the principal financial means by which the manager can formalize and express a plan. Moreover, once budgets are established they serve as a control technique by setting predetermined criteria against which managers can compare actual results. In addition, the budgeting process serves as a tool for coordinating the activities of various functions and operating segments of the firm.

Figure 10-1 shows that comprehensive budgeting consists of a number of budgets with the sales budget, based upon a sales forecast, usually serving as the starting point in the process. The production budget is based on the sales budget, and all others are, in turn, constructed on consistent assumptions concerning the future.

Responsibility for preparing and coordinating the budgets usually rests on the controller or some other staff executive; however, budgets must reflect joint planning of all operating segments. Budget committees, composed of responsible operating heads, usually make the planning decisions, because budgets established with the cooperation and understanding of all principal parties will be better understood and accepted as guides for future activities.

The period of time for which a budget will be made is the first issue for management to resolve. Two factors provide a range for the length of time: first, it should be short enough to permit the making of fairly

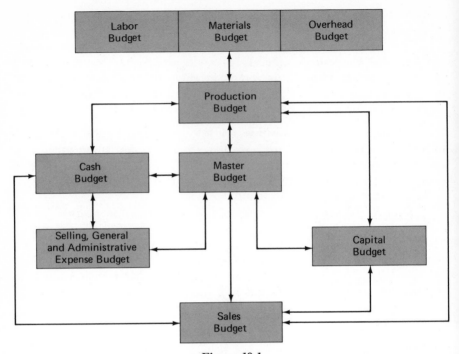

Figure 10-1
The Interdependence and Coordinating Nature of the Various
Budget Types as Indicated by the Connecting Arrows

accurate predictions; second, it should be long enough to raise significant problems of policy, strategy, and procedure. A number of factors can affect the length of the budget period: (1) the availability of factual information, (2) the stability of the market faced by the firm, (3) the rate of technological progress, (4) the seasonal characteristics of the industry, (5) the length of the production cycle, (6) the customary credit extension time for customers, and (7) delivery times of both raw materials and finished products. In addition, the budget period must coincide with the accounting period so that comparisons between actual results and budget amounts can be made routinely.

A budget for a stated future period of time that does not make allowance for cost changes due to possible changes in output is a **fixed budget**. A **flexible budget** shows expected costs of production at various levels of production. The prerequisite for flexible budgeting is the separation of fixed and variable costs. Once the flexible budget is formalized and reports are flowing to management, opportunities for analysis are opened. The advantages of flexible budgets are: (1) cost variations due to output changes are indicated; (2) the segregation of fixed and variable costs is useful for other management functions; and (3) standard costing (an important control technique) is more easily implemented.

The information provided by budgets enables managers to prepare *pro forma* (estimated) balance sheets and income statements. Financial results and commitments can be anticipated. Such estimates enable the manager to approach the future with less hesitancy than would be true otherwise.

CONTROL

As discussed previously, control involves the comparison of actual performance with some predetermined criterion. Obviously budgeting is a control device, because management compares the actual costs and revenues with the budgeted amounts. Other accounting techniques that provide management with control information are standard costs, distribution cost analysis, and responsibility accounting.

Standard Costs

Standard costs are predetermined costs developed from past experience, motion and time study, expected future manufacturing costs, or some combination of these. They contrast with *actual costs*, which are the amounts actually incurred in the manufacturing process.

In standard costing, the unit cost of a particular product would be computed as follows:

1. *Calculate Standard Labor Costs.* From a motion and time study it is found that the normal labor time required to produce one unit is four hours; the expected hourly wage cost for those workers responsible for its production is known to be $3.50. Thus, the standard labor cost is $14.00 (4 hours at $3.50 per hour).
2. *Calculate Standard Material Cost.* From a study of materials flow and handling, it is estimated that no more than ten pounds of raw materials should be used in the production of one unit; the expected cost of raw materials, given reasonably efficient purchasing, is $.80 per pound. Thus, the standard material cost is $8.00 (10 pounds at $.80 per pound).
3. *Calculate Standard Overhead Costs.* The unit overhead cost depends upon the expected (budgeted) production. A relationship is determined between expected overhead cost and some indicator of activity (usually a relation between overhead and labor costs). Thus, assuming that expected overhead is to be 80 percent of expected labor costs (as shown by the budget), the standard overhead is $11.20 (80 percent of $14.00).

4. *Add the Three Amounts.* In this example, the standard unit cost of a hypothetical product is:

Standard labor cost	$14.00
Standard material cost	8.00
Standard overhead cost	11.20
Standard unit cost	$33.20

As products are completed, the inventory of finished goods is charged with the standard costs of completely manufactured units. From the manager's point of view, the chief benefit of standard costing is the analysis of reasons for the difference between actual costs and standard costs.

The analysis of **manufacturing cost variances** (accounts that accumulate differences between actual and standard costs) is based on reports flowing routinely to management. As an example, assume that the actual labor cost for the preceding example is $16.00; the labor cost variance would be $2.00. There are two sources of the variance: (1) departure from the standard time and (2) departure from the standard wage cost. If the actual labor time is five hours (instead of the standard four) and the actual wage cost is $4.00 (instead of $3.50), management must determine the causes of the variation. Was a new man on the job? Is the standard time too tight? Did the supervisor use a higher paid person on the job than was supposed to be used? Material cost variances and overhead cost variances raise the same types of questions.

Responsibility Accounting

Effective implementation of the management by objectives (MBO) concept requires that performance be measured in a manner that will be meaningful to the individual. In **responsibility accounting,** costs are identified with those individuals who are responsible for their control. In determining costs *controllable* by a given manager, it is necessary to analyze each cost element separately. All variable costs cannot be assumed to be controllable, nor are all fixed costs *uncontrollable.* The authority of the person being considered must be recognized; thus, responsibility accounting classifications must fit the organization structure. Furthermore, a minimum of cost allocation should be employed; that is, consideration should be given only to those costs that are clearly influenced by a particular individual.

Closely related to the concept of responsibility accounting is the idea of **profit centers.** Here the concern is to assign responsibility for both revenue and expenses to a segment of a business. The establishment of profit centers requires the allocation of costs, revenues, and assets in order to evaluate the performance of a segment manager.

DECIDING   The manager can obtain accounting information designed to aid him in deciding between alternative courses of action in two ways: (1) The routinized collection of relevant data for certain types of anticipated decisions is called **programmed analysis**; (2) **nonprogrammed analysis** develops special cost information for specific decisions. The relevant cost information for decision making should pertain to those costs that will be different under alternative actions not yet taken. Thus the central idea in accounting for decision making, whether it be by programed or nonprogramed methods, is the incremental concept; that is, the analysis of *changes* in total costs and in total revenues.

Direct
Costing

Direct costing, or variable costing, is a product-costing technique that identifies only variable costs with products. All fixed costs are charged against revenue from the accounting period in which they are incurred and do not become a part of product costs for inventory valuation purposes.

The arbitrary allocation of fixed costs to products, called **absorption costing,** can result in confusion in some decisions. For example, the full cost of a product includes fixed-cost allocations and requires a special analysis to determine the increase in total costs if sales of that product increase. Direct costing attempts to eliminate the confusion by avoiding allocations and by presenting cost information that corresponds closely to incremental costs. The manager derives several benefits from direct costing: (1) cost-profit-volume relationships required for profit planning are obtained from regular accounting reports; (2) profit for a period varies with sales rather than with production; (3) relative appraisals of products are not obscured by allocations of common costs; and (4) incremental cost information for pricing and other product-oriented decisions is readily available.

Marginal
Income Analysis

Marginal income analysis is universally applicable in that it can be applied to any segment of business activity, that is, cause of costs (sales offices, operating departments, product lines, and so on), whereas direct costing is applicable only to production costs. Effective use of this technique requires that management carefully identify segments and segregate variable costs from escapable fixed costs of each segment.

Management systematically receives the type of data needed for short-run decisions involving changes in volume (variable costs) as well as the data needed for long-run decisions (variable costs and escapable fixed costs). Marginal income analysis is an attempt to measure the contribution of each segment to common fixed costs (fixed costs not applicable to any particular segment) and profits. No attempt is made to allocate common fixed costs or to require that each segment carry its "share of overhead." Rather, the relevant criterion is the ratio of marginal balance to the investment employed in the segment.

Special   Special cost studies—that is, non-
Cost Studies   programmed analyses—are prepared
for management as the occasion arises. Two general methods by which management can compare the relative profitability of alternatives are (1) **pro forma** (estimated) income statement or (2) analysis of cost changes. The two methods should lead to the same answers, but analyzing only cost changes has the advantage of being simpler to handle.

To illustrate the two methods, assume the position of a firm to be:

Sales revenue		$1,000
Cost of goods sold	$800	
Other costs (fixed)	300	1,100
	Loss	$ 100

The management is considering two alternatives that could decrease the loss and perhaps yield net income. Alternative A is to lower the price and increase sales; Alternative B is to raise the price and decrease sales, but, at the same time, decrease the cost due to a decrease in volume. *Pro forma* income statements prepared for both alternatives would show:

Sales revenue		$1,100	Sales revenue			$ 950
Cost of goods sold	$840		Cost of goods sold	$720		
Other costs (fixed)	300	1,140	Other costs (fixed)	300		1,020
Net loss		$ 40	Net loss			$ 70

Alternative A   *Alternative B*

According to the estimates, Alternative A reduces the loss by $60, whereas Alternative B reduces the loss by only $30. Other things being equal, Alternative A is better. Comparing changes in total costs and revenues lead to the same results gained by comparing *pro forma* income statements. The analysis of Alternative *A*, decreasing prices, would be:

Incremental revenue	$100
Incremental cost	40
Incremental income	$ 60

The analysis of Alternative *B*, increasing prices, would be:

Incremental costs (decrease in costs) $80	
Incremental revenue	
(decrease in revenue)	50
Incremental income	$30

The two approaches lead to the same conclusions, but comparing only *changes* in costs and revenue is simpler. Comparisons of incremental values also enable the manager to include the costs of decisions that are not recognized in accounting statements. Such costs include the loss of plant flexibility and the possibility of "spoiling the market" (the difficulty of raising the price back to its former level subsequent to a price decrease), both of which are possibilities of Alternative *A*.

ANALYSIS OF PAST PERFORMANCE

Financial accounting statements contain valuable information that managers can use to analyze past performance. In order to use such information, they must recognize the limitations of such data and apply techniques to overcome these weaknesses. At the same time, out of the great mass of financial information that is available, managers must sift out that which is relevant.

Financial Statement Analysis

Management can analyze financial data by (1) comparisons of two or more periods and (2) comparison within one period. The former includes the analysis of successive balance sheets and income statements to determine trends in individual items. The latter involves the analysis of current financial statements to determine the state of the firm with respect to its solvency, stability, and profitability. Good financial statement analysis uses both approaches. Individual items can be compared over a period of time, with increases and decreases expressed as percentage changes. A complementary technique is the ratio analysis of related data for a single period. (See Chapter 14 for additional discussion of ratios.)

Cash Flow   Another very useful technique of the *Analysis* managerial accountant is called **source and application of funds analysis.** This technique involves the determination of where funds have come from and how they were used, that is, a focus on cash flow. Although the term "funds" has a variety of meanings, in this analysis it means working capital; that is, current assets minus current liabilities. Most of the information needed for the analysis can be obtained from a comparison of two balance sheets plus some supplemental information added to reflect the flow of funds.

From management's point of view, the value of the analysis of source and use of funds is that it gives valuable insight on the efficiency of management in allocating funds. Table 10-1 illustrates a hypothetical example of the analysis.

From Table 10-1 it appears that the largest source of funds was the sale of capital stock; net income for the period provided a relatively small part. The decrease in working capital indicates that internal sources of funds were necessary to meet the requirements of long-term liabilities, dividend payment, and replacement of fixed assets. The entire analysis is straightforward, with the exception of depreciation, which does not require the outflow of cash. It is subtracted from revenue along with other expenses in the income statement, but, unlike other expenses, deprecia-

Table 10-1
Example of a Source and Application
of Funds Statement

Sources of Funds	
Proceeds from sale of stock	$10,000
Proceeds from sale of fixed assets	5,000
Net income from operations	4,000
Depreciation expense	1,000
Decrease in working capital	3,000
Total sources of funds	$23,000

Applications (Uses) of Funds	
Retirement of long-term debt	$16,000
Purchase of fixed assets	4,000
Payment of dividends	3,000
Total uses of funds	$23,000

tion does not involve an outlay of funds. Therefore, to obtain the correct amount by which funds are augmented by the firm's operations, it is necessary to add the depreciation as a source.

Source and application of funds statements accompany annual reports. They aid materially in the evaluation of management's ability to generate funds through normal business operations and to allocate the funds to various needs. As a management tool, the statement is valuable as a basis for forecasting future sources and uses of funds; however, such analyses will normally be a part of the formal budgeting process. The primary purpose of the analysis is to evaluate past performance and to raise issues regarding management's efficiency in managing its cash flow.

In the last thirty years, accounting techniques have been influenced heavily by managerial economics. Direct costing, for example, had gained some recognition in the late 1930s, but the intervention of World War II and price controls reestablished the need for full cost data. In the postwar era, the emergence of managerial economics reaffirmed the need for data that expressed marginal quantities. Thus, direct costing, marginal income analysis, and breakeven analysis have appeared as important elements of management accounting.

Management theorists and practicing managers who concentrate on the basic functions of management have pressed accountants to provide more data to aid in carrying out these functions. The emphasis on planning and controlling resulted in the establishment of standard costing, budgeting, responsibility accounting, internal control measures, financial statement analysis, and distribution cost analysis. These methods developed as management became convinced of their usefulness.

The developments in the behavioral sciences have already stimulated research on how accounting planning and control methods affect the behavior of people. For example, what is the reaction of workers to standard labor costs? How do supervisors react to unfavorable variance reports? Does the fact that the accounting department appears to be a "watchdog" over the operating personnel result in interpersonal frictions? Is this friction good or bad for the firm? The reaction of people to budgets and the motivational properties of budget variances have been examined in recent research.

Although the human element available to a firm has always been considered one of the most valuable resources, the accountant traditionally did not attempt to record a value for this resource. In the last decade, this omission has been faced through human asset accounting. **Human assets accounting** attempts to record the significant costs of recruiting, training, and servicing the human element and to recognize the long-term investment in human resources on the balance sheet. In short, the costs of the staffing function of management are being increasingly recognized by managerial accountants.

Developments in electronic data processing (EDP) have already gone far to relieve much of the detail of accounting work. For management accounting purposes, the significance of EDP is the flexibility of data accumulation and communication that is afforded. The management accountant will be able to supply information more quickly and for more varied needs in the future. The relief from detail should also encourage a broader view of the management accountant's position.

The use of statistical inference in management decision making has become a part of accounting techniques. For example, inventory valuation and accounts receivable verification by statistical sampling and manufacturing cost variance analysis based on probability concepts have moved out of the experimental stage. The results of these attempts have made a profound impact on management accounting techniques.

Accounting is, by intent, utilitarian; it is rooted in the pragmatic. As the primary accumulator and communicator of data within the firm, it must respond to the requirements of those using the information. Management will demand that the accountant prepare for interrelationships with disciplines that, on the surface, appear quite far removed from the accountant's experience and training. Some of these disciplines are the subject of the next chapter.

REFERENCES

ANTHONY, ROBERT N. and JAMES REECE, *Management Accounting Principles* (3rd ed.). Homewood, Ill.: Richard D. Irwin, Inc., 1975.

COPELAND, RONALD M. and PAUL E. DASCHER, *Managerial Accounting: An Introduction to Planning Information Processing and Control* (2nd ed.). Santa Barbara, Calif.: Hamilton Publishing Co., 1978.

GRAY, JACK and K. S. JOHNSTON, *Accounting and Management Action.* New York: McGraw-Hill Book Co., 1977.

HORNGREN, CHARLES T., *Cost Accounting: A Managerial Emphasis* (4th ed.). Englewood Cliffs, N.J.: Prentice-Hall, Inc., 1977.

LYNCH, RICHARD M. and ROBERT WILLIAMSON, *Accounting for Management, Planning and Control* (2nd ed.). New York: McGraw-Hill Book Co., 1976.

MCFARLAND, WALTER B., *Concepts for Management Accounting.* New York: National Association of Accountants, 1966.

MOORE, CARL and ROBERT K. JAEDICKE, *Managerial Accounting.* Cincinnati: South-Western Publishing Co., 1976.

THOMAS, W. E., *Readings in Cost Accounting, Budgeting, and Control.* Cincinnati: South-Western Publishing Co., 1973.

THE
BEHAVIORAL SCIENCES
IN MANAGEMENT

by Marc J. Wallace, Jr., University of Kentucky

⟸ **IDEAS TO BE FOUND** ⟹
IN THIS CHAPTER

- Human relations
- Motives
- Groups
- Job enrichment
- Motivation
- Herzberg's two-factor model of motivation
- Behaviorist reinforcement model of motivation
- Expectancy theory of motivation
- Equity theory of motivation
- Distributive justice
- Cognitive dissonance
- Leadership
- Leadership styles
- Contingency theories of leadership
- Organization behavior

The field of management has had a longstanding concern with the impact of individuals and groups on the effectiveness of organizations. It has been over 50 years since the beginning of the now-classic Hawthorne studies. These experiments are an excellent illustration of how scientific endeavor often leads to findings completely unexpected by the investigators at the outset.

What began in 1924 as an investigation of the impact of alternative lighting methods on employee productivity ended up ten years later providing the field of management with the knowledge that a number of psychological and sociological factors influenced productivity at least as much as such characteristics as physical conditions, work methods, technology, and organizational structures.

In the ensuing time period a great deal of effort has been expended by behavioral scientists in a variety of fields, building upon the Hawthorne findings and expanding our understanding of the impact of human behavior upon the effectiveness of organizations. The purpose of this chapter is to summarize these findings and to evaluate them in terms of how useful they are to the practicing manager interested in increasing his or her effectiveness. In other words, this chapter will limit itself to the question: What does the practicing manager need to know about the impact of individuals and groups upon organizational functioning and effectiveness?

BEHAVIORAL DISCIPLINES RELEVANT IN MANAGEMENT

Since the conclusion of the Hawthorne studies in the 1930s, investigators in a number of closely related scientific disciplines have explored the nature and dynamics of individuals and groups within work organizations. Of primary interest to us are the contributions made by the fields of psychology and sociology. The fields of history, economics, political science, and anthropology have also contributed (although in a secondary fashion) to this understanding.

Psychology, itself, is divided into a number of sub-disciplines, many of which have led to significant findings about the nature of individuals in organizations. *Motivational* psychologists, for example, have concentrated their efforts on identifying the kinds of needs or motives that influence work behavior. In addition, they and other psychologists interested in the phenomenon of *learning* have examined the processes by which behavior occurs and is changed over time. Still other psychologists engaged in the field of *personality* have attempted to predict and understand the influences of moods, interests, needs, tendencies, intelligence, aptitudes, capacities, and values on work behavior. Those psychologists who have applied basic knowledge in the sub-disciplines of *motivation, learning,* and *personality* to an understanding of work behavior in organizations have identified themselves as **industrial psychologists** and, in fact, constitute a formal division within the American Psychological Association, the professional body of practicing psychologists in the U.S.

Overlapping somewhat with the interests of industrial psychologists are the concerns of **industrial sociologists**, who have applied basic knowledge in the field of sociology to an understanding of the behavior of individuals in formal and informal groups. The difference between industrial psychology and sociology is a matter of degree rather than any fundamental qualitative distinction. We might say that the primary focus of the psychologist is on the employee as an individual. In contrast, the sociologist focuses on that individual employee's interactions with others, formally and informally. Industrial sociologists have tended to define their field in a combination of three position statements:

1. Sociology is the study of *interactions* between people. Interactions can involve power, influence, status, authority, affiliation, support, or common interests and objectives.

2. Sociology is the study of *group behavior*. Two or more people, whether joined formally or informally, have a joint impact on organization.

3. Sociology is the study of *social systems* or *organizations*. These may be formal (e.g., having a written charter) or informal (e.g., a clique of co-workers). Such organizations have a variety of characteristics that influence the behavior of individual employees. These include values, norms, communication channels, and roles.

THREE ILLUSTRATIONS OF APPLIED BEHAVIORAL RESEARCH A complete examination of industrial psychology and sociology's contributions since the Hawthorne studies is well beyond the scope of this chapter. Instead, three cases of behavioral research will illustrate the kinds of efforts made between the 1930s and the present.

Human Relations —A Case of Applied Sociology The recognition of the importance of individual and group dimensions of behavior led to a series of investigations carried out by William F. Whyte and his associates during the 1940s and 1950s that have collectively become known as the **human relations** school of thought.

Analyzing individual responses to a number of management policies, including incentive payment programs, Whyte and his co-workers were impressed by the formal work group's influence on individual behavior. In fact, they concluded that informal work-group norms are more important than formal organizational rules in influencing individual decisions about level of work performance.

Investigators in the human relations tradition, including Whyte, Leonard Sayles, George Strauss, Orvis Collins, Melville Dalton, and Douglas McGregor, concluded that two sets of factors are critical as determinants of employee work behavior:

1. *Individual Motives*: The human relations school reacted sharply to the earlier premise that employees have an inherent dislike of work and must be closely supervised and directed. In addition, they rejected the earlier belief that money is the only basis for motivating work behavior. McGregor characterized these assumptions as Theory X. In contrast, he proposed a set of premises, labeled Theory Y, that best summarize the human relations school beliefs concerning the individual. McGregor believed that physical and mental effort is as natural to an individual employee as play or rest. Furthermore, if allowed, an employee will exercise self-direction and self-control in his or her work behavior. Indeed, the opportu-

nity to take on responsibility, exercise discretion, and direct one's own actions in the completion of meaningful tasks is far more powerful as a motivator than threats, coercion, or money rewards.

2. *Informal Groups*: The human relations school concluded that the informal group is the greatest single source of influence on an employee's behavior. Informal work groups establish very important rules or norms regarding appropriate and inappropriate behavior. In addition, according to this reasoning, informal groups can dispense or withhold very attractive rewards in order to assure compliance with such norms. These rewards include: (a) the satisfaction of *affiliation* needs, (b) a sense of *identity* with a recognized and respected group, (c) a confirmation of *self-esteem*, (d) a means for *testing reality*, and (e) a means for *assistance* in accomplishing work tasks.

Recognizing the importance of individual motives and informal work groups, the human relations school of thought rapidly developed into the human relations *movement*, a strongly expressed set of managerial prescriptions for designing and directing work organizations. This set of prescriptions focused principally on three areas of managerial activity: (1) encouraging employees to *participate* in decisions regarding their work and the operations of the organization, (2) implementing job *enlargement* or *enrichment*, i.e., redesigning jobs to allow for a broader degree of discretion and breadth of activities, and (3) improving the flow of *communications* between managers and subordinates as well as all employees.

The early work of the human relations school is an excellent example of industrial sociology, especially in their research of small group dynamics. Unfortunately, the field slipped prematurely away from description and understanding to prescription. Subsequent analysis critical of the human relations school has cited a number of important weaknesses in such prescriptions:

1. They tend to oversimplify the complexity of human behavior and group dynamics. They do not take account of the varying situations under which work is carried out.
2. Their assumptions about the nature of human motives are as simple and sterile as those they sought to replace. Money, for example, remains an important work-related incentive for employees.
3. They lack an underlying model of sufficient richness to allow testing major human relations propositions or extending knowledge gained in one administrative setting to another.

Although its impact was felt through the 1960s, the human relations school is more an item of historical interest than a modern, contributing body of theory and knowledge about work behavior. It did, however, make an important and lasting contribution in (a) demonstrating that employees are motivated by a variety of needs, not just monetary needs, (b) discovering the importance of informal work groups in organizations, and (c) recognizing the importance of communication channels in influencing employee behavior and performance.

Work Motivation– *A Case of* *Applied Psychology* The sociological approach of the human relations school over the past 40 years has been paralleled by the efforts of industrial psychologists to understand the nature and operation of motives in influencing work behavior and performance. Industrial psychologists' efforts originated in an attempt to identify the specific needs that motivate work behavior; in effect, they concentrated on the *content* of work motivation. More recently, they have begun to address themselves to *process* questions, that is, issues regarding the dynamics or mechanics by which motives influence work behavior and performance.

Industrial psychologists, then, initially undertook the task of identifying those work-related motives that influence work behavior. Several hundred attempts have been made to identify and classify the multitude of work-related motives. Out of these, three or four have emerged to influence managerial thought and practice. The first of these is the work of Abraham Maslow, who introduced the notion of a **Need Hierarchy**. Maslow's principal argument is that employee needs emerge in a hierarchical fashion; lower-order needs are experienced first and must be satisfied by the work environment before higher-order needs are perceived. The implication is that rewards of higher-order needs will have no incentive effect upon employee motivation until lower-order needs are satisfied (Maslow labeled this phenomenon the concept of **prepotency of needs**).

Maslow's hierarchy is illustrated in Figure 11-1. From lowest to highest, the needs are defined as:

Physiological needs: These include hunger, sex, thirst;

Safety needs: These represent the need to be free of bodily threat;

Social needs: These represent the need to love and be loved. They include affection, friendship, and affiliation;

Esteem needs: These include an employee's need for self-respect and respect from others;

Self-actualization: This need has never adequately been defined either by Maslow or subsequent theorists. In an existential sense, the term refers to becoming all that one chooses and is capable of becoming.

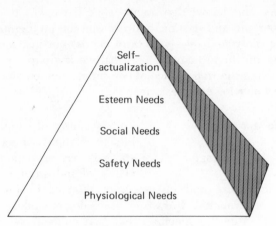

Figure 11-1
Maslow's Need Hierarchy

Most industrial psychologists agree that Maslow identified several classes of needs that are important sources of work motivation. The theory has been faulted, however, over the prepotency issue. Very few management theorists believe anymore that a strict ordering exists in the sequence in which needs are felt (except, possibly, for physiological and safety needs). Perhaps the most important managerial implication emerging from Maslow's work is that most employees experience a variety of needs motivating them to come to work and perform at a given level of effort. It is important for a manager to consider each employee's unique profile of felt needs when explaining his or her response to the organization.

A second famous statement of employee needs was made by Frederick Herzberg and his associates. Herzberg is credited with a **two-factor** model of motives that (like Maslow's) was adequate in describing the content of work motives but failed to describe adequately their impact on work behavior and performance. Herzberg and his associates analyzed the content of interviews carried out with approximately 200 employees about their jobs. Respondents were asked to think of times when they felt particularly good and particularly bad about their jobs, and to describe the conditions leading to these feelings in as much detail as possible.

An analysis of these interviews led Herzberg to propose that the conditions leading to positive feelings about the job were fundamentally different from those leading to negative feelings. The former were called satisfiers and the latter were labeled dissatisfiers. He inferred from these findings that needs were discontinuous as far as their impact on motivation and performance is concerned. Positive work motivation (factors leading to enhanced performance) would only be influenced by **satisfiers** (e.g., the satisfaction of achievement needs, recognition, advancement, the work itself, personal growth). Later theorists agreeing with Herzberg considered these factors **intrinsic** because they exist primarily within the context of the work being carried out.

Dissatisfiers, according to Herzberg, could only lead to dissatisfaction with the job, and therefore could not positively motivate job performance. Dissatisfiers include such factors as company policy and administration, technical supervision, interpersonal relations with supervisors and peers, salary, job security, work conditions, and status. Later theorists referred to these elements as **extrinsic factors**, because they exist outside the context of the immediate work being performed on the job.

As was the case with Maslow, Herzberg's ideas gave us an interesting and a useful framework for considering a variety of needs and rewards that are important to employee motivation. His model, however, has failed as an accurate statement of the process by which these needs influence behavior and performance. Few serious students of management today accept the notion of a discontinuity between satisfiers and dissatisfiers. These constitute two opposite ends of the same continuum, and both have measurable impacts on employee motivation and performance.

In recent years the field of psychology has given us three models of motivation that focus on the process (as opposed to the content) of motivation. When combined, these have provided a rich and fruitful approach to understanding employee effort, behavior, and performance. These are: (1) the **behaviorist-reinforcement model**, (2) **expectancy theory**, and (3) **equity theory**.[1]

The behaviorist-reinforcement model is a product of over 70 years of scientific investigation, beginning with the work of John Watson at the turn of the twentieth century, continuing with the work of Clark Hull during the 1930s, 1940s, and 1950s, and developing further in the more recent work of B. F. Skinner in the 1960s and 1970s.

Three concepts are fundamental to the behaviorist model diagrammed in Figure 11-2:

1. *Drive* is an internal state of need. It can be started by a variety of conditions, including the needs described above in the content models of motivation. Under conditions of drive, an individual is aroused—his or her behavior is energized. Needs then arouse the drive that motivates behavior. Needs, furthermore, fall into two classes: (a) primary and (b) secondary. Primary needs (like hunger

---

[1]Much of the discussion is drawn from W. Haynes, J. Massie, and M. Wallace, *Management: Analysis, Concepts, and Cases*, 3rd Ed. (Englewood Cliffs: Prentice-Hall, 1975), Chapter 5.

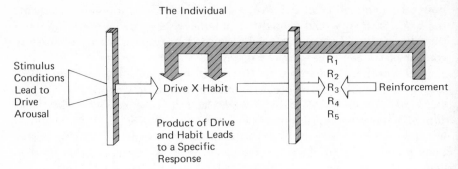

Figure 11-2
An Outline of Hull's Model

and thirst) are unlearned. Secondary needs (like money, power) are learned; they must be acquired through experience.

2. *Habit* is a learned connection between a condition or event in the employee's environment and a response (behavior) to that event. Behaviorist psychologists label the event S and the response R. The habit itself is denoted as "S-R," indicating a stimulus-response connection. The habit (S-R connection) determines the *choice* and *direction* of employee behavior. If an employee, for example, has learned that he can reduce the need for money by working at a given level of performance, the next time he has been aroused by a need for money he can be expected to work at the same level of performance.

The notions of drive and habit combine in multiplicative fashion to result in observed behavior. The *product* of drive times habit (S-R) leads to the selection of a specific behavior or response in a *given* set of stimulus conditions. Note that the S-R model deals explicitly with the issues of strength and direction of employee effort and performance. Without the presence of drive, performance would not be energized. Without the presence of habit (S-R), behavior and performance would be random, unorganized, and not directed toward specific actions.

3. *Reinforcement* is an event (stimulus) that follows a response or action. A reinforcer or reward has two impacts on the employee: (1) Reinforcement reduces drive; that is, the employee's need is satisfied. Most psychologists add, therefore, that the experience of reinforcement is pleasurable and attractive to the individual. (2) Reinforcement strengthens habit (S-R) connections. Through the process of reinforcement, therefore, new habits are learned.

Understanding of the behaviorist model is central to an explanation of a great deal of employee behavior and employee learning. The experience of a need or set of needs leads to the arousal of drive. Such arousal energizes behavior—makes the employee capable of performance. Habits (both learned and unlearned) serve to direct behavior and make it predictable under the same need conditions. Finally, reinforcement is a powerful force that (a) reduces a felt need and (b) leads to both learning new behaviors and retaining other behaviors under similar circumstances.

B. F. Skinner has made a valuable contribution to our understanding of reinforcement as a powerful managerial tool for controlling and shaping patterns of employee behavior. Two generalizations about reinforcement emerge from his work. First, the timing or *scheduling* of reinforcements is at least as important as the absolute level of reinforcement. He has demonstrated, for example, that intermittent reinforcement (rewarding the desired behavior only part of the time) is more effective than constant reinforcement (rewarding the desired behavior each time that it occurs). Second, Skinner has demonstrated a vital distinction between the notion of *reinforcement* on one hand, and that of *punishment* on the other:

> Reinforcement can be positive or negative. Positive reinforcement is the presentation of an attractive stimulus following the desired behavior. Negative reinforcement is the *removal* of an aversive or unpleasant stimulus following the desired response.
>
> Punishment, on the other hand, consists of *removing* a pleasant event following an undesired behavior or *presenting* an aversive or unpleasant stimulus following an undesired response.

Note the important differences between reinforcement and punishment. According to strict Skinnerian logic, behavior can only be positively influenced and learned under conditions of reinforcement (positive or negative). The reason for this is that reinforcement focuses upon the desired behavior, and therefore gives the employee a great deal of information. Punishment, in contrast, can only serve to disrupt an undesired behavior. It carries no informational content about the desired behavior. Under conditions of punishment, the employee only knows that whatever he or she is doing is wrong.

The behaviorist-reinforcement model has two major qualities associated with it. First, it has been developed and thoroughly tested in a rigorous scientific fashion. Generalizations made from it to applied settings are on firm theoretical and empirical ground. Second, much of the content of the model lends itself directly to one of the most cogent and pressing concerns of managers: how does one influence the behavior and performance of others? This model is only now influencing the applied field of management. We should expect to see a great deal more influence and application of the model in future years.

The major weakness of the behaviorist-reinforcement model is that it tends to be mechanistic in its conception of the human mind and thought processes. Indeed, strict Skinnerian thinking downplays the necessity even to be very explicit about what goes on in the mind of a person in the process of motivation. According to such thinking, the scientist need only predict tangible behavior (observable actions) from tangible events (stimuli) in order to understand motivation. In a sense, therefore, the individual is quite passive in the behaviorist model. In contrast to the behaviorist-reinforcement models, **cognitive** models focus directly on the individual employee as an active and conscious agent in his or her work environment. A basic premise of the cognitive models we are about to examine is that the individual is a conscious decision maker. Indeed, these models propose that an employee's decision is a result of (1) the outcomes he or she believes will result from the response, and (2) the value or importance of such outcomes to the person.

Although early cognitive models of behavior are credited to the work of such psychologists as Kurt Lewin and E. C. Tolman during the 1930s and 1940s, the work of Victor Vroom has had the most pronounced effect upon management's thinking about employee motivation in recent years. In 1964, he published what has become a standard reference statement about the process of employee motivation. His model has become known as **Expectancy Theory** and represents the translation of a normative statistical decision model (often found in economics) into the language of psychology.

Expectancy theory focuses directly on the process of human decision making and emphasizes the cognitive processes by which alternatives are evaluated in terms of valued outcomes and likelihoods that such outcomes will occur if a given alternative is chosen. Accordingly, Vroom argues that an employee's motivation is the effort or force driving a person to a specific act. In the case of employment the act will most likely be some level of job performance. The motivation or force behind a specific level of work performance will be a function of two perceptions on the part of the employee:

1. the probability or perceived likelihood that certain outcomes will result from the person's effort; and,
2. the value or utility of such outcomes to the employee.

Figure 11-3 outlines the way an expectancy theorist explains employee behavior. Before expending a given level of effort, a worker will likely ask, "If I make a strong effort on this job, will a superior level of performance be achieved? And, if I do achieve such an outstanding level of performance, what kinds of rewards (or negative outcomes) will occur?"

The answer to this line of questioning is what Vroom characterizes as an **expectancy**, that is, the personal probability estimate that a given level of effort will result in a given outcome (superior performance). The expectancy alone, however, is not all the employee needs to know before acting. The person also needs to know how valuable that outcome or performance level is to him or her. Vroom calls this value a **valence** and argues that the valence associated with a first-level outcome (like performance) is in turn determined by the personal probability that the performance will lead to a series of **second-level outcomes** together with the valences associated with those outcomes (e.g., income, social approval, job security, promotion, and accomplishment).

The employee described in Figure 11-3, for example, may believe that performance at a high level (first-level outcome) will result in being paid a higher wage (second-level outcome). The degree to which the worker believes that high performance will lead to higher pay is also a subjective guess or probability, which Vroom calls an **instrumentality** perception. In addition, high pay has some value or valence associated with it. The combination of the valence of secondary outcomes and the instrumentality that first-level outcomes (such as high performance level) will result in a secondary outcome (e.g., higher pay) determines the valence associated with first-level outcomes. Finally, the force, effort, or motivation to achieve first-level outcomes is determined by the valence of the first-level outcome combined with the expectancy that a given level of effort will actually result in the desired first-level outcome.

A final note on expectancy theory relates to the notion of **job satisfaction** or **morale**, a topic that has long been discussed by students of

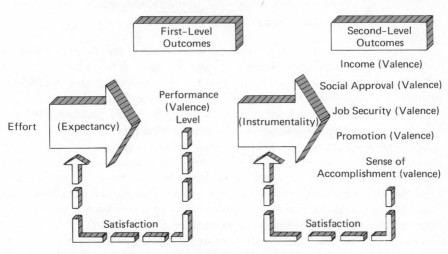

Figure 11-3
An Outline of Expectancy Theory

management. Job satisfaction is characterized most frequently by behavioral scientists as an attitudinal reaction to the job. It represents a reflection on the employee's part about how happy or unhappy he or she is with various aspects of the job, including the work itself, supervision, pay, and other, peripheral matters. Psychologists call such a reaction an **affective reaction** or attitude. The concept of satisfaction fits in very nicely in expectancy theory. Accordingly, employees consciously evaluate the results of their behavior. If the outcomes experienced confirm the expectancies and instrumentalitites originally experienced, satisfaction will result. If not, dissatisfaction will result. Note the close similarity between the behaviorists' notion of reinforcement and that of satisfaction. Both are rewarding, both tend to reinforce learning. Indeed, satisfaction plays an extremely important role as feedback (indicated by the dotted line in Figure 11-3), which causes the individual to readjust efforts and behavior in response to changing work conditions.

In addition to the behaviorist and expectancy models, a third area of theory development has influenced management thought about employee motivation during the late 1960s and 1970s. This model has been named **Equity Theory** and brings together two quite different lines of theoretical development: the notion of Distributive Justice and the concept of Cognitive Dissonance. The name most often cited for developing the equity model is J. Stacy Adams. According to equity theory, each employee constantly engages in a form of social comparison. In this process employees attempt to evaluate each other's returns from the work experience relative to the contribution each has made. This kind of comparison can be represented as follows:

$$\frac{\text{Person's Outcomes}}{\text{Person's Inputs}} \quad \text{vs.} \quad \frac{\text{Others' Outcomes}}{\text{Others' Inputs}}$$

If these two ratios are equal (that is, returns are proportionate to inputs), then **distributive justice** is said to exist. The achievement of distributive justice (or equity) is said to be a powerful and overriding motive for employees. If these two ratios diverge in either direction, a state of cognitive dissonance is said to develop. Social psychologists use the term **cognitive dissonance** to describe a situation in which a person experiences something that he or she neither expects nor desires to experience. The experience of dissonance is a motivating event, very similar to the behaviorist's notion of drive. Its experience is unpleasant, and the individual will behave in ways expected to reduce dissonance. In fact, the reduction of dissonance following some action on the employee's part serves the same purpose as reward or reinforcement. It is experienced as pleasurable, and it will reinforce whatever behavior preceded it. Hence, dissonance reduction influences the direction of behavior—it serves to shape behavior.

All three process theories we have considered so far—the behaviorist-reinforcement model, expectancy theory, and equity theory—are complementary to each other; they fit nicely together to provide a rounded view of employee motivation. This comparison is illustrated in Figure 11-4. Basically, questions of employee motivation boil down to three major issues:

What arouses or energizes behavior?

What directs behavior?

What outcomes that occur as a result of behavior tend to feedback and influence subsequent behavior?

Figure 11-4 illustrates the complementary ways in which the three theories address these three questions. With respect to arousal, the behaviorist model proposes drive, while the expectancy model describes valence and equity theory discusses cognitive dissonance.

Similarly, direction of behavior is explained by habit in the behaviorist model and by expectancy and instrumentality in expectancy theory. This is the only motivational question not directly addressed in equity theory. Finally reinforcement, satisfaction, and equity all play similar roles in addressing the question of outcomes that feedback and influence subsequent behavior.

The great contribution of the process theories of motivation has been in increasing our understanding of the processes or mechanisms by which employee behavior occurs. Both the behaviorist and expectancy

**Aspect of
Motivation**

	Arousal	Direction	Outcome
Behavioral Model	Drive	Habit	Reinforcement
Expectancy Model	Valence	Expectancy and Instrumentality	Satisfaction
Equity Model	Dissonance	—	Equity or Distributive Justice

Figure 11-4
Integrating the Behaviorist, Expectancy, and Equity Models

models suggest specific mechanisms by which individual responses to the work environment are aroused and directed. When combined with the content theories which suggest specific kinds of needs or motives operating among employees, the process theories show a great deal of promise as sources of information to guide practicing managers in directing the activities of employees.

Leadership–
A Case Combining
Applied Sociology
and Psychology

A third important line of research and theoretical development over the last 30 years combines the work of applied sociologists and psychologists: the study of leadership. Leadership has long been considered one of the most important factors influencing organizational performance and achievement of goals.

Although a variety of definitions of leadership have been proposed over the years, we can say that leadership is the practice of influence. Thus, **leadership** is a process through which the performance of others is influenced by a person occupying a leadership role. Leadership is thus an important part of study in management, though it is by no means synonymous with management.

The primary emphasis of early research on leadership was psychological in nature and focused on the *traits* or personality characteristics typically found among successful leaders. Such researchers began a long task of "laundry-listing" all conceivable personal characteristics of so-called "great" leaders. Such compilations included the following kinds of characteristics:

Age
Maturity
Intelligence
Physical bearing
Height
Education
Decisiveness
Extroversion
Verbal skills
Prestige
Attractiveness
Charisma
Popularity
Aggressiveness

The problem with these early efforts was that they left too many questions about leadership unanswered. For example, is there any optimal combination of traits that is most critical in determining one's success as a leader? In what ways do such characteristics influence one's ability to lead? Are these characteristics that one can learn, or must one be born with them? Although such qualities might have fit popular stereotypes characterizing popular leaders or great personalities, their citation did little to expand our knowledge about the *process* of leadership.

It was not until a sociological view of the problem was combined with the psychological approach that headway was made in understanding leadership. Characteristic of these efforts was work carried out by researchers at Ohio State University in the 1950s. They recognized that leadership involves an interpersonal *relationship* between a leader and subordinates. Furthermore, the most critical element in this relationship is the *behavior* of the leader toward the subordinates.

This realization led them to focus their research efforts on the set of behaviors or actions that constituted leader behavior. Their basic approach was to isolate and measure the dimensions underlying leader behavior that could be used to define leadership; it was an empirical approach. A questionnaire was designed, with over 100 specific kinds of acts or behaviors a manager might engage in while supervising the work of others. The leader's subordinates were asked to use the questionnaire to describe the leader's behavior. The following is an illustration of the kinds of questions contained in the instrument that has come to be known as the **Leader Behavior Description Questionnaire** (LBDQ).

The subordinate indicates the degree to which each of the following statements describes the actions of the supervisor:

Refuses to give in when people disagree with him
Is easy to understand
Refuses to explain his actions
Encourages overtime work
Tries out his new ideas
Assigns people under him to specific tasks

Subsequent analysis of several thousand subordinates' responses to such questions consistently yielded two dimensions or factors that underlie subordinates' descriptions of their leaders: **Initiating Structure** and **Consideration**. In other words, the actions a leader takes regarding subordinates tend to cluster in one of these two major kinds of leader activities. Consideration is the extent to which the leader's behavior toward subordinates is characterized by mutual trust, mutual respect, support for subordinates' ideas, a climate of rapport, and two-way communication. A low score on consideration reflects an impersonal way of dealing with subordinates.

Initiating Structure, on the other hand, is the extent to which a leader defines and structures his role and those of subordinates. A high score reflects a leader who is likely to play a very active role in directing, planning, and scheduling the group's activities. Initiating Structure and Consideration have come to refer to kinds of leadership behavior that constitute a leader's **style**, the way the person influences subordinates.

As so often happens with attractive models, the work of the Ohio State researchers was prematurely applied by others as a set of **normative prescriptions** for leaders to follow, rather than being used as a model to be tested further in order to enhance our understanding of leadership. Many entrepreneurs traveled the country assessing supervisors on their measures of initiating structure and consideration. For some reason, they presumed that the ideal leader is one who is high on both leadership dimensions.

For a fee, they would then provide two kinds of services: (1) diagnose a particular leader's style, using this two-dimension framework; and (2) propose changes (usually involving expensive training programs) in leadership style that should lead to improved leader effectiveness.

In all this entrepreneurial flurry two major questions went unanswered: (1) How do we know when a leader is effective? and (2) What factors determine whether or not a given style of leadership behavior will be effective? Reliable answers to the first question remain the subject of continuing research. The problem is that the goals of a leader are many, and each constitutes a valid dimension of leader effectiveness. At the very least, we can say that the following are elements of leader effectiveness: (a) individual effectiveness of subordinates in accomplishing their tasks, (b) the morale or satisfaction of subordinates, (c) the productivity or efficiency of groups of subordinates in accomplishing their tasks, (d) the quality of products or services generated by subordinate groups.

Fortunately, research on what constitutes the most effective leadership style has become the topic of serious research efforts during the 1970s. Two such efforts deserve our particular attention: (1) the work of Fred Fiedler and (2) the path-goal theory of leadership. Building upon the results of the Ohio State studies, Fiedler reasoned, as was mentioned in Chapter 8, that there was probably no single best leader style to fit all work situations. His research has identified three major situational factors that determine the appropriateness of a given style of leadership:

1. *Leader-member relations*: the quality of the leader's relations with subordinates, the confidence they have in the leader, and their loyalty. It is generally measured by asking the leader to rate the

atmosphere of the group on a number of dimensions.

2. *Task structure*: the degree to which the work tasks are routinized. This is generally measured by asking observers to rate the degree of routine observed in carrying out assigned tasks.

3. *Position power*: the amount of formal authority vested in the leader's formal position, including the degree of control over rewards and the degree to which upper management supports the leader in the use of authority.

Fiedler collapsed the original Ohio State dimensions into a single dimension of leader style with employee-oriented behaviors (high consideration) at one extreme and task-oriented behaviors (high initiating structure) at the other extreme. His research (as well as that of subsequent investigators) has found that the most successful style of leader behavior depends upon the situation defined by the three conditions just listed. These contingencies are summarized in Table 11-1. A task-oriented style, for example, appears to be most effective where leader member relations are good and the task is structured. A task-oriented style is best, furthermore, when leader-member relations are good, the task is unstructured, and the leader's position power is strong. Under similar conditions, however, if the leader's position power is weak, an employee-oriented style is more effective. An examination of Table 11-1 will reveal the varying situational conditions under which two entirely different styles of leader behavior can be equally effective.

The major importance of Fiedler's work lies in the discovery that the situation surrounding the leadership role has a critical bearing upon the success of any given leadership style. Subsequent management students have credited Fiedler with introducing a **contingency** or **situational** approach to the study of leadership.

Table 11-1
Summary of Research Findings Regarding Fiedler's Theory

Situational factor			
Leader-member relations	Task structure	Position power	Most effective leadership style
Good	Structured	Strong	Task-oriented
Good	Structured	Weak	Task-oriented
Good	Unstructured	Strong	Task-oriented
Good	Unstructured	Weak	Employer-oriented
Moderately poor	Unstructured	Strong	Employee-oriented
Moderately poor	Structured	Weak	Employee-oriented
Moderately poor	Structured	Strong	Employee-oriented
Moderately poor	Unstructured	Weak	Task-oriented

A second theory of leader effectiveness also concentrates on contingencies as they influence the effectiveness of various leader behavior styles. According to the work of House and his colleagues, leaders can choose the degree to which they engage in four kinds of leader behaviors:

1. *Instrumental Behavior*: very similar to Initiating Structure, consisting of planning, organizing, controlling, and coordinating subordinates closely in their tasks;

2. *Supportive Behavior*: very similar to Consideration, consisting of displaying concern for the interests, needs, and well-being of subordinates;

3. *Participative Behavior*: characterized by sharing information and an emphasis on consultation with subordinates;

4. *Achievement-Oriented Behavior*: setting challenging goals, expecting subordinates to perform at the highest level, and continually seeking improvement in performance.

This model has been labeled a **Path-Goal Theory** of leadership effectiveness, because it proposes that a leader's choice of these behaviors should be premised upon a goal of increasing personal payoffs to subordinates for work-goal attainment, and making the path to these payoffs as free of obstacles as possible. The path-goal model, furthermore, is a contingency model, in that it posits that the appropriate mix of such leader behaviors depends on two major sets of factors: (a) the individuals being supervised, and (b) the characteristics of the work environment.

Individual characteristics influencing the impact of leader behaviors include: (1) Ability—the greater the employee's perceived level of ability to accomplish a task, the less the individual will accept direction or instrumental behavior on the part of the leader. (2) Locus of control—this is the degree to which employees believe they have control over what happens to them. Those who believe that they have a great deal of control over what happens to them are said to react more favorably to a participative leader, and others would prefer a more directive leader. (3) Needs and motives—the particular set of needs that are felt strongly by an employee will affect the impact of a particular set of leader behaviors on that person's performance. People with a high need for autonomy will probably react negatively to instrumental kinds of leader behavior.

A number of organizational characteristics, in addition to subordinates', are also proposed by path-goal theory as influences on the effectiveness of leader behavior. Specifically, three broad groups of work environment properties have been studied: (1) subordinates' tasks—the degree of structure involved in work operations; (2) the work group—

informal work group norms and cohesiveness; and (3) organizational factors—stress levels in the work situation, situations involving high uncertainty, and the degree to which rules, procedures, and policies govern an employee's work.

A full explication of contingency leadership theories is beyond the scope of this chapter. It is important, however, to note that present research on the topic of leadership is just now beginning to yield an understanding of the complexities of leadership phenomena. The practice of leadership involves elements of the leader's own personality and behavior, complex relationships between the leader and subordinates, informal group characteristics, and a variety of characteristics of the formal environment within which work activities are carried out. Any formula, then, that proposes to make one an effective leader by adopting a single ideal leader style is hopelessly wrong, and anyone purporting to sell such a formula is no more of a help than were the snake oil salesmen of 70 or more years ago.

ORGANIZATIONAL BEHAVIOR: A SUMMARY CONCEPT We have examined three illustrations of theoretical development and research in the behavioral sciences that are important and representative of the work this field has contributed to the field of management. Furthermore, we have said that the fields of industrial psychology and industrial sociology have contributed heavily to this tradition.

Actually the 1970s has seen a blending and integration of such efforts into a recognizable field that is now called **organizational behavior (OB)**. Organizational behavior is a field that is primarily concerned with an understanding and prediction of *performance* at the organizational, group, and individual level. To accomplish this, the field focuses on a study of three broad areas: (1) formal organizations and their processes, (2) informal groups and their dynamics, and (3) individual behavior (including the topics of motivation, perception, learning, and personality). Finally, the field of organizational behavior can be identified by its emphasis on the employment of scientific method in conducting investigations and accumulating knowledge. The term *scientific method* implies that a heavy reliance is placed on logically consistent models in developing questions for research and that all such models are submitted to the test of data; that is, all propositions about individual and organizational behavior are subjected to carefully controlled empirical studies. Only after a model or proposition has passed the test of data is it considered confirmed and treated as knowledge.

REFERENCES

ARGYRIS, C., *Interpersonal Competence and Organizational Effectiveness*. Homewood, Ill.: Richard D. Irwin, Inc., 1962.

FIEDLER, FRED, *A Theory of Leadership Effectiveness*. New York: McGraw-Hill Book Co., 1967.

HAYNES, W., J. MASSIE and M. WALLACE, *Management: Analysis, Concepts, and Cases* (3rd ed.). Englewood Cliffs: Prentice-Hall, Inc., 1975.

HERZBERG, FREDERICK, *Work and the Nature of Man*. New York: World Publishing Co., 1966.

HILGARD, ERNEST and GORDON BOWER, *Theories of Learning*. Englewood Cliffs: Prentice-Hall, Inc., 1966.

HOUSE, ROBERT J., "A Path-Goal Theory of Leader Effectiveness," *Administrative Science Quarterly* (1971), pp. 301-332.

IVANCEVICH, J. M., A. D. SZILAGYI, JR. and M. J. WALLACE, JR., *Organizational Behavior and Performance*. Santa Monica, Calif.: Goodyear Publishing Co., Inc., 1977.

MCGREGOR, DOUGLAS, *The Human Side of Enterprise*. New York: McGraw-Hill Book Co., 1960.

NORD, WALTER, "Beyond the Teaching Machine: The Neglected Area of Operant Conditioning in the Theory and Practice of Management," *Organizational Behavior and Human Performance*, 4 (1960), pp. 375-401.

ROETHLISBERGER, F. J. and W. J. DICKSON, *Management and the Worker*. Cambridge, Mass.: Harvard University Press, 1939.

STOGDILL, R. M., *Handbook of Leadership*. New York: Free Press, 1974.

VROOM, VICTOR, *Work and Motivation*. New York: John Wiley & Sons, Inc., 1964.

WHYTE, WILLIAM F., *Money and Motivation*. New York: Harper and Brothers, 1955.

QUANTITATIVE
METHODS
OF
ANALYSIS

by Martin B. Solomon, Jr., University of Kentucky

⟵ **IDEAS TO BE FOUND** ⟶
IN THIS CHAPTER

- Symbols and models
- Strategies and states of nature
- Risk and uncertainty
- Linear programing
- Payoff tables
- Decision trees
- Simulation
- Network analysis (PERT)

Some of the greatest advances in fields fundamental to management have been made in the quantitative disciplines: mathematics and statistics. Although some managers do not possess the necessary background to make the calculations that refined decision-making techniques require, it is becoming increasingly clear that managers must be able to understand the quantitative approach well enough to: (1) *state* their problems in forms that will facilitate the use of specialists in handling quantitative data and (2) *communicate* with specialists in the interpretation of the answers obtained by refined methods.

The general framework for decision making, outlined in Chapter 5, remains useful when quantitative methods are used, but some refinements must be made. These are: (1) the problem must be stated in *quantitative* terms, (2) the relationships must be expressed in *symbols* that facilitate mathematical manipulations, and (3) results of actions must be *measurable*. The modern manager should develop a viewpoint that encourages trials of some of the newer methods. This chapter discusses the fundamental concepts of this viewpoint and introduces some of the methods. A number of books are now available which describe the details of the techniques; therefore, the reader is encouraged to use those books, several of which are listed in the references at the end of this chapter.

SYMBOLS AND MODELS

Symbols   Management involves many complex relationships among numerous factors. These relationships can be expressed vaguely in qualitative terms, but it is often more meaningful to state them in quantitative form. For example, a manager could say that sales increase with costs (qualitative), but it is more helpful to state: Costs consist of two types—fixed and variable; fixed costs are about $50,000 and variable costs increase $.62 for every dollar of sales.

Complex relationships are often difficult without some simplifying means of description and classification. Symbols can be useful for explicitly stating relationships and for making mathematical calculations. For example, the preceding problem could be stated as follows:

$$C = \$50,000 + .62S$$

where C equals total costs and S equals total sales.

If one is not accustomed to their use, symbols may at first appear to be difficult. Actually, they simplify and make explicit the basic factors relating to a problem. Stating thoughts in symbols also makes it possible for the manager to communicate with mathematical specialists, who may then be able to help in the analysis of relationships with tools not otherwise available. Furthermore, the increased use of electronic computers makes it desirable for the manager to become accustomed to the use of symbols.

Models   The manager bases actions on theories about the interrelationships among variables. These theories may be implicit in the actions or they may be stated explicitly as assumptions in words or in symbols. A manager who has several variables to consider simultaneously may find that it is easier to represent them with symbols. The manager may develop a model for the problem. A model is merely a representation of some part of real life. A **mathematical model** is an attempt to represent the important aspects of the real world in an equation, or series of equations, in order to understand or predict real-world events.

Some models are simple, others are complex; the degree of complexity depends upon how much of the real world is included. For example, a complete model of a firm would include detailed descriptions of each individual customer. The simplified model would describe general patterns of consumer behavior.

Mathematical models are powerful tools of analysis in decision making because each symbol representing a variable can be explicitly defined and the relationships of the most relevant variables can be stated. Typically, a decision model consists of the most important assumptions, variables, and relationships relevant to a decision. In short, a symbolic model focuses on the quantitative aspects of a problem and restricts one's consideration to a stated group of factors by clearly stating assumptions. Thus, by treating the situation as a closed system, limited by explicit assumption, the decision maker can determine more rigorously the relevant factors, available alternatives, and possible outcomes.

Any decision model consists of (1) an *objective function*—a symbolic statement of an objective of the decision making, such as maximizing profits or minimizing costs; (2) a set of *contraints* or relevant factors that are important for consideration; and (3) *hypotheses* of the relationships among the factors. Management scientists refer to those factors that are not within one's control as **states of nature**, the uncontrollable possible events that affect outcomes of alternatives. On the other hand, the decision maker has control over the choice of a *strategy*, a statement of preference for a certain pattern of response, and can identify certain guidelines for decisions, which are called *decision rules*. For example, the head of a business may select a marketing strategy of providing a full line of products, with a clear-cut decision rule of dropping any product that does not cover variable costs.

Conditions under which managers make decisions vary along a continuum from those of perfect certainty to those of complete uncertainty. A manager can assume certainty and use a **deterministic model**, one in which all the factors are assumed exact, with chance playing no role. On the other hand, to treat chance quantitatively in the model, a **probabilistic model** may be constructed, one in which a quantitative representation of probability is included.

A business model will never completely describe the real world. Its purpose is to help direct attention to the most important variables, but the assumptions of the model need not be completely realistic; it is more important that the model yield useful or accurate predictions. The necessary precision desired by the user of the model, therefore, is an important factor determining the type of model. In other words, a model useful to one firm may be useless to another.

CERTAINTY, RISK, AND UNCERTAINTY

Being oriented toward the future, a manager necessarily faces problems with various degrees of uncertainty. In some cases, however, it may be desirable to assume conditions of certainty. For example, the cost per mile of driving a truck between two towns will vary for each trip, but the variability may be so slight that, for practical purposes, a manager may assume that the cost is known. It may be useful to build a model, assuming **conditions of certainty** in which it is assumed that the outcome can be predicted perfectly from the knowledge at hand. Although few situations exist in which the manager posesses perfect information, it is often useful to assume specific values for some variables in order to analyze the effect of other variables.

Problems that face a manager vary with the existing degree of uncertainty. In many problems, even without sufficient information to predict the outcome, it may be possible to determine the chances that different outcomes may result. Those situations in which the manager knows only the *probability* of the occurrence of the events are called **conditions of risk**. Cases in which the manager possesses neither perfect nor probabilistic information about the occurrence of possible events are referred to as **conditions of uncertainty**. This classification tends to over-simplify the numerous degrees of uncertainty, but it is useful as a concep-tual device for distinguishing types of models and for introducing the concept of probability. Models that include elements of probability are sometimes called **stochastic models**.

Probability (usually represented by the symbol P) can be defined as the percentage of times in which a specific outcome would occur if an event were repeated a very large number of times. Two methods of determining probability are *a priori* and *empirical*. In the cases of **a priori probability**, management would, through deduction from as-sumed principles, obtain information about probability. For example, one knows that the probability of a head on the flip of a fair coin is .5. It is not necessary to toss the coin a large number of times in order to predict that in about one-half of the cases the outcome will be heads. Through knowledge of the conditions of the coin, one can deduce the probability of the results, without being able to predict with certainty the outcome of any single toss.

Empirical probability is based on recording actual experience over a period of time and computing the percentage of times that each event occurred. Management usually has considerable historical data that can be used in computing such a percentage. For example, the insurance industry is based on probabilities developed from past experience. Through use of its experience tables, a life insurance company can predict the percentage of 40-year-old policy holders who will die in the next year. Although the company cannot predict whether or not a specific 40-year-old person will die, it operates on the basis of the **law of large numbers** (which states that mass phenomena tend toward regularity of behavior).

Attitudes concerning uncertainty differ from one person to the next. This subjective element should be recognized; yet, it does not eliminate the possibility of employing a systematic approach to managerial problems. Manager A may dislike taking risks; Manager B may be venturesome. Manager A may not feel like taking a "fair" gamble—not be willing to pay $1.00 for a one-tenth chance of winning $10. Manager B may be willing to pay $1.50 for a one-tenth chance of winning $10. This difference in attitudes may be caused by numerous factors: (1) past successes in taking chances, (2) familiarity with the basic arithmetic of computing odds, (3) available resources (A may not have the $1.00), and (4) the disutility of losing the money that is bet compared with the utility of potential winnings. Many managers seem to require some premium above the fair odds before they will take risks. One firm may be large enough to risk large sums of money, the loss of which would not create a threat to its existence, whereas a small firm may not be able to undertake some project with highly favorable odds of success because a loss may mean bankruptcy.

The differences in the subjective reaction to risk taking create many interesting problems that are beyond the scope of this book. One example, however, will illustrate the need for quantifying subjective probabilities, that is, assigning definite values of P for various alternatives even though the values are merely estimates in the mind of the manager. Within the same firm, managers have different feelings about assuming risks. Competing projects that are considered by these managers have different chances for success. The quantification of the subjective probabilities by each manager offers a means of communication among the managers about probabilities. If there is no method of comparing the probability estimates, how can it be determined which manager's attitude is consistent with the policies of the firm regarding risk taking?

Because managers must make decisions under conditions of risks and uncertainty, they cannot avoid developing some criteria for their decisions. If they wait until they have complete knowledge, they will forego opportunities for profitable actions. If they can estimate the probabilities of outcomes, they can systematically make the decisions that they think will maximize their profits.

SOME ILLUSTRATIONS OF QUANTITATIVE TECHNIQUES

Numerous quantitative techniques are available to managers. Some of these are listed in Table 12-1. The remaining sections of this chapter will concentrate on four of the most important techniques: (1) linear programing, (2) stochastic methods, (3) simulation techniques, and (4) network analysis. These four techniques may be used in a wide range of problems and are typical of the newer methods being used in research and business.

Linear Programing

A fundamental technique for allocating available resources under conditions of certainty, developed since World War II, is called linear programing. **Linear programing** is a mathematical procedure for optimizing the use of resources, given an objective and resource limitations that are stated as linear functions. The actual calculations used in this technique are often complicated but can be handled by a general procedure called the simplex method. Although the details of this method are too involved to discuss here, it is possible to demonstrate the use of linear programing by a graphical illustration.

Table 12-1
Checklist of Quantitative Techniques

Name of Technique	Applications	Description
Sampling	Market research. Work sampling. Inventory control. Auditing.	Through the use of various designs, sampling makes possible inferences about population characteristics with specified degrees of reliability.
Linear programing	Used to allocate scarce resources in an optimum manner in problems of scheduling, product mix, and so on.	Key factors include an objective function, choice among several alternatives, limits or constraints stated in symbols, and variables assumed to be linear.
Decision theory	Used to select the best course of action when information is given in probabilistic form.	Developments in Bayesian statistics allow the executive's judgment to be systematically brought into the analysis of problems.
Correlation	The study of the degree of functional relationship among two or more variables.	One variable can be estimated if the value of another variable is known. Key factors: regression analysis, correlation coefficients, and scatter diagrams.
Game theory	Used to determine the optimum strategy in a competitive situation.	Most solutions involve two persons, in sum zero competitive situations (ones in which two people are involved and one person wins exactly what the other loses). More complex situations become extremely involved.

Table 12-1 (cont'd.)

Name of Technique	Applications	Description
Index numbers	Measurement of fluctuations in prices, volume, economic activity, or other variables over a period of time, relative to a base.	Important factors include the choice of the base period, the method of weighting, and the selection of the components to be included in the index.
Time series analysis	Interpretation of sales, production, price, or other variables over a period of time.	Series of data over a period of time are analyzed as to their chief types of fluctuations such as trend, cyclical, seasonal, and irregular.
Simulation	Used to imitate an operation or process prior to actual performance. Business games are popular applications.	Long periods of time are simulated in short trials. Complex groups of variables can be handled when no mathematical method is available.
Waiting-line theory	To analyze the feasibility of adding facilities and to assess the amount and cost of waiting time.	Most models assume a specific distribution of arrivals and service times. Sometimes called queueing theory.
PERT (Program evaluation review technique)	Planning and control of a complex set of activities, functions, and relationships.	Key concepts include: (1) network of events and activities; (2) resource allocation; (3) time and cost considerations; (4) network paths; and (5) critical paths.
Statistical quality control charts	To distinguish those variations due to chance from those due to assignable causes in production.	Results of samples (e.g., means and ranges) are plotted, on charts having upper and lower control limits. If values for the sample fall within these limits, the production process is considered under control. If outside, management should look for a cause of the variations.
Inventory models	Determine when and how much inventory to carry.	Simple models assume no delivery delay and that demand is known. Probabilistic models handle situations of risk and uncertainty.

Suppose that a firm can produce either one or both of two products: toothpicks and matchsticks. At capacity, the available machines can produce either 15 million toothpicks per day or 10 million matchsticks per day, or any combination of both, subject to the limitation:

$$2T + 3M = 30,000,000$$

where T equals the number of toothpicks and M equals the number of matchsticks.

If we substitute zero for toothpicks, it can be seen that we could produce 10 million matchsticks. If the firm produced 9 million toothpicks, how many matchsticks could also be produced? Substituting 9,000,000 for T in the equation and solving for M (the equation would read: $2(9,000,000) + 3M = 30,000,000$) we get 4,000,000 matchsticks per day.

Suppose that as a further limitation the firm must (because of a labor contract) operate eight hours a day and hire exactly 100 workers (800 man-hours per day). These workers are needed to carry wood to the machines and to package the finished product. Assume that the workers can haul and pack 20 million toothpicks or 8 million matchsticks per day, or any combination of both. These assumptions could be stated as:

$$8T + 20M = 160,000,000$$

The above two equations could be shown graphically as a machine constraint and a labor constraint (see Figure 12-1). Assume that our objective is to maximize profit.

If matchsticks return a profit of $100 per million produced and toothpicks $60 per million produced, we could state an objective function as:

$$\$60\,\frac{T}{1\text{ million}} + \$100\,\frac{M}{1\text{ million}} = \text{Maximum}$$

In other words, we want to produce the optimum quantity of toothpicks and matchsticks that will maximize our profit. Two illustrations of our objective function are plotted on Figure 12-1. Notice that an objective function can be drawn for any level of production, representing various combinations of toothpicks and matchsticks that yield equal profit (hence, each is called an iso-profit line).

Because our problem is to maximize profit, we will push the objective function as far from the origin as possible and still remain under or on the constraint lines, i.e., inside the feasibility space. (Notice that iso-profit lines represent larger profits as they move away from the origin.) The solution will always be found at some intersection. In this case, we can push the objective function out until we reach the point 5 million matchsticks and 7.5 million toothpicks. At that point our profit would be

$$\$60\,\frac{(7.5\text{ million})}{1\text{ million}} + \$100\,\frac{(5\text{ million})}{1\text{ million}} = \$950\text{ per day.}$$

This simplified example serves only to indicate the class of problems that are solvable by means of linear programing. If we had additional constraints, we might find that some other combination of matchsticks and

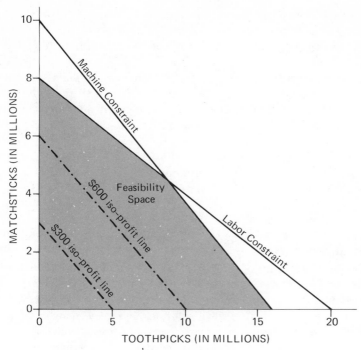

Figure 12-1
Graphical Illustration of Linear Programing

toothpicks would prove more profitable. If we had additional products and additional constraints, it would be impossible to show the relationships in a simple two-dimensional graph.

Multiple Criteria Problems in Linear Programing* A primary difficulty in modern decision analysis is the treatment of multiple objectives. The question becomes one of value trade-offs in the social structure of varying interests. A formal decision analysis capable of handling such situations is a new entrant in the field of management technology.

The organizational goals depend very much on the character and type of organization, the philosophy of management, and environmental conditions. Profit maximization, which is regarded as the sole objective of the business firm, is one of the most widely accepted goals of management, but is not always the only goal. The various formal solution techniques that have been needed for decision analysis are concerned

*Contribution by Sridhar Kadaba, Doctoral Candidate, University of Kentucky.

primarily with making the right selection from a set of alternatives. However, in recent years, the nature of major decision problems has changed drastically and the adequacy of many solution techniques has been questioned.

Goal programming is a special extension of linear programming which is capable of handling a decision problem with multiple goals and multiple subgoals. Often goals set by management are achievable only at the expense of other goals. In goal programming, instead of trying to maximize or minimize the objective criterion directly, as in linear programming, the deviations between goals and what can be achieved within the given set of constraints are minimized. Thus the objective function becomes the minimization of these deviations, based on the relative importance of priority assigned to them. The true value of goal programming lies in its ability to solve problems involving multiple, conflicting goals according to the manager's priority structure, with a greater emphasis on "satisfying" rather than "maximizing."

Another extension of **linear programming** is in the solution of problems involving multiple objectives and is termed **multiple objective linear programming**. In this technique the ordering of the objectives is very crucial in obtaining the optimal solution. Forestry management, manpower allocation, water resource problems, and media selection problems in advertising are some of the areas in which the techniques mentioned above are being used.

Stochastic Methods In many management problems, *the probability* of the occurrence of an event can be assumed to be known, even when a particular outcome is unpredictable. Under these conditions of risk, stochastic methods will be useful. Actually, stochastic methods merely systematize the thinking about assumptions, facts, and goals that is involved in decisions under conditions of risk.

Three steps are basic to formalizing the factors to be considered in a decision involving probabilities: (1) The decision maker should first lay out, in tabular form, all the possible *actions* that seem reasonable to consider and all the possible *outcomes* of these actions. (2) The decision maker must then state in quantitative form a "probability distribution" projecting chances of each outcome that might result from each act. In this step, a priori or empirical methods may be used, or it may only be possible to assign probabilities that are reasonable estimates. The key to this step is to state explicitly the various probabilities that might be attached to each act-outcome situation. (3) Finally, the decision maker must use some quantitative yardstick of value (usually dollars) that measures the value of each outcome. It is then possible to calculate an average of the outcome-values weighted by the assigned probabilities; the result is called the **expected monetary value.**

To illustrate the use of these steps, suppose that a store manager must decide whether to stock Brand A or Brand B. Either brand can be stocked, but not both. If A is stocked and it is a success, the manager can make $200, but if it is a failure, there can be a loss of $500. If Brand B is stocked and it is a success, the manager can make $400, but if it is a failure, there can be a loss of $300. Which brand should be stocked? Without some idea of the probabilities of success and failure of these brands, the manager's thinking cannot be quantified. But assume that the manager's feelings about the probabilities of each outcome are:

Probability of	Brand A	Brand B
Success	.80	.50
Failure	.20	.50

Payoff Table The store manager can present the above information in tabular form, showing the conditional values for each **strategy** (choice of brand) under each **state of nature** (the combination of uncontrollable factors, such as demand, that determine success or failure). The simplest payoff table is illustrated in Table 12-2 as the first step in stating strategies and possible outcomes.

Table 12-2 Payoff Table

Strategy	State of Nature (Demand)	
	Success	Failure
Stock Brand A	$200	−$500
Stock Brand B	$400	−$300

With the information in Table 12-2, the store manager can use subjective estimates of risks assumed above and multiply the conditional values by their probability of occurrence. This calculation will result in *expected values*. Table 12-3 shows the expected value payoffs, using the assumed payoff in Table 12-2 and the above feelings about the probability of success for Brands A and B.

Table 12-3 Expected Value Payoff Table

Strategy	State of Nature	
	Success	Failure
Stock Brand A	$200 × .80 = $160	−$500 × .20 = −$100
Stock Brand B	$400 × .50 = $200	−$300 × .50 = −$150

From the expected value payoff table, the store manager can determine the total expected value for each strategy by obtaining the sum of

165

the expected values for each state of nature. If Brand A is stocked, the total expected value is $60 ($160-$100); if Brand B is stocked, the total expected value is $50 ($200-$150); therefore, under the assumptions in this case, the store manager would decide to stock Brand A, because its total expected value is $10 more than if Brand B were stocked. Obviously, if the total expected value for stocking each brand had been negative, the manager would decide not to stock either, because there would probably be a loss under either strategy.

Decision Trees In order to examine problems of this type better, a *tree diagram* is useful. With it, extremely complex problems can be analyzed. A tree diagram shows each choice situation together with each payoff and each probability. A tree diagram for the problem of the choice of brands appears in Figure 12-2.

To interpret the tree in Figure 12-2, we would start at the origin or trunk of the tree. If we choose Brand A we have an 80 percent chance of making $200 and a 20 percent chance of losing $500. Our expected value is $60. If we choose Brand B we have a 50 percent chance of making $400 and a 50 percent chance of losing $300. Our expected profit is $50. If we can choose only one product, we would pick Brand A.

The manager should be aware of the possibility of using such a technique but must also interpret the results correctly. It is altogether possible that in the problem of the choice of brands, the manager will lose money. It is important to remember that an expected monetary profit of $60 does not mean an assured profit of $60. It merely means that if this decision is made many times, on the average there would be $60 profit if the choice was Brand A and on the average there would be $50 profit each time the choice was Brand B. If Brand A is stocked only once, there may be a loss of $500, but the chances of a greater profit are better by choosing Brand A.

With the help of a person specialized in stochastic model-building, some of the manager's most pressing problems are capable of analysis. The prerequisite, however, is for the manager to be able to state beliefs in a concise manner (in terms of probabilities) so that the model builder can handle the factors mathematically.

**Simulation
Techniques** Often, when a management problem is too complex to be answered by a series of mathematical equations, it is possible to simulate the probable outcomes before taking action. In this way, the manager may rapidly try out on paper (or with a computer) the results of proposed actions before the actions are taken. By trying out several policies, it is possible to determine which one has the best chance of providing the optimum result.

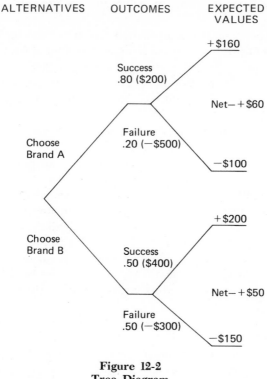

ALTERNATIVES	OUTCOMES	EXPECTED VALUES

+$160

Success
.80 ($200)

Net— +$60

Choose
Brand A

Failure
.20 (−$500)

−$100

+$200

Choose
Brand B

Success
.50 ($400)

Net— +$50

Failure
.50 (−$300)

−$150

Figure 12-2
Tree Diagram

The idea of randomness represented by random numbers is at the heart of simulation. **Random numbers** are numbers, each of which has the same chance of being selected. Tables of random numbers are now readily available.

One type of simulation is used in queueing problems, ones in which the need for personnel or equipment varies over a time period but the determination of the peak demands cannot be estimated because the occurrence is random or due to chance. With simulation, the manager can try out available strategies as they might result in different outcomes, depending upon probabilities from a table of random numbers. For example, the store manager may wish to determine the work schedules for three salespeople to serve customers and to decide whether to add a fourth salesperson. The problem arises from not knowing when customers may appear in the store. Experience may indicate the probabilities that at some hours of the day all three salespeople will be serving customers, but that at other times the salespeople will be idle. In simulating the traffic for a day, the manager may wish to use subjective probabilites for those times in which there are no data from experience; but even if there are no experience data, it is still possible to simulate an activity by using random numbers.

In practice, simulation is carried out by electronic computers. In seconds, a computer can perform thousands of simulation trials and at the same time compile all costs. At the present time, inventory decision rules are commonly tested on computers. The executive specifies such things as reorder points and order quantities, and the computer generates the total cost for, say, five years. Then the executive specifies a different reorder point and order quantity and the computer determines the costs of that policy over the same period of time. After many different policies are put through the series of simulation runs, the best policy can be selected.

Network Analysis

Network analysis is a general-purpose schematic technique used to identify all the interconnecting links in a system. The technique is useful for describing the elements in a complex situation for the purpose of designing, planning, coordinating, controlling, and making decisions. The network approach has many applications; we shall discuss one which focuses on the critical path in scheduling.

Critical path analysis uses network analysis for scheduling production, construction projects, and research and development activities and in other situations that require estimates of time and performance. A sophisticated version of this technique (PERT—Program Evaluation and Review Technique) was first developed for use in defense projects, specifically in the development of the Polaris missile program, but it can be used in many scheduling situations.

The first step in network analysis is to separate each element, or link, and describe it in terms of other elements in the system. In order to present a network pictorially, one must distinguish the activities and events involved. An **activity** is a *time-consuming* effort necessary to complete a particular part of the total project; it is represented by an arrow (————▶) that shows the direction of the sequential activities. An **event** is a specific *instant of time* that denotes the beginning and end of an activity; an event is represented by an ellipse or circle. An event cannot be accomplished until all activities preceding it have been completed. All activities begin and end with an event. The event is a "milestone," or signal for dependent succeeding activities to begin. Events usually are assigned numbers sequentially for identification and analysis. In thinking through the process, one must repeatedly check three questions about the events and activities: (1) which must be accomplished before a given event? (2) which cannot be accomplished until an event is completed? and (3) which can be accomplished concurrently?

After a network has been prepared and times for each activity have been noted, it is possible to determine the path that consists of those events and activities that require the maximum time (by adding the times for all activities along the path). This path is "critical," since it identifies the sequence of activities that will determine the minimum time in which the project can be completed. The **critical path** requires greater attention on the part of management for a number of reasons: (1) Any delay along this path will postpone the final completion date of the project. (2) Special study of each of the activities along the path may result in methods by which more resources or more concurrent activities or a change in the technology used may reduce the time required, which in turn would reduce the overall project time. (3) Advance planning and improvements along the critical path may cause another path to become critical. In short, the critical path approach directs management's attention to the "exceptional" and most significant facts, spots potential bottlenecks early, and avoids unnecessary pressure on the other paths that will not result in an earlier final completion date. Figure 12-3 illustrates a skeleton network and the critical path.

The **Program Evaluation and Review Technique (PERT)**, a special application of network analysis, has received the greatest amount of attention, because it has developed statistical refinements for estimating the time required for each activity and because it is of greatest help in new projects for which little past experience is available. In these cases, PERT has refined the network technique (usually with the help of electronic computers) and has provided danger signals for management that

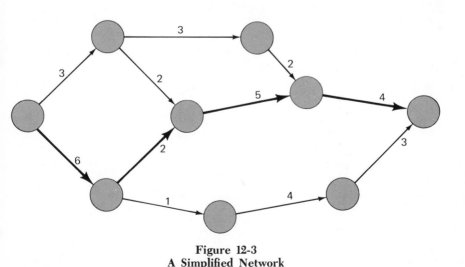

Figure 12-3
A Simplified Network

require decisions for trade-offs in times required, resources allocated, or quality specifications.

In handling the times for an activity in a network, a single best estimate may not be reliable when compared with the time that the activities actually take. In order to arrive at a more reliable estimate, three time values are usually employed: the optimistic estimate (t_o), the most likely time (t_m), and the pessimistic estimate (t_p). The optimistic time is the shortest time possible if everything goes perfectly, with no complications; the chance of this optimum's actually occurring might be one in a hundred. The pessimistic time is the longest time conceivable; it includes time for unusual delays, and thus the chance of its happening might be only one in a hundred. The most likely time would be the best estimate of what normally would occur. If only one time were used, it would be the most likely time (t_m). The difference in the three time estimates gives a measure of the relative uncertainty involved in the activity. From these times, the expected time (t_e) can be computed by applying statistical techniques. The expected time (t_e) is the weighted arithmetic mean of the times. It may or may not be the same as the most likely estimate (t_m), since the differences between the optimistic and most likely and between the pessimistic and most likely would not necessarily be equal. The calculation of t_e is based on a statistical distribution of probabilities and can become quite complicated. However, it has been found that the formula

$$t_e = \frac{t_o + 4t_m + t_p}{6}$$

provides approximate results that are usable. The t_e provides the time in which there is a 50-50 chance of the project's being completed. The time required for each activity is shown on the arrow representing the activity; at times, it may be desirable to record t_o, t_m, and t_p, in which case the numbers are noted in that order along the arrow representing the activity.

A primary reason to estimate more than one time for an activity is to provide data by which management may determine the probabilities that each activity will be completed in a certain time. Moreover, most projects are assigned target dates, which may or may not be the same as the computed expected time (t_e) for the entire project. Slack is the difference between the target and the length of any path. Slack may be positive or negative, and it does not necessarily mean that there is time to spare. If the critical path has a time length that equals the target time, other paths will have positive slack. With these concepts, management has available information for making decisions for a variety of actions that will improve the chances of meeting the desired target.

SUMMARY The most important function of quantitative techniques is that of forcing managers to state a problem in explicit form. At least when one attempts to build a model, one tends to develop an understanding of just what the problem is. Models permit a systematic analysis of problems. Good highways may prove useless without a good roadmap, and a systematic approach provides a roadmap for the manager. Models do not nullify the need for sound judgment, but they do help pinpoint the areas in which valuable managerial talent can be profitably spent in making these judgments.

REFERENCES

ACKOFF, RUSSELL L. and MAURICE W. SASIENI, *Fundamentals of Operations Research*. New York: John Wiley & Sons, Inc., 1968.

BIERMAN, HAROLD, JR., CHARLES P. BONINI and WARREN H. HAUSMAN, *Quantitative Analysis for Business Decisions* (5th ed.). Homewood, Ill.: Richard D. Irwin, Inc., 1977.

CHURCHMAN, C. WEST, RUSSELL L. ACKOFF and E. LEONARD ARNOFF, *Introduction to Operations Research*. New York: John Wiley & Sons, Inc., 1957.

GORDON, G., *System Simulation*. Englewood Cliffs, N. J.: Prentice-Hall, Inc., 1978.

GRAYSON, C. J. "Management Science and Business Practice," *Harvard Business Review*, July-August, 1973, pp. 41-48.

HADLEY, G., *Linear Programming*. Reading, Mass.: Addison-Wesley Publishing Company Inc., 1962.

HILLIER, FREDERICK S. and GERALD J. LIEBERMAN, *Introduction to Operations Research* (2nd ed.). San Francisco: Holden-Day, Inc., 1974.

LEVIN, RICHARD I. and C. O. KIRKPATRICK, *Quantitative Approaches to Management* (3rd ed.). New York: McGraw-Hill Book Company, 1975.

LEVIN, RICHARD I. and RUDOLPH P. LAMONE, *Linear Programming for Management Decisions*. Homewood, Ill.: Richard D. Irwin, Inc., 1969.

LOOMBA, N. PAUL, *Linear Programming, An Introductory Analysis*. New York: McGraw-Hill Book Company, 1964.

NAYLOR, THOMAS H. and EUGENE T. BYRNE, *Linear Programming, Methods and Cases*. Belmont, Calif.: Wadsworth Publishing Company, Inc., 1963.

RICHMOND, SAMUEL B., *Operations Research for Management Decisions*. New York: The Ronald Press Company, 1968.

MANAGEMENT INFORMATION SYSTEMS AND COMPUTERS

by Martin B. Solomon, Jr., University of Kentucky

<== **IDEAS TO BE FOUND** ==>
IN THIS CHAPTER

- Categories of management information
- Evolution of computer systems
- Hardware for computer systems
- Modes for computer processing
- Problems in the development of computerized systems
- Economic and social implications

This chapter will summarize some basic concepts of management information systems and introduce the terminology and concepts employed when computers serve as the means of implementing these systems.

Management information systems (MIS) can be thought of as any systematic process for providing reports, data, or other outputs. A spy is a type of information system, as is a group of clerks who process checks and deposits in a bank. An information system has inputs, processes, and outputs. The creation and storage of inputs, performance of processes, and creation and storage of outputs are the functions of an information system.

While information systems have existed as long as life on this planet, until recently they have been severely restricted in the ability to assimilate a large volume of data. The advent of the computer allowed management to expand its horizons and expectations concerning the possibilities of such systems. Prior to computers, limited types of analyses and correlations of business data could be extracted from the vast amount of information gathered in most business environments. This chapter will cover categories of information, a brief history of the development of computer systems, a short description of computers, some major problems usually encountered in computer systems, and some social and economic implications of computerized information systems.

MANAGEMENT INFORMATION CATEGORIES

Management information can be conveniently categorized into three main areas:

1. Strategic planning information,
2. Management control information,
3. Operational information.

Strategic planning information relates to the top management tasks of deciding on objectives of the organization, on the levels and the kinds of resources required to attain the objectives, and on the policies that govern the acquisition, use, and disposition of resources. Strategic planning depends heavily upon information external to a specific organization. When this is combined with internal data, management can make estimates of expected results. The specifics of this information are often unique and tailor-made to particular strategic problems.

Management control information sheds light on goal congruence; it helps managers take those actions which are in the best interests of the organization; it enables managers to see that resources are being used efficiently and effectively in meeting the organizational goals. Robert Anthony pinpoints three types of information needed for management control: costs by responsibility centers, direct program costs, and full program costs (including allocations for indirect costs). Management control information ties together various subactivities in a coherent way so that managers can gauge resource utilization and compare expected with actual results. Management control information is often interdepartmental, in that the inputs come from various organizational groups, cutting across established functional boundaries.

Operational information pertains to the day-to-day activities of the organization and helps assure that specific tasks are performed effectively and efficiently. It also includes the production of routine and necessary information, such as financial accounting, payrolls, personnel rosters, equipment inventories, and logistics. Operational information, such as scheduling work flow through a department or producing a payroll, generally originates in one department.

Systems for handling each of these categories differ as a result of the varying degrees to which the tasks can be well defined. Operational information can be well defined and easily reduced to a routine of a series of instructions, whereas strategic information is difficult to define; control information falls in between.

EVOLUTION OF COMPUTER SYSTEMS DESIGN

Although computers were originally designed for mathematical calculation, the twelve business firms which used computers in 1954 used them primarily to process accounting and statistical data and to perform **data reduction** (summarizing or reducing large volumes of data to a significantly smaller amount). Since 1954, computer use in business has expanded rapidly. More than 100,000 computers are now operating in the United States. What caused this dramatic investment of billions of dollars?

Shortly after their introduction to the business world, it became obvious that computers could produce substantial cost savings in areas where large volumes of repetitive paperwork were required. Payrolls, order recordings, shipping documents, invoice preparation, accounts receivables, and many other high-volume operations, such as loan processing in banks, provided ample justification for early computers. In other words, the production of operational information was the initial impetus for computer acquisition by commercial firms.

The first units were termed **first generation computers**, because they utilized vacuum tubes in their electronic circuitry. With the advent of the transistor, the **second generation computers** were born. The use of transistors represented a technological breakthrough in the cost of producing computers, and their prices reflected this. While a first generation computer with a specific set of capabilities rented for, say, $8,000 per month, a similar second generation machine rented for less than half that amount. This means that using computers for many information processing applications that were economically marginal before is now economically feasible. How were these applications for information processing automated? **Computer programmers** (people who write instructions for computers) and **systems analysts** (people who analyze problems and recommend solutions) designed and implemented the applications by studying the problems, designing new systems, and creating computer programs to perform essentially the same tasks that clerks previously performed.

An important element of operational information is that it generally relates to one department—luckily so, since the designer of the system can obtain most or all of the system requirements from that one department. Also, the same department can be responsible for the control of the accuracy, timeliness, security, and policies regarding the inputs to the

174

process. But serious problems existed: many operational systems involved too many separate steps to provide output on time, accuracy of inputs was insufficient, input information was lost, and extraneous inputs were accidentally introduced into the system. Perhaps even more serious, however, was the relative inflexibility of these systems. As changes in requirements occurred in the firm, computer programs and systems required redesign and reprograming, which often required rather long periods. Worse yet, programs and systems were poorly documented, so that when changes became necessary, computer people found it difficult to remember or to determine how to introduce changes without disrupting the portions of the process which performed adequately. All of these problems were compounded by the fact that computers were being produced and installed at a faster rate than programers and systems analysts were being trained.

All of these problems are still present in differing degrees. Several reasons explain why they have not been solved. First, there is a shortage of qualified personnel. Second, because of this shortage, most qualified personnel spend all of their time in new development projects or modifications of existing processes rather than in trying to solve the decade-old problems. Third, even the "qualified" personnel in the field have generally gained their credentials through experience on the job, with little or no formal training in system design. Fourth, educational institutions have provided limited amounts of formal training, because little theory and few generalizations have evolved; even if the existing body of knowledge were taught, the institutions could not easily staff such curricula. Fifth, since personnel are scarce, employees change jobs often, induced by salary increments; the result is a lack of continuity in the development of specific systems. Sixth, the management of information-processing activities is often lacking in management sophistication, since most such managers were promoted from exclusively technical occupations. In spite of these problems, thousands of operational information systems are in existence, and they seemingly perform economically.

During this same period (the 1950s and the 1960s), managers, systems analysts, and clever programers began working to create more sophisticated systems. The integrated order entry represents such a system. A customer order is entered into the computer. The inventory is checked for availability; if no inventory exists, production scheduling is notified. If inventory exists, shipping is notified and inventory reduced. In either case, sooner or later an accounts receivable record is created, an invoice produced, and shipping information generated. The single entry of the order triggers many other events; this was a big step forward in routinization of a large number of interrelated tasks. The costs were reduced, but even more important was the routinization, because it eliminated the need for the training of people and the development of procedures and elaborate controls to ensure that each subtask was performed. Newer, simpler controls sufficed.

In 1964, IBM announced a new line of computers termed the System/360 (the name being derived from the 360 degrees of a compass, implying that the system was universally applicable). Because the circuitry was microminiaturized, the **third generation computers** were born. In addition to another level of economic effectiveness over the second generation, these computers permitted moderately inexpensive communication between a computer and other devices such as teletypes, typewriters, or even other computers. This advance represented the first generally recognized, economical, commercially available computer system of such capability. Consequently, designers began to envision extremely elaborate systems in which any imaginable sort of information could be extracted as quickly as one could negotiate a telephone call. People began planning for computerized information systems in which all company transactions were entered into storage units accessible to computers, then classified, tabulated, and cataloged in such a way that any arrangement of information was easily retrievable. "Total information systems" became theoretically possible.

At this point in time, computer people were just beginning to learn how to design and implement good operational information systems, and some were doing respectable work in management control information systems. But most of the previous problems still existed and the new task was infinitely more complex; firms simply were not prepared to meet the challenge. The reasons seem apparent. Designers had gained most of their experience in operational information systems which obtained inputs from one or a few departments and were designed to solve specific operational or reporting needs. Most computer systems began on that premise and were special-purpose systems. The current vision is to tie together several of the existing operational systems to gain from the computer the ability to interrelate different kinds of information which can prove useful to a number of departments. One approach is to systematize "islands" or blocks of operational data and then to tie the blocks together; however, it is a big step from interrelating specific information to producing a generalized total information system. Another approach, i.e., the *systems approach*, begins with a comprehension of an overall design and finally fits each individual operational system into the grand plan. An all-encompassing system design requires a first look from the top, in the strategic planning area, since this information is the most comprehensive. Next, designers might view management control, because it is next most comprehensive. Lastly, the operational area requires attention. Herein lies a paradox. While one might desire to study comprehensively an organization from the top down, it is the operational information needs which are invariably met first, because they can be economically evaluated and justified; planning and control information are much more elusive and often difficult to evaluate. Therefore, the designer is torn between the existing, necessary, already-operating information systems with major omissions and the desire to design a new, more comprehensive system. The old systems cannot be abandoned, because they fill operational needs, and for the same reason the new, more global system cannot easily be implemented without temporarily duplicating many functions at unusually high costs.

New complexities emerge. Now instead of coping with inputs and requirements from one department, designers must be asked to consider all the needs of all departments simultaneously, as well as those of all levels of management. Human beings have difficulty in comprehending the complexities. In addition, security problems present themselves, because now a department is essentially providing its information for the use of others. Coordination of all various inputs is necessary, with differing cycles, accuracy levels, and distances. The fact is that we do not know how to solve all of these new problems; the old ones haven't yet been solved.

The **fourth generation computers** were developed using large scale integration (LSI) technology, whereby massive amounts of electronics could be placed on "chips" smaller than the eraser on a pencil, and these units could be mass produced very economically. The powerful hand-held computers retailing for only a few dollars are an example of this development. This breakthrough has allowed microcomputers to be used to control every imaginable type of device, including automobile gasoline-air mixtures, electronic ovens, typewriters, and even clocks.

In the 1980s the rapid development of computer systems will continue, not only in ever more complex large, powerful computers but also in minicomputers for industrial process control, data communication, and medical/scientific lab analysis and microcomputers for personal, flexible use in the home, available for a few dollars. This evolution will affect the daily life of managers in diverse ways.

COMPUTER SYSTEMS   Computer systems are composed of three main parts:

1. Storage.
2. Processor.
3. Input and output devices.

Computer storage takes many forms, but the common element is the ability to record and retain information such as letters and numbers. The main storage of a computer is composed of a large number of storage locations, each with a unique address and each possessing the ability to hold a specific number of letters or numbers. These storage locations are analogous to post office boxes, each with an address, each with storage capacity. The analogy is extremely close. The storage can hold names, addresses, part numbers, account balances, or even literary works. In short, any combination of letters, numbers, or special characters which can be written can be stored in computer storage. These kinds of information are referred to as **data.** Of course, computers with larger storage capacities are accompanied by larger price tags.

In addition to data, computer storage holds instructions, which are also combinations of numbers, letters, and special characters. These **instructions** command the computer to perform certain basic operations, such as add two numbers, compare two names, read or write information. Computers have an instruction repertoire of from 30 to over 1,000 different commands which can be understood. The ability to retain and comprehend these instructions is what differentiates the computer from other simple devices such as adding machines and is also the primary characteristic that gives it so much power. A set of these instructions, written in some computer language, is called a **program** and is written by a computer programer. The two most popular computer languages in use today are **COBOL** (*Co*mmon *B*usiness *O*riented *L*anguage), heavily used by business and administrative programers, and **FORTRAN** (*For*mula *Tran*slator) generally used in scientific environments.

The ability of a computer program to modify itself gives rise to activity which closely parallels human thought. For example, computer programs designed to play checkers actually learn (refine themselves) through experience. As they play more and more games, they become better checker players. This is done not by figuring out all possible moves, which is impossible, but by acting very much like a human, remembering poor strategies and refraining from making the same mistake again. Secondary storage units usually possess the ability to store information (programs or data) but cannot retrieve the information as quickly as main storage; consequently, the monthly rental for such units is much less.

Processor units house the control unit (which interprets and executes the instructions) and an adder (which performs addition rapidly). The adder can also perform subtraction, multiplication, and division through simple variations of addition. The processor is analogous to a brain which performs interpretive functions.

Input and output units provide an ability to enter into computer storage information in the form of punched cards, magnetic tape, paper tape, or written documents or to convert internal computer representation into a form suitable for either human interpretation, such as printed pages, or further processing or temporary storage, such as magnetic tape, paper tape, or punched cards. Figure 13-1 shows a schematic of a computer system.

In the past, computers were operated as **batch** or **sequential** machines:

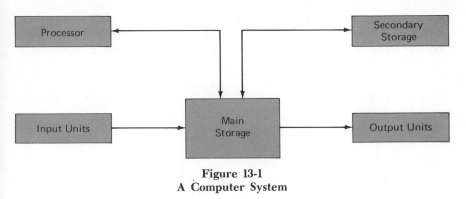

Figure 13-1
A Computer System

only one job was processed at a time. Consider the sequential processor shown in Figure 13-2.

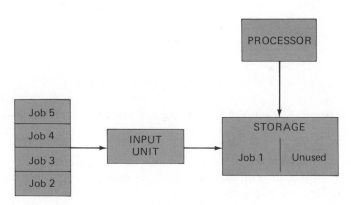

Figure 13-2
Sequential (Batch) Computer System

The sequential machine concept adapted an extremely flexible general purpose computer to that of a special purpose machine at any point in time. As shown in Figure 13-2, Job 1 is in control of the computer while Jobs 2 through 5 wait. Three consequences of this scheme result. Total capacity remains unused, since seldom does any one job use all the facilities of the computer. Storage may be partially used as indicated; some of the input or output devices are undesired by any one job and the processor has spare time that is unused by any one job. In addition, any one job blocks others until it is finished processing. Present generation computers are generally built to overcome these difficulties. The technology employed is called **multiprogramming**, whereby multiple jobs reside in storage and an attempt is made to utilize fully the capacity of the processor. As shown in Figure 13-3, the processor picks among the jobs to be accomplished those which will most fully use the processor's resources. In this case three jobs reside simultaneously in storage. When Job 1 does not use some of the processor capability, Job 2 does, and so forth.

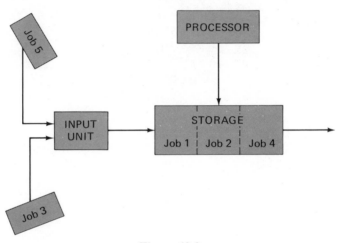

Figure 13-3
Multiprogramming Computer System

The results of a multiprogramming system have revolutionized system design concepts. A great deal more flexibility exists. Since the computer can process multiple jobs, it can process operational work while remaining available for unpredicted demands for management-control and strategic-planning information. For example, suppose that the computer is processing its regular work of payroll, inventories, etc., and a manager decides to examine the production records for the year as of that day. If such records are available to the computer, the manager may gain access to them in on-line mode, i.e., can immediately query the computer system through direct coupling without waiting for the present work to terminate or aborting the work in process. If the receipt of information is within a very short period—say, seconds—the processing can be thought of as occurring in real time. In short, **on-line** implies a direct connection to the computer and **real-time** implies an extremely fast response. This is illustrated in Figure 13-4. Suppose that Jobs 1 through 3 are actively being processed, Job 4 is dormant or inactive, and Jobs 5, 6, and 7 are waiting. A manager at a **remote terminal** (a device to receive or transmit information to or

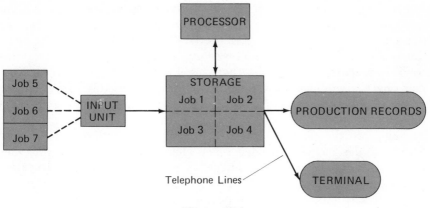

Figure 13-4
Time Sharing Process

from a computer which is located at a geographically distant location) can direct a query to Job 4, which immediately becomes active and makes the production records available. The request to Job 4 can be processed and the information retrieved without substantially interfering with Jobs 1 through 3, which are in operation. Under the sequential processor concept, the jobs being executed would complete execution before any such inquiry could be processed.

A variant of multiprogramming is called **time-sharing**, where several computer programs are each given a "slice" of computer time in a round-robin fashion. In this manner, several users can each simultaneously receive a small amount of computer service.

An additional development is large-scale storage, which can retain large volumes of information less expensively than ever before. This large, economical storage promises further advancements in computer systems. A large amount of data is often called a **data base.**

The three features of multiprogramming, remote computing, and large-scale storage remove serious barriers and raise the horizons of the production of timely and accurate management-control and strategic-planning information.

DEVELOPMENT OF COMPUTERIZED SYSTEMS

Cartoons and jokes often scoff at the ability of computer systems to make ridiculous or even gigantic mistakes. Computer systems sometimes do not function at all; this section will categorize and discuss the reasons.

Systems
Design
After the problem to be solved by the computer is defined, a **system definition** and a **system design** are written which define the goals, objectives, and specifications relating to the problems to be solved and precisely how the system is to operate when it becomes operational. There are five basic steps involved: (1) A **flow chart** (a graphical explanation of the problem-solving procedures) is prepared to ensure efficient processing. (2) A program is written in one of the general programing languages, which can then be translated by the machine into the machine language used by the specific computer. (3) Forms are designed and needed reports finalized. (4) After the programs have been written, they are **debugged** (the process by which all evident errors are removed). (5) Documentation is prepared to describe how the programs and the system are to operate.

Next the system goes into *production*, whereby the actual work is performed. If an obsolete, existing system was in operation prior to this step, **parallel operations** are often performed, in which the old and the new systems operate concurrently and the results are compared to detect errors in the new system. Finally, the system enters a **maintenance state,** in which minor modifications and corrections are made from time to time.

Problems
with
Computer Systems
At least four major categories of computer system malfunctions exist: they may be (1) **hardware** related, whereby the actual computing machine does not operate properly; (2) **software** related, whereby the instructions or programs provided to the computer are incorrect or inadequate; (3) **computer operations** related, whereby the computer processing procedures are not followed or are incorrect or the workload is not properly scheduled; (4) **system** related, whereby the input was incorrect or missing, the information produced not relevant, or the output not timely.

Hardware Problems   Computer reliability may be a source of problems in the sense that a job may not be completed when it is desired because the computer malfunctioned. In this case, the job can be run properly later. Seldom do computers produce incorrect answers because of electronic or mechanical failure; instead, such failures normally result in no information at all being produced at the appointed time.

Computers are composed of many electronic, electrical, and mechanical components. Each component is subject to failure, in much the same manner as parts of an automobile. Some computers fail less frequently than others, sometimes because of a superior engineering design but more often because of the smaller number of different components required. A computer with millions of components will probably fail more frequently than one with, say, ten thousand components.

Computer reliability must be carefully examined before automating an information system. Information system requirements do not usually require unusually high levels of hardware reliability, because most work is performed in the batch processing mode, whereby the job is submitted to a computer and the results are available at a much later time. On the other hand, some information systems imply on-line processing, whereby input data is sent to the computer as soon as the data are available. At this point the continuing availability of computers is important. A higher level of interaction between people and computers occurs in real-time processing, whereby not only inputs but the processing and outputs are performed almost immediately. In this last case, continuous availability of computers is essential.

Some examples may better explain the differences among these modes.

A typical payroll consists of input data, which is punched onto tabulating cards, with historical information on magnetic tape. At an appropriate time prior to payday, the computer run is performed, which produces paychecks. This run usually takes between ten and sixty minutes of computer time. If the computer system fails, there is usually enough time to rerun the payroll and still produce paychecks in time for normal distribution.

An *on-line* system involves a process in which input data are often sent directly to a computer without the need for intermediate recording. For example, in a manufacturing plant, the defects found on an assembly by an inspector can be typed directly into a computer without any other paperwork.

A *real-time* process involves performing calculations and/or controls at the same time an external activity is taking place. An airlines reservation system is both on-line and real-time; reservation requests are typed directly into the computer (on-line) and seat availability is typed back to the airline clerk immediately (real-time).

The level of computer reliability required depends partly upon the mode of operation. The reliability requirement for batch processing is the lowest; airline reservation systems, on the other hand, utilize two interconnected computers, to allow operation even if one of the computers malfunctions. Additional computer availability provides a significantly reduced probability of complete failure.

A very different sort of computer hardware problem relates to undercapacity of the computer itself. One cannot expect to go at a speed of 100 miles per hour in a car with only 30 horsepower; similarly, sufficient computer power must be available to process the expected workload. Because the procurement cycle for computers is so long (often from one to three years), by the time a computer is actually installed, it is sometimes too small to process the then-required workload.

Software Problems   Complex computer programs contain thousands or even millions of individual instructions to the computer. The number of possible logic paths through these instructions may reach millions or billions. In short, there are too many possible logic paths in complex computer programs to be able to test them for 100 percent accuracy. Only satisfactory testing (95 percent to 99 percent accuracy) is possible. The power of computers is largely derived from their ability to make many decisions rapidly. Suppose in a program ten different types of individuals can be processed, each with twenty possible categories; there are 10×20 or 200 different types of people involved. If each of these can be subcategorized into five areas, we have 1,000 different situations. Part of the job of the programer is to anticipate what the computer is to do in every possible case. Clearly this is impossible to do with complete accuracy when large numbers of possible situations or decisions arise.

Large computer programs may never be completely error free, because of their extreme complexity. Consequently, sometimes computer software failure occurs because of incorrect logic in programs, discovered long after they were thought to be error free. For example, if when the computer program was written, the programer did not anticipate that a West Coast salesperson would pay New York City occupational taxes, and one did, there would be an error in the payroll program. In actual cases some errors have shown themselves four or five years after a system was in the production state, simply because some unusual conditions never occurred until then.

Because software errors are not unusual, a staff of maintenance programers is required in any large computing installation, to locate quickly and to correct errors when they become known. A careful and thorough testing requirement imposed by management can reduce software errors; however, no one knows how to eliminate them completely. It is in this area that highly experienced professional programers pay for their higher salaries by experiencing much lower software failure rates than beginning programers.

But because the logic in computer programs can be so complex, programing under extreme time-pressures inevitably induces additional errors which may not have otherwise occurred. Even the best professional will err under these conditions. On the other hand, a well-planned computer program will usually result in higher reliability. In actual practice, the specifications for a program are often changed after a great deal of the planning has been done; consequently errors in logic generally result.

Operations Problems   The computer workload must be scheduled so that there is a sufficiently high probability that the needed processing can be done. Realistic times for job completion must be known, realistic amounts of time provided for reruns (where the first computer run was incorrect for some reason), and realistic estimates made of when accurate inputs will be available for processing. Without proper planning of computer operation, no insurance exists that all of the required workload will be processed when it is needed.

In addition to scheduling various procedures (e.g., selecting the proper computer program to be run or the proper forms upon which output is to be printed), the proper sequencing of computer programs must be determined. If other types of malfunctions occur, computer operations must be capable of determining the proper corrective action to take. Poor procedures or inexperienced personnel can induce severe errors at this point by selecting an improper course of corrective action in the case of hardware, software, or system failure. Good procedures, thorough training, and adequate supervision are the cures for these problems.

Systems Problems   A successful system must make the inputs to the computer available when needed, ensure the proper controls over accuracy and timing of the inputs and outputs, and ensure that the specifications for the software and operations are correct. Computers usually do what they are told, but the specifications which were originally provided may be incorrect or obsolete. One often hears, "The darned computer will not provide me with the information I need." While this assertion may well be true, these particular requirements may have never been included in the original specifications. Further, as time passes, new requirements occur which make existing systems obsolete and render them less useful. These types of needs must be respecified in a logical manner in order to initiate responsive system change.

Reports are often late or not timely because the proper inputs were not available for computer processing when they should have been. Or the inputs were available but they were so inaccurate that they were returned to data preparations for further checking and corrections. Then by the time they are actually available, the report is late.

Over-zealous computer systems designers do not always appreciate human weaknesses or realistic time requirements. Billing systems demonstrate this problem where, for example, automatic credit cancellations are issued by a computer some time after initial billing has taken place. But often payments are received by the firm well in advance of the payment deadline. The problem frequently centers upon the long (and perhaps necessary) time lag between receipt of payment and notifying the computer system of the fact. In the meantime the firm may have incurred serious ill-will by withdrawing credit from a good, long-standing customer. The error here is that some human observation must still be ensured when harsh or severe actions are "recommended" by a computer system.

Economic and Social Implications   It is clear that the rapid change in
of Some Operational   information processing has created
Information Systems   the need for revising some of the
operational and control approaches within organizations. Furthermore, this rapid change will have a tremendous impact on economic and social factors.

Many extremely sophisticated informations systems exist; most of them provide operational information and some management control information, but few, if any, strategic information systems are in operation. The American Airlines SABRE system was the first attempt to develop a highly complex commercial reservation system. The system made a significant impact on the entire travel industry. Most airlines and many hotel-motel chains have developed similar reservation systems and vastly improved customer service. In fact, the implication now is that no airlines or hotel chain may be able to effectively compete without similar services. This information revolution may create serious barriers to entry into certain industries and may reduce the capacity of some small firms to compete. Yet, the development of minicomputers and microcomputers has made computing capability available to even the smallest businesses.

The use of computers raises questions about decentralization of authority. A number of writers do not believe that centralized information will result in less decentralization of authority. The fact that a great volume of centrally stored information can be distributed widely may enable a greater number of managers to make better decisions in their own area of responsibility. The U.S. Internal Revenue's system allows certain checks on tax returns. The result is that more people now accurately complete federal tax returns and elaborate audit procedures, which was previously impossible because of volume.

On the horizon are Hospital Information Systems. In such a setting, all patient records are computerized, along with most of the procedures involved in a hospital. When the patient is admitted, his initial record is entered into a computer system. From that time forth, each activity related to that patient is typed into the system and recorded by computer. Plans are so extensive that they call for computers to remind nurses when it is time to administer medicine and even to check patient food lists to ensure that those with special dietary needs are cared for properly. These systems will revolutionize hospital care, improve the quality of services, and relieve the pressing shortage of technical hospital personnel.

Federal data banks to store large amounts of data about citizens are now common. The implications of such systems are far-reaching. The scheme has a chance of producing significant cost savings, but an argument centers around fears of losing privacy through the access to complete personnel records by any single body. Consequently a variety of state and federal laws have been enacted to protect the rights of citizens.

The technical problems of developing comprehensive information systems are being answered rapidly. The development of management thought, which might make full use of the technical developments, has been slower. Of one thing we can be sure: management will devote much time and creative thinking to making such systems operational.

One of the pioneers in computer technology, Norbert Wiener, expressed concern about the ability of human beings to remain in control of electronic computers: "It is my thesis that machines can and do transcend some of the limitations of their designers, and that in doing so they may be both effective and dangerous." His concern was based on the speed at which computers operate relative to the reactions of human beings. Even assuming that computers are governed by the programs given them by humans (and H. A. Simon and others have raised questions about this assumption), Wiener argued that computer systems may take actions at such speeds that the human control may be too late to ward off disastrous consequences. He cited the analogy of a driver of a speeding automobile being unable to correct the path of the machine before it hits a wall. Management faces a similar challenge of remaining in control of the equipment that it has introduced.

TRENDS IN COMPUTERIZED INFORMATION SYSTEMS

The technical advancements in computer hardware have forced improvements in software. This rapid progress has made possible economical and comprehensive information systems that are certain to have a strong impact on all functions of management in the future. Whereas in the past slide rules were essential for engIneers and ccwlator were important to accountants, the modern computers now serve as the powerful foundation for management information systems. At first the use of computers was of particular value for large organizations; in the future, as a result of the growing availability of **data processing centers**, which sell computer service to small users, and the development of small, inexpensive computers, managements of firms of all sizes find the use of computerized systems within their capabilities. The only obstacle to universal use of computer information systems is the lack of awareness on the part of human beings of the tremendous power now available to them. Managers need not understand the technical matters of computers to gain this power, any more than an automobile driver needs to be a mechanic or a child turning on a light or starting a toy needs to understand electricity.

REFERENCES

ANTHONY, ROBERT, *Planning and Control Systems: A Framework for Analysis.* Boston, Mass.: Division of Research, Harvard Business School, 1965.

AWAD, ELIAS, *Introduction to Computers in Business.* Englewood Cliffs, N.J.: Prentice-Hall, Inc., 1977.

BURCK, GILBERT, ed., *The Computer Age.* New York: Harper Torchbooks, 1965.

COOPER, J. W., *The Minicomputer in the Laboratory.* New York: John Wiley and Sons, 1977.

DEARDEN, JOHN and F. W. MCFARLAN, *Management Information Systems.* Homewood, Ill.: Richard D. Irwin, Inc., 1966.

DOLL, D. R., *Data Communications: Facilities, Network and Systems Design.* New York: John Wiley and Sons, 1977.

EDITORS, *Scientific American Information.* San Francisco: W. H. Freeman & Co., 1966.

HOLOIEN, MARTIN, *Computers and Their Societal Impact.* New York: John Wiley and Sons, 1977.

KENNEDY, MICHAEL and MARTIN B. SOLOMON, *Ten Statement Fortran with Fortran IV* (2nd ed.). Englewood Cliffs, N.J.: Prentice-Hall, Inc., 1975.

LI, DAVID H., *Accounting Computers, Management Information Systems.* New York: McGraw-Hill Book Company, 1968.

MARTIN, JAMES, *Telecommunications and the Computer* (2nd ed.). Englewood Cliffs, N.J.: Prentice-Hall, Inc., 1976.

SANDERS, DONALD H., *Computers in Business* (3rd ed.). New York: McGraw-Hill Book Company, 1975.

SHARPE, WILLIAM F., *The Economies of Computers.* New York: Columbia University Press, 1969.

PART

4

APPLICATIONS OF MANAGERIAL FUNCTIONS IN OPERATIONS

Management concepts and analytical techniques are fundamental to a large number of varied activities. Government agencies, religious institutions, health delivery systems, nonprofit organizations, civic groups, and educational institutions require that the functions studied in Part 2 be performed; contributions from the disciplines summarized in Part 3 are useful in these various applications. In Part 4 we outline the applications of managerial functions in the major sectors: the private business sector and the public sector.

Management in a business firm can be classified in several ways: (1) by the size of the firm; (2) by levels of the hierarchy—that is, top management, middle management, and supervisory management; and (3) by special functional activities. The last viewpoint has received the most attention ever since F. W. Taylor emphasized the functional phases of operations. For this reason, Chapter 14 focuses on three of the classical functional activities that have developed a distinct literature in business management.

In the last several decades, renewed attention has been given to improving management in not-for-profit organizations. Yet public administration received early attention by Henri Fayol and others, and a number of the newer techniques have originated in public agencies and then been transferred to the private sector. Chapter 15 focuses on key techniques and issues of particular significance to public administration.

APPLICATIONS IN BUSINESS OPERATIONAL AREAS

⟸ IDEAS TO BE FOUND ⟹
IN THIS CHAPTER

- Functions of production planning and control
- Work improvement
- Work standards
- Financial ratio analysis
- Cash flow
- Evaluation of investment opportunities
- Cost of capital
- Pricing
- Product planning
- Promotion
- Channels of distribution
- Marketing research
- Consumerism
- Environmentalism

A business firm applies managerial functions in three major operational areas. Consequently, education and applications in management receive specialized attention under these areas: operations management (also referred to as production or manufacturing management), financial management, and marketing management. Each of these employs ideas and techniques discussed earlier; however, a focus on the specialized applications in each area will further illustrate how managerial concepts are applied in actual operations of a business firm. This chapter will discuss some of the most important applications in these operational areas.

OPERATIONS MANAGEMENT   Operations management concentrates on the technical aspects of an industrial firm. In performing the managerial functions, the operations or production manager employs the tools of analysis provided by economists, accountants, mathematicians, behavioral scientists, and engineers. Early scientific managers expanded concepts originating in industrial engineering. The focus was on such topics as description and analysis of individual jobs, the technology of manufacturing, work flows, specifications of raw materials and the final product, location of plants, layout of work, methods for increasing productivity, standards, and planning and control of production. While these topics remain central to operations management, in the last two decades the new developments have been in systems thinking and quantitative methods of analysis. Therefore, much of the knowledge needed by production managers in modern operations has been outlined in Chapters 12 and 13.

This section summarizes three techniques that remain essential in applications by operating managers: production planning and control, work improvement, and work measurement. These techniques provided the foundation for modern industrial expansion in the United States and other industrial countries and are of critical importance to developing countries today in their efforts to establish an industrial base for their economic development. The essence of the job of operations manager is in increasing productivity—processing of inputs in an optimum manner so as to add value to output or finished product.

Production Planning and Control

The operations manager is in charge of producing items that the marketing department can sell to customers. He must handle a vast amount of information that flows to him from other departments, and he must plan and control his own internal operations. If his plant is large, he does not have time to handle these details himself. Production planning and control often is performed by a separate functional department and serves as the nervous system for the production department. Its chief functions are processing of information and planning work to be performed by operating departments.

The production control department serves the manufacturing departments. Figure 14-1 summarizes the principal relationships between the production control department and other departments and indicates some of the important documents handled.

Production planning and control typically consists of five functions: routing, loading, scheduling, dispatching, and expediting. The first three are planning functions that take place before any production occurs; the last two are action functions that provide control.

1. **Routing** determines the operations to be performed, their sequence, and the path or flow of materials through a series of operations. The chief paper that describes what is to be done and how it will be done is called the *route sheet*, or operations sheet.
2. **Loading** is the function of assigning work to a machine or department in advance. The number of machines available and their operating characteristics, such as speeds and capabilities, are facts

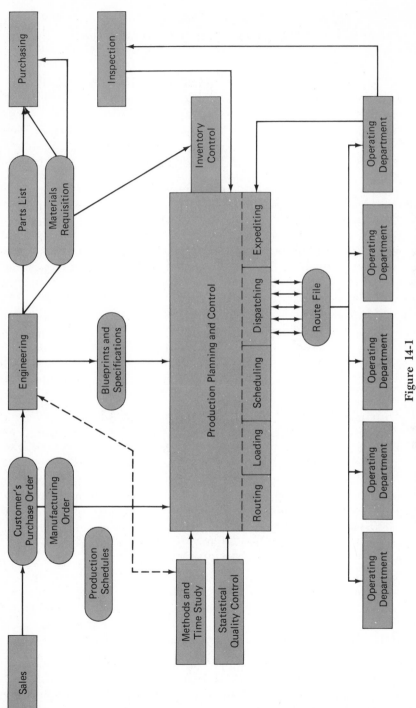

Figure 14-1

Relationship of Production Planning and Control to Other Departments of a Manufacturing Company

kept by the production control department so that it can develop an optimum plan for using plant facilities. The selection of the best machine, or the best substitute machine in case of breakdown, is a part of the loading function.

3. **Scheduling** of production determines the time at which each operation is to take place. Master schedules show the dates on which delivery is promised to the customer. Detailed schedules are needed for each of the semifinished parts, so that all components will arrive at the proper place in time for the next operations. Assembly schedules depend on availability of all parts to be included in the finished product.

A useful tool of scheduling is a chart which portrays planned production and actual performance over a period of time for any or all of the factors that require planning and control. A **Gantt chart** is merely a bar chart with time on the horizontal axis and the factor to be scheduled on the vertical axis. Some are "progress charts" that show the various articles to be produced on the vertical scale and the planned time for production on the horizontal scale. Others are: "machine record" charts, which show the available machines and the time at which different jobs are planned; "order charts," which indicate the time to start different orders and the time of completion; and "man charts," which show the work planned for each person or group of people. In addition, network and critical path analysis (discussed in Chapter 12) have become powerful scheduling devices.

4. **Dispatching** is the process of actually ordering work to be done. If the previously mentioned planning functions have been accomplished properly, the dispatching function may be merely a routine one of issuing authorizations to start operations. In some systems, dispatching is left to the head of the operating departments; in other systems, all orders are issued by the production control department. If the necessary information is available to the department head, greater flexibility might result from decentralizing the dispatching function, even if all the planning functions are centralized.

5. **Expediting** is a follow-up activity that checks whether plans are actually being executed. Expediting can be accomplished by routine reports and oral communications with operating departments. At times, specialists, known as expediters, may spend all their time insuring that key orders are being finished on schedule.

The control of inventory is critical to the functions of production control. Often, the same department handles both inventory control and production control, because production directly affects the three main types of inventories: raw materials and parts, work in process, and finished goods. Raw materials must be ordered to arrive in time for production; the nature of the production process determines the size of work in process; the output of production must go either into finished goods inventory or directly to the customer.

Inventory control handles the following questions: (1) what is the optimum amount of inventory to carry? (2) what is the economic lot size for an order from a supplier or from a production department? and (3) what system of controlling inventory should be used?

1. The optimum size of inventory depends on the needs of the production department. Some parts, materials, and completed products have to be kept on hand in order to absorb discontinuities in production and to handle uncertainty. Some inventory must be held, if only for the purpose of having something to work on. At times, inventory may be kept as speculation on future price changes. Finished stocks may be held to provide better service for customers.

2. The **economic lot size** depends upon two groups of costs: preparation costs and carrying costs. *Preparation costs* are primarily fixed costs relating to the starting of production or the writing of an order for a purchase and do not vary with the number of items in the lot; *carrying costs* vary directly with the number of items involved. Examples of typical preparation costs are the setup costs of machines, the clerical cost for writing an order, and the administrative costs of executive attention in placing a lot into production; examples of carrying costs are interest on capital, insurance, obsolescence, deterioration, handling, inventory taking, and so on.

Numerous formulas have been developed that weigh preparation costs, carrying costs, and rate of usage. One of the oldest and best known is:

$$Q = \sqrt{\frac{2RS}{I}}$$

in which: Q = economic lot size
R = annual use of the items in units per year
S = setup cost each time a new lot is started
I = carrying cost per unit per year.

Other formulas incorporate probability estimates for handling uncertainty—especially the uncertainty of the rate of usage and the uncertainty about the amount of time it will take to deliver the new order.

3. A number of systems of inventory control are available. A most popular one is the *periodic-order system,* in which cards indicate

the pertinent information concerning usage rate, items on order, items reserved for specific usage, and balance on hand. In this system, four quantities serve as critical decision rules: maximum inventory (the most items ever to be stocked), minimum inventory (the safety reserve below which inventory should not fall), the reorder point (the level of inventory at which an order should be made so that receipt can be accomplished before the minimum level is reached), and the order size (the standard amount to be ordered). This system assumes that the picture of usage and ordering is that shown in Figure 14-2.

The subject of inventory management has received much attention in recent years. New techniques are helping to answer inventory questions. Because inventory is a very important problem, each manager should give considerable time to the development of a tailored system that will best answer his needs.

Work
Improvement
The goal of work improvement is the economizing of effort. The key to the attainment of this goal is an awareness of exactly what an operation involves, the details of what must be done, and an inquiring mind that searches for "the best way."

The inquiring mind needs certain questions to guide its thinking. Four such questions have proved useful in all work improvement: (1) Can some element of the work be *eliminated?* If there is any step that need not be done at all or any motion that is completely a wasted one, it should be eliminated. (2) Can some parts of the operation be *combined?*

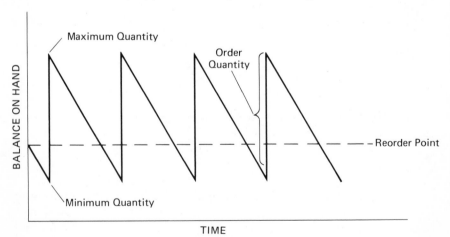

Figure 14-2
Routine Inventory Control in a Stable Situation

If two parts of an operation can be done jointly, combining them will improve it. (3) Can the *sequence be changed?* Anyone who has purchased disassembled furniture and has failed to follow the enclosed instructions will be especially conscious of failing to give proper consideration to sequence. (4) Can the operation be *simplified?* The simple way is usually the easiest, least expensive, and best way.

In using the four questions, it is mandatory to describe in detail exactly what is being done. One cannot improve an operation that one does not visualize and analyze.

Certain key ideas have helped guide thought about work improvement. Use *symmetrical* motions which have corresponding size, shape, and relative position when viewed from the center. The numeral "8" and the letter "S" are symmetrical when divided by a horizontal line through the center. *Opposite* motions contribute to the balancing of members of the body. *Ballistic motions* in which movement is "free"—uncontrolled— are best. *Continuous, curved* motions require less effort. *Rhythm,* a term generally understood from its musical usage, is generally applicable in motion study. *Momentum* can help once an item is in motion. *Gravity* is a basic law of nature that is very beneficial to a worker if he finds out how to use it to his advantage instead of having to fight it. The *definite location* for tools, materials, persons, and work in process is particularly important in planning the workplace.

Considerable research indicates that the design of machines to fit the physical, intellectual, and psychological characteristics of people greatly affects the improvement of work. Results of this research can be summarized.

1. The human body is so constructed that its best position for work is an erect one. When a person is standing or walking, a perpendicular line best describes the relationship of the leg, back, neck and head. In carrying a load, it was found that the primitive yoke method proved superior because it distributed the load over a large area, making use of the strongest muscles. In lifting materials, the back should be kept straight and the legs bent because the back is relatively weak compared with the muscles in the thighs. Chairs that support the back in an erect position are universally considered to be superior.
2. The human body needs to change position. Equipment that permits the operator to either sit or stand reduces fatigue and increases productivity. A job that includes the use of different muscles, from time to time, will enable the worker to rest one set of muscles while continuing to work with another set.
3. Equipment should be adjustable to suit persons of different sizes. Because workers differ in height, weight, length of arms, and other

physical characteristics, seats should be adjustable to the unique contours of the individual. The movable front seat of automobiles is an example of a use of this principle.

4. Controls and dials should be as simple and realistic as possible. For example, if an object is to be moved to the right, the control lever should move to the right. Dials with the fewest markings have proved to give the best results. Controls should be spaced to prevent mistaking one lever for another and should be grouped according to similar functions. A large number of individual controls increases the strain on the operator.

Work Standards

The improvement of work should precede the setting of work standards. Obviously, if changes are made in the method of performing an operation, the time required for the performance will be changed. Once the improved method is found, it should be standardized and all workers should be trained in using the improved method.

Managers use time standards to answer a number of important questions:

1. What is the time required for each operation in the *scheduling* of production?
2. How can production in one department, or at one machine, be *balanced* with other departments and machines in the plant?
3. How can the company develop a solid basis for a standard *cost accounting* system?
4. What amount of time will a job take for the purpose of estimating the *price* to place in a bid?
5. What basis is best for an *incentive* system?

The original method of setting time standards is F. W. Taylor's procedure of using a stopwatch to time a representative man actually working on a given job. Stopwatch time study continues to be used in setting standards.

The steps in making a stopwatch time study are:

1. Select and describe the exact repetitive-type operations to be studied. (A standard method is assumed.)
2. Collect the necessary supplies to be used, including a stopwatch, a clip board, and observation sheets.
3. Select the operator to be observed and obtain the cooperation of the line supervisor.
4. Precisely identify the timing points and elements of the operation.

5. Determine the number of cycles to be timed.
6. Make the actual observations and record them on the observation sheet. Rate the performance of the worker simultaneously.
7. Compute the measure of central tendency, which will represent the detailed time values. (The result is called the "base time.")
8. Compute "normal time" by using the performance rating of the observed worker.
9. Compute the "standard time" by providing "allowances."

Because stopwatch time study has received considerable criticism, other methods of setting standards have been developed. Several of these (methods-time measurement, work factor, basic motion time study) make use of catalogues of motions, with a table of time values for each. The catalogues contain time data that have been developed through detailed research in laboratories. They are the basis for setting time standards without the use of a stopwatch.

Another technique of work measurement that has received increased attention is work sampling. It can be used for two purposes: (1) to determine the percent of time that workers are engaged in different activities (or not engaged in any productive effort), in order to find the proper allowances to be added to normal time, and (2) to set standards for irregular work and for indirect labor.

Work sampling depends upon random sampling theory. It involves the breaking down of the total working time of all workers who perform the operation into *instants* of time that are used as the basic unit for sampling. The exact instants of time for actual observations are determined by some random method. After the observer tallies the action occurring at a large number of different instants of time, the total number of instants at which each type of activity has been observed is divided by the total number of observations. The results are the percentages of instants at which each type of activity was observed. These percentages are the basic data provided by work sampling. They yield directly the information needed for determining allowances.

The setting of time standards is a difficult and important problem for management. Because time standards have many valuable applications, it is worth considerable effort to make them as sound as possible.

If a time standard is set hastily, management will have difficulty instilling confidence not only in that standard but also in the entire standards program. A "loose" standard is difficult to change once it has been adopted. A worker on a job having a "loose" standard becomes accustomed to the low requirements. If management tries to "tighten" the standard, the worker will charge that it is attempting to "speed up" and that there is no reason to try to meet or exceed the standard if management is going to take this as evidence that the standard needs raising. It is for this reason that a basic policy of management should be that once a time standard is set for an operation, it will not be changed unless the operation has been changed in some significant manner. With such a policy, management is faced with the problem of determining just what type of a change is significant. Typically, workers tend to make a number of small improvements in a job, none of which warrants a restudy. Accurate description of the job when it was timed, therefore, becomes especially important as a basis for determining just when a job has changed enough to need a new standard. Comparison of the description at the time of the previous study with the description of the current operation will provide a means of showing workers the reason for the new study.

This section has outlined only a few of the major topics of importance to the operations manager. The operations manager daily handles the technical aspects of a business firm, and therefore usually must be acquainted with the technological details and often is an engineer. This overview can only outline some major topics. A manager entering production and operations thus needs to refer to the more specialized books listed in the references.

FINANCIAL MANAGEMENT*

Financial management is the operational activity of a business that is responsible for obtaining and effectively utilizing the funds necessary for efficient operations. The objective of financial management is to see that adequate cash is on hand to meet required current and capital expenditures and otherwise to assist in maximizing profits.

A financial manager usually is located at a high level in an organization, and is one of those who advise the president and board of directors, under whose authority policies are formulated and final decisions are made. Typically, the chief financial officer carries the title of vice-president, serves as chairman of the finance committee, and reports directly to the president and board of directors.

Recent developments have changed the environment in which the financial manager functions. The rise of large-scale business units, increased product and market diversification, acceleration of corporate mergers, increased governmental regulation, and innovations in information-processing techniques have significantly broadened the responsibility and usefulness of financial control. Hence, the demands for careful planning and control, incident to the realization of profit goals, have made the

---

*This section is based upon the original work of Dr. H. A. Ellis, University of Kentucky.

financial officer a key executive. Three functions of the financial manager are financial forecasting and planning, acquisition of funds, and assistance in valuation decisions.

Financial Forecasting and Planning The financial planning function involves long-range plans for plant expansion, replacement of machinery and equipment, and a miscellany of expenditures, causing large cash drains. The financial manager assists in the analysis of cash flows over the planning period.

Financial forecasting and planning involve: (1) financial analysis ascertaining the capabilities and needs of the concern; (2) prediction of the needs for funds over the short-run operating period, including cash flow, cash budgets, and sources of current capital; (3) prediction of the need for funds over a long-run period including investment fund flow, capital budgets, alternative capital expenditure proposals, cost of capital, and conditions of the capital market.

Financial analysis consists of a comparison of a company's current status with industry standards. It points out the firm's operating weaknesses, its potential capacity, and the volume and types of financing needed to enable the company to accomplish the objectives of the management. The raw material for this analysis consists of the historical accounting records of the company and appropriate industry standards. Financial ratios serve as guideposts for management by helping to spotlight the areas that call for financial attention. A check list for comparing the performance of a company with norms for the industry is presented in Table 14-1. Data for several consecutive accounting periods will strengthen the usefulness of these comparisons. The norms used in the table are for illustrative purposes only; in practice they should be obtained from sources that collect information on the specific industry concerned.

Prediction of the short-term needs for funds is interrelated with long-term requirements. A combined short- and long-run cash flow analysis, the framework for which is illustrated in Figure 14-3, may be helpful in judging future cash needs. Cash and capital budgets may further facilitate decision making with respect to the sources and expenditure of funds.

The **cash budget** is basically a tool by which the analyst attempts to predict the various additions and withdrawals from the cash reservoir over a normal operating period. It aims to discover the extent of funds needed to meet current operating expenses. The cash budget is a part of the master budget discussed in Chapter 10.

Other aids for the prediction of short-term needs include pro forma income and balance sheet statements, pro forma statements of working

Table 14-1
Check List for Financial Ratio Analysis

Name of Ratio	Formula	Industry Norm (assumed merely as illustration)
I. Liquidity Ratios (measuring the ability of the firm to meet its maturing obligations)		
Current ratio	$\dfrac{\text{Current assets}}{\text{Current liabilities}}$	2.6
Acid-test ratio	$\dfrac{\text{Cash and equivalent}}{\text{Current liability}}$	1.0
II. Leverage Ratios (measuring the contributions of financing by owners compared with financing provided by creditors)		
Debt to equity	$\dfrac{\text{Total debt}}{\text{Equity}}$	56%
Coverage of fixed charges	$\dfrac{\text{Net profit before fixed charges}}{\text{Fixed charges}}$	6 times
Current liability to equity	$\dfrac{\text{Current liability}}{\text{Equity}}$	32%
III. Activities Ratios (measuring the effectiveness of the employment of resources)		
Inventory turnover	$\dfrac{\text{Sales}}{\text{Inventory}}$	7 times
Net working capital turnover	$\dfrac{\text{Sales}}{\text{Net working capital}}$	5 times
Fixed-assets turnover	$\dfrac{\text{Sales}}{\text{Fixed assets}}$	6 times
Average collection period	$\dfrac{\text{Receivables}}{\text{Average sales per day}}$	20 days
Equity capital turnover	$\dfrac{\text{Sales}}{\text{Equity}}$	3 times
IV. Profitability Ratios (including degree of success in achieving desired profit levels)		
Gross operating margin	$\dfrac{\text{Gross operating profit}}{\text{Sales}}$	30%
Net operating margin	$\dfrac{\text{Net operating profit}}{\text{Sales}}$	6.5%
Sales margin	$\dfrac{\text{Net profit after taxes}}{\text{Sales}}$	3.2%
Productivity of assets	$\dfrac{\text{Gross income less taxes}}{\text{Total assets}}$	10%
Return on capital	$\dfrac{\text{Net profit after taxes}}{\text{Equity}}$	7.5%

capital and source and use of funds, and breakeven charts. These devices facilitate the comparison of actual results with expected results, pointing up the strong and weak points of the periodic performance.

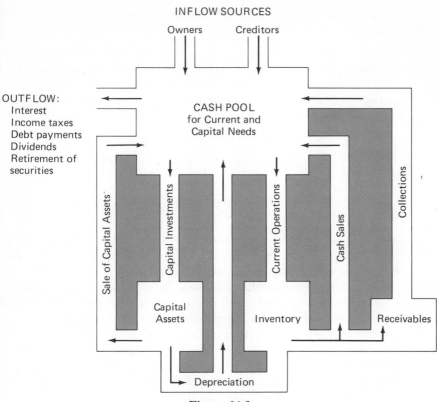

Figure 14-3
Flow of Cash Through a Business

Long-term differs from short-term planning primarily in the purpose to be achieved. Accountants distinguish between the two terms by separating cash uses into capital expenditures and current expenditures. Generally, a **current expenditure** is one from which principal benefits are realized within a year, and a **capital expenditure** is one from which benefits are realized over a period longer than a year.

Long-term financial planning starts with the preparation of a capital budget. **Capital budgeting** is an attempt to appraise the long-range monetary benefits of alternative capital expenditures. The first step in this process is for each department head to determine the various capital expenditures he believes to be desirable. Each department head faces three problems: (1) the determination of available alternatives, (2) the classification of proposals according to purpose, and (3) the final selection.

Several approaches may be useful in the evaluation of investment opportunities. The job in all approaches is to find the difference between the net benefits that accrue from each alternative and the financial burden incurred to secure the benefits. The following three methods may be used:

1. *Payback Period.* An estimate is made of how long it will take for the investment to pay for itself, called the payback period. Then the period is compared with some standard period. If the asset would pay for itself in less time than the standard period, the investment would be made. The payback formula is simple:

$$P = \frac{C}{R}$$

where P represents the payback period, *C* the cost of the investment, and *R* the expected net annual return from the investment.

2. *Present Value.* A more precise method of evaluating capital expenditures is to calculate the present value of the net cash benefits discounted at the company's cost of capital rate (the weighted average annual cost computed as a percentage of present total capitalization). If the amount computed is greater than the new investment, monetary gain should result from the outlay. To illustrate: Assume that the cost of capital is 10 percent after taxes and that the benefits after taxes from a $10,000 investment are $4,500 per year for three years. Using present-value tables, the present value of this stream of income discounted at 10 percent is $11,192 or a net realizable gain of $1,192. The basic formula is

$$P = \frac{R_1}{(1 + i)} + \frac{R_2}{(1 + i)^2} \cdots \frac{R_n}{(1 + i)^n}$$

in which P = present value of the investment; $R_1, R_2 \ldots R_n$ = expected dollar returns in each year; i = the appropriate interest rate.

3. *Discounted Rate of Return.* The object in a third method of evaluation is to find the rate of return that will discount those returns to equal the cost of the proposed investment when applied to the future-dollar returns. Using the same assumptions as in the present-value illustration, the rate that will equate the stream of $4,500 per year for three years with the required investment of $10,000 is computed. A series of trial calculations will reveal that a net cash inflow of $4,500 for three years is equivalent to a rate of return of approximately 16.6 percent. If this exceeds the present cost of capital, the investment should be profitable as compared with overall past performance.

*Acquisition
of
Funds*
The acquisition of funds involves a consideration of the available sources and the time period for which they are needed. A first step for these considerations is the determination of the types of funds to be used and the mix best suited to the situation.

Broadly speaking, there are two basic types of funds: **debt** (fixed claims by outsiders) and **equity** (ownership). Four factors influence the choice between the two types:

1. Maturity of the obligating agreement.
2. Priority of claim on income.
3. Priority of claim on assets.
4. Voice in management.

Some considerations that influence the types of funds to use are:

1. *Suitability.* The types of funds must harmonize with the kinds of assets being financed.
2. *Volume and stability of income.* The more substantial and reliable the flow of income, the more feasible is the adoption of financial leverage (debt financing).
3. *Control.* The types of funds used reflect the residual owners' desire to maintain control of the company.
4. *Flexibility.* The ability to adjust the source and nature of the funds in response to changes in needs for funds.
5. Characteristics of *the economy*, including the level of business activity, money, capital markets, and tax developments.
6. Characteristics of *the industry*, including seasonal variations, nature of competition, regulation, and growth potentials.
7. Characteristics of *the organization*, including legal form, size, status in the industry, credit status, and management attitudes and policies.
8. *Economic and social responsibilities.*

Acquisition of funds is affected by whether the funds are anticipated for short-term, intermediate, or long-term use. One general rule is to match the maturity of the obligation with the income-producing life of the asset being financed. A second rule is that regular working capital should be derived from long-term sources, whereas fluctuating working capital normally requires short-term debt financing.

A major portion of the funds employed by a successful business is generated by the business itself in the form of depreciation allowances and retained earnings. Outside sources include the sale of equity shares, long-term debt securities for investment purposes, and the use of various credit facilities for short-term and intermediate-term financing. Trade creditors, finance companies, insurance companies, commercial paper houses, factoring companies, government agencies, and commercial banks are some possible outside sources. Circumstances prevailing at the time of the need will dictate the final choice.

For most businesses, commercial banks are relied upon heavily for current funds. Firms generally maintain a close working relationship with one or more commercial banks to provide depositories for the company's monies, meet payrolls, distribute interest and dividend payments, and handle other money matters; the financial manager turns to commercial banks for aid when short-term credit is needed.

In the early stages of a company's life, banks normally demand extensive information before extending credit, including personal information about the borrower, information about the business, historical accounting data, and facts about the need and use of the loan. After credit is granted, it is expected that the bank will be furnished a record of the borrower's subsequent business performance.

Successful acquisition of long-term (capital) funds depends upon the competence of the financial manager in knowing who the principal buyers are, the best contacts with the capital market, and the factors that underlie a good capital structure. The manager must keep informed of recent trends in the market for corporate securities (such as the increasing importance of pension and retirement funds) and of the impact of institutional buyers on the market. He should know the important classes of buyers such as life insurance companies, commercial and mutual savings banks, investment companies, and individual investors.

Various methods may be employed in contacting potential buyers of securities. The most important are: (1) contractual underwriting arrangements with investment bankers; (2) offers to existing shareholders on a preemptive (prior-privilege) basis; (3) direct placement with an institutional buyer or trust fund administrator; and (4) competitive bid by all prospective purchasers. The final selection of the method of contacting buyers depends on the relative cost, conditions prevailing in the capital market, effects of the issue on capital structure, effects on stockholder relations, and the amount of government regulation involved.

In building the capital structure of a company, the following policies may be helpful:

1. Don't use bonds unless the estimated earnings will give a *factor of safety* of at least 100 percent. (Ratio of what is left after interest payments to the amount of the interest.)
2. Keep the capital structure as *simple* and *conservative* as is feasible.

3. Keep the contracts between the security holder and the corporation as flexible as possible.
4. Safeguard the control of the company.
5. Keep the annual cost to a minimum.
6. Keep the best security (most appealing; minimum risk) for emergency financing.

Of critical importance in investment analysis is the determination of the *cost of capital*. Since capital may be raised by selling shares of equity and by long-term debt (leverage), a firm's cost of capital must involve a weighted average from both sources. It is important for two main reasons: first it provides a basis for evaluation of investment opportunities; second, it emphasizes how the degree of leverage is useful in the development of a balanced capital structure. The *cost of capital*, therefore, is a weighted, after-tax average computed on the combined capital structure mix. The future cash payments that must be made on the entire mix of capital sources constitute the cost of capital. Estimating the average cost of capital involves three steps:

1. Determine the optimum capital structure.
2. Determine the after-tax cost of each type of fund used or sought.
3. Weight the cost of each type of fund by its proportion in the optimal capital structure.

Although the idea of cost of capital is clear, there is considerable controversy concerning the average cost of capital when the degree of financial leverage (debt) increases. The Miller-Modigliani view suggests that the average cost of capital decreases as debt increases, because the interest on debt is tax deductible. The traditional view stated that the average cost of capital increases because the cost of debt and equity increases. Recent research in financial management has been devoted to simulations of models of different capital structures. The general manager, therefore, is well advised to check assumptions carefully and consult recent literature before employing a figure for cost of capital.

Valuation Methods of a Firm

The financial manager from time to time must participate in decisions relative to the purchase of major assets and to consolidations and mergers. During the negotiations for acquiring parts or all of other companies, he has the job of arriving at the dollar value of going concerns. The job is made more difficult inasmuch as value must be based not only on present or past value but on careful forecasts of future income-producing ability under conditions of uncertainty. Some of the conventional methods of valuation are:

1. *Original asset cost less depreciation* is based on the theory that an asset is worth what was paid for it, less the value lost through useful wear and tear. Objections are raised to this method because prior cost is no measure of present worth.

2. *Asset replacement cost less depreciation* avoids the question of changing price levels, but is objected to because of the lack of agreement on what replacement means (for example, identical replacement or present worth of replacement).

3. *Total book value of claims on assets* is another way of saying that the value of the claim is represented by the value of the asset to which the claim applies.

4. *Market value of outstanding securities* constitutes a composite expression of value incorporating all the factors that influence investment decisions. Wide fluctuations in security prices, however, do not facilitate a sound estimate of established values.

5. *Capitalization of earnings* is based on the proposition that, in the final analysis, an asset is worth what it will produce in the form of a stream of income over a period of years, discounted at a "fair" rate of return. For example, the assets of a given company may be capable of producing "normal" annual earnings of $217,333. A capitalization rate of, say, 12½ percent is judged reasonable for a business of this character, considering the degree of risks inherent in the venture. Thus, through the simplest capitalization formula, $.12\frac{1}{2}V = \$217,333$, the value of the business would be $1,738,665. At a capitalization rate of 15 percent the estimated value would be $1,448,890, and at 10 percent the value would be $2,173,330. Of course, the valuation decision would be no more reliable than the accuracy of the estimated future earnings, and the acceptability of the capitalization rate. Furthermore, better but more complicated formulas are available in more rigorous studies of financial management.

The financial manager sits on the horns of a dilemma, being charged with the responsibility of having money ready to *spend* for current and investment purposes and at the same time having to get and *keep* sufficient money on hand to enable the business to achieve its profit objective. A workable balance between cash inflow and cash outflow must be constantly maintained. This calls for continuous planning, controlling, and maintaining relationships with the source of current and capital funds. A sound business rests on a sound financial foundation, the construction of which is the foremost responsibility of the financial manager.

**MARKETING
MANAGEMENT***
Marketing management is a third
major field of business for applying
the concepts and analytical devices
covered in earlier chapters. Its special orientation is toward the consumer
of products and services offered by the firm.

As a result of fundamental changes in the overall economy, marketing and marketing management today occupy a more strategic place in
business than they did prior to World War II. The **marketing concept**
which has emerged from these changes refers to making all decisions in
terms of a marketing orientation, with special attention to the consumer.
All activities of the firm are integrated and balanced in terms of what is
best for the company in the marketplace.

An important distinction should be made between marketing management and marketing. **Marketing** can be defined as the performance of
business activities that direct the flow of goods and services from the
producer to the consumer and includes selling, buying, transportation,
storage, standardization, grading, financing, and risk taking. **Marketing
management** is that area of company management that is concerned with
decisions and *policies* relating to the marketing *activities* of the firm.

The marketing manager is responsible for the firm's marketing program. A **marketing program** can be defined as a plan for guiding a
company's marketing activities toward specific objectives. It tells what is
to be done, when it is to be done, and who is to be responsible for
carrying out the various activities. The objectives of the marketing program are usually set by top-level management, and the plan covers a
definite time period, usually one year.

Marketing *policies* form the heart of the marketing program. They
provide a framework for the decisions of the marketing manager and his
subordinates that will better enable them to achieve their stated objectives. The principal marketing policies usually concern such matters as (1)
pricing, (2) advertising, (3) service, (4) warranty, (5) credit, (6) product-
line, (7) branding, (8) terms of sale, (9) reciprocity, (10) sales personnel,
(11) distribution channels, and (12) market coverage.

The *activities* that are part of the firm's marketing program will be
discussed under five categories: (1) pricing, (2) product, (3) promotion, (4)
channels of distribution, and (5) marketing research. When any of these
are combined, they are called a marketing mix. The **marketing mix** refers
to the apportionment of effort, and the combination, design, and integration of the elements of marketing into a program that, on the basis of
appraisal of the market forces, will best achieve the objectives of an

*This section is based on the original work for the first edition by Dr. Lawrence X.
Tarpey, University of Kentucky.

enterprise in a given time period. The elements of a marketing program can be combined in many ways, and the successful marketing manager is the one who can find the most profitable mix for the company through careful study of the five activities.

Pricing

The marketing manager's most important task probably is pricing, because prices are the firm's prime source of current revenue. Pricing is a difficult task, because it requires the decision maker to make judgments concerning consumer income, business conditions, competitive reaction, and so on.

Prices represent *values*. The manufacturer, in setting prices, is really translating into quantitative terms (that is, dollars and cents) the value of products to customers at a point in time. From the standpoint of the purchaser, *value* is a personal thing; it is what the consumer feels the product is worth and what he is willing to give up (exchange) in order to obtain the good. The marketing manager has to be able to do two things to be an effective price setter: (1) estimate value, and secure a suitable product in line with this estimate and (2) convince the consuming public that the product is worth the price (money) being asked.

In making pricing decisions, the marketing manager must take into account six main factors: (1) the nature and extent of consumer demand; (2) the costs of manufacturing and selling the product; (3) the competitive reaction; (4) the antitrust laws; (5) the promotional strategy; and (6) the channels of distribution.

Price policies are those decisions that relate the actual pricing decisions to the objectives of the firm. These policies also function to describe the marketing philosophy of the company. One policy might be, "We will not be undersold." A more sophisticated price policy would be to sell at relatively high prices and skim the market, recognizing that all segments of the market have different elasticities of demand and attempting to exploit that part of the market that is relatively price inelastic. Sometimes high prices are charged to "try the market" when there is little or no information to be had concerning the price elasticity of demand. This policy assumes that it is easier to lower a price than to raise it.

The firm's policies help determine how the prices are established, but most companies have formulas for determining the actual dollars-and-cents figure to place on products. In economics, the forces of demand and supply set the price (market price) that consumers pay; however, in practice, prices are determined by the company's management. Thus, the price that the consumer pays for a product is usually an *administered price*.

Many pricing formulas can be reduced to two basic approaches: (1) the cost approach and (2) the market or competitive approach. The cost approach is easy to understand but very difficult to apply accurately, because costs are difficult to ascertain. Three commonly accepted price formulas are:

1. Prices equal to allocated total firm costs, plus a certain standard percentage markup. Under this formula every product is presumed to contribute equally to the net profit of the firm.
2. Prices equal to a certain percentage of a major cost component. This is the basic method in the retail and wholesale trade. In certain manufacturing industries, where material costs loom large, this method is easy to understand and calculate.
3. Prices equal to direct costs plus some amount added to cover allocated overhead and profit contribution.

Using the cost-plus approach, management must decide two questions. What to use as the base (full costs or variable costs)—and how large to make the margin. If a company prices some products on the basis of variable costs rather than full costs, it is using *incremental cost pricing*, a policy which is economically sound but legally questionable.

A competitive approach is the reverse of the cost-plus approach. Here the marketing manager takes as the starting point the customer. For example, suppose a hardware manufacturer wants to price a new kind of screwdriver for the home workshop. The established price for this kind of product might be $1.98. If it is sold through hardware stores and variety chains, a markup of about 40 percent must be allowed for the retailer. The manufacturer's selling price could not be more than 60 percent of retail or about $1.19 per unit. If the manufacturer's marketing expense, administrative overhead, and net profit added up to 30 percent, the allowable cost of manufacture would be about $.83 ($1.19 × 70 percent). The product design and production personnel are expected to come up with an attractively packaged item with sales appeal that can be manufactured for 83 cents. (The pricing of this book employed this type of thinking.)

The market or competitive approach directly considers such things as market structure, consumer income, tastes, and habits. The policy of quoting prices in odd cents (for example, 99 cents) is an attempt to take advantage of the consumer's psychological desire for a bargain and is quite common in retailing. Certain products (for example, chewing gum and candy bars) are sold at prices the consumer is accustomed to paying, and marketing managers will alter the product rather than raise the price. Some products (for example, consumer durables) are highly sensitive to changes in income—that is, income elastic—and a sharp drop in personal income can radically affect sales. Also, certain industries are so structured that lower prices will always be matched by the competitor, whereas higher prices will be ignored; raising the price will only cause the firm to lose business. This is the normal situation in an oligopoly with fairly homogeneous products.

Prices are often structured, which means that the company has no flat price that is charged to everyone, but instead, a system of discounts permits certain customers to buy for less than other customers. Sometimes prices are reduced if the product is purchased in larger quantities, by allowing quantity discounts that reflect cost savings by selling larger amounts. **Trade discounts** are reductions from the list price based on the buyer's position in the channel of distribution (for example, wholesaler, retailer). Trade discounts are supposed to compensate the middlemen for performing their marketing tasks. In establishing a system of discounts, the marketing manager must determine whether they are adequate to secure the necessary cooperation from the various middlemen, and whether they are nondiscriminatory from the standpoint of the laws.

Prices are always under pressure either from costs, competition, the law, or the consumer. Authority to change prices is not usually delegated to the sales force but remains a top-management responsibility, because of the direct connection between prices and profits. Generally, a vice-president will decide when and how much to charge. Sometimes a marketing committee is given this authority. In any case, the changes are made only after much deliberation. An important part of marketing management is to review constantly the price structure to see that it is in line with costs, competition, and the other policies and objectives of the company.

Product

A company's product is what it has to sell. In a very narrow sense of the word, a product is the physical thing that comes off the assembly line. However, under the marketing concept, the idea of a product is given a broader meaning. Here **product** is viewed as the satisfactions that accrue to the owner of the product from possession or use. These satisfactions include such things as esthetic qualities, convenience in use, economic status, and so forth. For example, the relative decline of railroads as a transportation agency can be explained largely by the belief they were in the railroad business. Actually, the increasing demand for transportation was filled by others because railroads conceived their product narrowly (railroad transportation) rather than broadly (movement service).

A product is the company's main link connecting it with the consuming public. Through their products, most firms enjoy their greatest opportunity to stimulate demand. The task of developing products and product lines to satisfy the needs of the ever-changing consumer is called **merchandising.**

Three basic strategies available to the marketing manager are product differentiation, market segmentation, and planned obsolescence.

Product differentiation seeks to direct new consumer demand toward an existing or slightly modified product. Promotion tries to convince the consumer of the superiority and advantages of a product that is closely similar to others, as in the case of cigarettes and aspirin. **Market segmentation** seeks to adjust the physical and total product to consumer demand. In contrast to product differentiation, a market segmentation policy recognizes the existence of many submarkets that could lead to a substantial expansion of the product line, as in the introduction of the compact automobile. **Planned obsolescence** deliberately creates new products, supposedly with minor and superficial variations, in order to make the older models obsolete. In some cases, the product is designed to wear out faster. A policy of planned obsolescence is often criticized as being wasteful; however, it appears that this marketing strategy does satisfy consumer needs. In fashion, for example, this year's style will probably not be popular next year, and it is the happy merchant who is able to second guess public fashion whims.

Product design and packaging are two of the more important aspects of a firm's product program. Designing a product should start with an idea that has been verified by market research. Design should be consumer oriented rather than production oriented; yet it must be compatible with the company's overall product policy in order to make most effective use of the firm's resources. A good package should (1) protect the product, (2) inform the consumer, (3) advertise and stimulate sales, (4) lower marketing costs, and (5) facilitate use of the product.

One of the most important subjects of product management is brands. A **brand** is a name, term, symbol, or design (or a combination of these) that identifies the goods of one seller or group of sellers, and distinguishes them from those of competitors. In a very general sense, branding usually includes all of the printed matter that appears on the product. Brands are so closely related to the product and the individual producer that they are protected by law (the Lanham Act of 1946). Some manufacturers produce and sell merchandise using their own brands; others allow wholesalers or large chains to place their own brand name on the merchandise (private brands). Sometimes the same brand is used for many products (family brands) so that the goodwill attached to one product will carry over to similar products, such as Betty Crocker, Allstate, and Ann Page.

Today, new-product management is an important part of a firm's competitive strategy. When a company selects and develops a product, it is choosing the kind of business it is going to be; therefore, a new-product program is a top-management responsibility. Within industry a number of organizational arrangements have recently evolved: (1) a product manager is charged with the responsibility of keeping the product up to date; (2) a new-product manager (also called the product planner or product development manager) may have the task of maintaining a steady stream of new products for the various product managers; (3) a product planning committee, composed of top executives representing the functional areas of business, may contribute to new-product development.

Channels *of* *Distribution*   Managing the channels of distribution is a major line responsibility of the marketing manager. A **channel of distribution** is the route that the product follows in its passage from the producer to the consumer. This route can be very simple or very complex, depending on such things as: (1) the nature of the product (convenience good, specialty good, or industrial good); (2) the nature and location of the market; (3) the price of the product; (4) the availability of distributors willing to handle the product; (5) the sales effort required; and (6) the resources and capabilities of the producer. Thus a bar of soap may be sold by a manufacturer to a broker, wholesaler, retailer, or customer, whereas an electronic computer may be sold direct from the factory to the user.

Channel management involves two basic problems: the selection of the proper channel for the product and maintaining the channel. Four policy alternatives may be considered in the selection of the channel: (1) the policy of *general or intensive distribution,* whereby the firm seeks to obtain the widest possible distribution for its product by allowing it to be sold everywhere by anyone willing to stock it; (2) the policy of *selective distribution,* where the manufacturer chooses only those outlets that are able best to serve that company's needs; (3) the policy of using *exclusive dealerships,* which allows only *one* distributor to stock and sell the product in a given market; (4) the policy of *leasing,* under which the manufacturer (lessor) gives possession and use of the equipment to the customer (lessee), but the title to the equipment remains with the manufacturer.

A company may use more than one channel, particularly if its market is diversified. Grocery manufacturers, for example, sell direct to the chain stores but also sell to the independents through brokers and wholesalers. If a company feels that its product is of a very high quality, it may not want it to be sold in a 5- and 10-cent store because it may adversely affect the product image.

The second problem of channel management is that of maintaining the channel so that no blockages develop that can adversely affect the company's competitive and profit position. If a firm is selling part of its product by means of its own sales force, the channel maintenance problem is one of directing the outside sales force. When other types of middlemen are employed (such as agents and wholesalers), the marketing manager has to do three things: (1) see to it that the terms of the contract are followed by all parties; (2) maintain good relations with the middlemen and encourage them to cooperate fully; and (3) represent his company to the middlemen by seeing to it that sufficient cooperation and assistance are provided to enable them to market the product successfully.

Promotion **Promotion** refers to the nonprice selling activities of the firm. Three important types are advertising, personal selling, and sales promotion. **Advertising** is any paid form of nonpersonal presentation of merchandise to a group by an identified sponsor. **Personal selling** is the process of assisting and persuading a prospect to buy a commodity in a face-to-face situation. **Sales promotion** includes such devices as trading stamps, dealer aids, incentive travel, premiums, contests, and so on. In practice, sales promotion activities are used primarily to supplement either advertising or personal selling.

Advertising and personal selling are different means to the same end—increasing sales. Usually they are employed together and are not in competition. Advertising appeals to the mass mind, whereas personal salesmanship is directed to the individual. Advertising assists salespeople and makes their efforts more productive by giving preliminary information about the product to prospects.

The successful marketing manager is always aware of the fact that the promotional activities are a cost to the firm. Therefore, selling expenditures have to be justified in terms of increased sales and profits. There must always be some standard by which the worth of the promotional effort can be measured; otherwise the company's money may be wasted.

The advertising manager is usually in charge of a firm's advertising program, and has the responsibility to plan the entire advertising program, to draw up a budget, and to justify the request for funds—often with valuable help from an advertising agency. The **advertising agency** is a type of service institution composed of specialists that assist clients in planning, preparing, and placing advertising. Agencies are paid by the various media (usually a 15 percent commission).

Personal selling is usually the responsibility of the sales manager, who hires, fires, trains, and supervises the sales force. Some personal selling is directed to the middleman and some to the ultimate consumer. Some selling is creative in nature because it involves the process of arousing demand and persuading the buyer, whereas some is simply routine selling because the customer has already decided to buy.

The sales manager must organize the sales force for maximum effectiveness. Bases for organization include: (1) the geographic area; (2) the type of product; (3) the kind of customer (consumer or industrial); (4) the channel of distribution (middlemen versus direct buyers); or (5) the nature of the selling task (new business or servicing old accounts). The marketing vice-president makes the important decisions regarding the amount and kinds of promotion to be included in the marketing mix, and harmonizes the advertising efforts of the company with the other selling programs and vice versa. For example, it is the marketing vice-president's responsibility to see that the sales manager is informed ahead of time of any new advertising campaigns so that the salespeople in the field can inform the dealers to build up sufficient inventories.

Market Research

Market research can be defined as the systematic gathering, recording, and analyzing of data about problems relating to the distribution and sale of goods. The market research department is a staff function that serves the entire organization, because the need for market research information is pervasive. The justification for market research is that it helps to keep the executive informed and thus serves as a basis for making decisions.

Market research departments usually are headed by a director who reports to the top marketing executive. Research personnel are specialists (for example, statisticians, psychologists, economists) in the technical tools of their work. If a company cannot afford to maintain a full-time marketing research department, the responsibility for research will be assigned to one of the marketing executives and an outside agency will be relied upon to provide the actual technical research. These external agencies are varied as to mode of operation, but in general there are eight basic types: (1) consulting firms that work for the company as independent contractors; (2) syndicated data services (for example, A. C. Nielson, Daniel Starch) that assemble certain types of data and sell them on a subscription basis; (3) specialized service organizations that perform limited functions such as tabulating, interviewing, printing, and sample design; (4) trade associations that serve an entire industry, supported by contributions from firms in the industry; (5) media that have full-time research staffs to perform certain kinds of marketing studies on a continuing basis and perform specialized services only upon request; (6) advertising agencies that perform marketing research studies for clients on a fee-plus-expense basis; (7) universities that have bureaus of business research that contract to do studies for businesspeople or industries; and (8) government agencies (for example, Small Business Administration, the Agricultural Market Service) that sponsor or perform research for an industry or for a certain kind of business.

Below are listed some typical market research projects and applications:

1. *Product studies*, which include developing and testing new products, measuring product preference, and testing package design.

2. *Consumer studies*, which identify potential consumers, measure characteristics (income, habits, attitudes, etc.), and study and explain their behavior.

3. *Market analysis*, which tries to measure current sales potential and sales trends and to forecast sales.

4. *Sales analysis*, which appraises sales policies, measures distributor and dealer performance, evaluates sales territories, appraises salespeople's performance, and so forth.

5. *Advertising studies*, which attempt to measure the effectiveness of advertising campaigns, determine advertising appeals, and measure media audiences.

6. *Distribution cost analysis*, which seeks to measure the actual cost of marketing a product.

Marketing managers must know enough about research techniques to be able to evaluate reports and to communicate with the market research personnel. A working knowledge of statistics and accounting is vital in the interpretation of market research information. For example, almost all market surveys are based on some type of probability sample, and sales forecasting relies heavily on trend analysis and statistical correlation. The marketing executive is not expected to be an expert in every field, but has to know enough about methodology to ask intelligent questions of the researcher.

MARKETING TRENDS AND CHANGES* Marketing has undergone radical changes in the past decade. Rapid economic growth, once the impetus for marketing practice, has developed into marketing's "problem child." The emphasis on materialism and high-powered technology in the 1950s and early 1960s has resulted in an extremely costly venture for society. New factors in the marketing environment posed some interesting challenges to marketers in the 1970s. Such factors as consumerism, environmentalism, shortages, economic uncertainty, and public sector needs have contributed to more socially responsible marketing.

(1) *Consumerism.* A better educated population, increasingly complex and hazardous products, and the general public's disenchantment with big business are the primary reasons for the organized involvement of private citizens and government in attempting to enhance the rights and power of buyers in relation to sellers. Marketers who recognize consumerism as an opportunity to serve their publics

*This section was contributed by Mary Joyce, graduate student, University of Kentucky.

better through providing more education, information, and protection will realize the success in the long-run that can only be realized through a consumer orientation.

(2) *Environmentalism.* Quality of life has become a predominant concern in society. Organizations must be held responsible for their actions. Minimizing the harm done by marketing practices is important to the consuming public in the long run. When societal costs outweigh the benefits of satisfying individual consumer needs and wants, society's interests should be considered foremost.

(3) *Shortages.* There is little doubt that shortages have forced an alteration in the strategic programing of the marketing mix. The guiding principle during a shortage period should be one of consumer orientation. During shortage periods, the major asset that an organization has is its loyal customers.

(4) *Economic uncertainty.* Rapid inflation and recession have been responsible for creating more problems for marketing. Rampant inflation, coupled with government's attempt to discourage excessive prices, has presented marketers with a somewhat paradoxical situation. The major solution has been product simplification. Cost increases are offset without passing on price increases to consumers. Recessions have also contributed significantly to a change in marketing. More sensible purchasing behavior has resulted in a redefining of the needs of markets.

(5) *Public Sector Needs.* The growth in private goods has not been matched by a corresponding growth in public goods. The issue of what to produce in capitalist economies is left mainly to be determined in the marketplace. As a result, public services tend to be underfinanced and neglected. Nonprofit organizations responsible for satisfying public sector needs have just recently begun to improve their services by adopting a marketing orientation.

Marketing has indeed evolved into a field which involves more than the directing of goods and services. An ever-changing environment has broadened the scope of marketing to include not just a consumer orientation, but also a societal orientation. This broadened scope will present a continual challenge to marketing managers in the future.

SUMMARY   This chapter has summarized some of the specific applications of managerial functions, using the relevant disciplinary foundations discussed in Part 3 in the principal operational areas of a business firm: operations or manufacturing (production) management, financial management, and marketing management. These three areas typically serve as the basis for functional specialization in a business firm.

The operations manager concentrates on producing products, using special techniques for planning and control of production and improving the methods of production, and using standards which serve as measures of efficiency and productivity. A person in this position usually has a technical background and is well acquainted with various topics that have an engineering base.

The financial manager is charged with the responsibility of having money ready to spend for current and investment purposes, and must keep a workable balance between cash inflows and cash outflows. These activities call for continuous planning, controlling, and maintaining relationships with the source of current and capital funds. In short, the financial manager is the chief functional manager oriented to keeping the business on a sound financial foundation.

The marketing manager focuses on distributing the product and services to customers, with emphasis on pricing, promoting, identifying products, establishing channels of distribution, and researching the market.

Each of these functions is essential to profitable operations and therefore each has its own area of specialization. However, the performance of all these functions must be coordinated, and in the final analysis it is a team effort; no one is more or less indispensable than any other.

REFERENCES

Operations Management

BARNES, RALPH M., *Motion and Time Study* (6th ed.). New York: John Wiley & Sons, 1968.

BOWMAN, E. H. and R. B. FETTER, *Analysis for Production and Operations Management* (3rd ed.). Homewood, Ill.: Richard D. Irwin, Inc., 1967.

BUFFA, ELWOOD S., *Modern Production Management* (5th ed.). New York: John Wiley & Sons, 1977.

CHASE, R. B. and N. J. AQUILANO, *Production and Operations Management.* Homewood, Ill.: Richard D. Irwin, Inc., 1977.

MOORE, FRANKLIN G. and T. E. HENDRICK, *Production/Operations Management.* Homewood, Ill.: Richard D. Irwin, Inc., 1977.

PLOSSL, G. W. and O. W. WIGHT, *Production and Inventory Control.* Englewood Cliffs, N.J.: Prentice-Hall, Inc., 1967.

TIMMS, H. L., *Introduction to Operations Management.* Homewood, Ill.: Richard D. Irwin, Inc., 1967.

Financial Management

BRIGHAM, EUGENE and RAMON JOHNSON, *Issues in Managerial Finance*. Hinsdale, Ill.: Dryden Press, 1976.

GITMAN, L. J., *Principles of Managerial Finance*. New York: Harper & Row, 1976.

HELFERT, ERICH, *Techniques of Financial Analysis* (5th ed.). Homewood, Ill.: Richard D. Irwin, Inc., 1977.

JOHNSON, ROBERT W., *Financial Management* (4th ed.). Boston: Allyn and Bacon, Inc., 1971.

SCHWARTZMAN, S. D. and R. E. BALL, *Elements of Financial Analysis*. New York: D. Van Nostrand Company, 1977.

SEITZ, NEIL, *Financial Analysis: A Programmed Approach*. Reston, Va.: Reston Publishing Co., 1976.

VAN HORNE, JAMES, *Financial Management and Policy* (4th ed.). Englewood Cliffs, N.J.: Prentice-Hall Inc., 1977.

WESTON, FRED and EUGENE BRIGHAM, *Essentials of Managerial Finance* (4th ed.). Hinsdale, Ill.: Dryden Press, 1977.

Marketing Management

ENIS, BEN M., *Marketing Principles* (2nd ed.). Santa Monica, Cal.: Goodyear Publishing Co., 1977.

MCCARTHY, E. J., *Basic Marketing* (6th ed.). Homewood, Ill.: Richard D. Irwin, Inc., 1978.

ROSENBERG, L. J., *Marketing*. Englewood Cliffs, N.J.: Prentice-Hall, Inc., 1977.

SCHWARTZ, D. J., *Marketing Today: a Basic Approach* (2nd ed.). New York: Harcourt Brace Jovanovich, Inc., 1977.

15

MANAGEMENT
OF
PUBLIC
ORGANIZATIONS

by Lawrence K. Lynch, University of Kentucky

⟸ **IDEAS TO BE FOUND** ⟹
IN THIS CHAPTER

- Cost effectiveness
- Planning-Programing-Budgeting Systems
- Benefit/cost analysis
- Zero-base budgeting
- Merit systems

Public administration—management of public organizations—emphasizes goals which differ significantly from the goals emphasized by business organizations. The functions and disciplines of management described in earlier chapters apply to both private and public organizations, but have some unique orientations in the public sector because of problems created by this difference in goal emphasis.

Recall that business firms primarily seek to earn profits, although they have other goals such as growth, stability, and public service. Public organizations have public service as their primary goal, with efficiency (and perhaps growth) as secondary goals. Public organizations include federal, state, and local government agencies, school systems, public colleges and universities, and "independent" quasi-governmental agencies such as the Postal Service, the Tennessee Valley Authority, and the Federal Reserve System.

The work of early management scholars, especially Henri Fayol, was adopted by public administrators in the 1930s, largely through the work of Luther Gulick, who coined the acronym POSDCORB to describe the critical functions performed by administrators (planning, organizing, staffing, directing, coordinating, reporting, and budgeting). More recent developments in public sector management include the introduction of "cost effectiveness" analysis in the Department of Defense by Robert McNamara under President Kennedy, the adoption of Planning-Programing-Budgeting-Systems (PPBS) by the federal government in the Johnson Administration, and the requirement for Management by Objectives imposed on federal agencies by the Nixon Administration. The influence of each of those planning tools, which will be discussed further below, has peaked and declined, but each has left its mark on the way public administrators think. The newest decision making technique is zero-base budgeting, which was introduced by the Carter Administration.

GOALS AND MEASUREMENT

Business firms have one tremendous advantage over public organizations: it is easy to *measure* profits. Public organizations, for which the major goals must be articulated in phrases such as "reduce crime," "improve public health," "protect the country from nuclear attack," and "issue Social Security checks to all qualified people," have a much harder time in measuring goal attainment.

The fundamental goal of any public organization is a legislatively prescribed impact on society, or on some subpopulation of society. Some quantitative measures of impacts have been developed (such as number of crimes in different categories, numbers and percentages of people with various diseases, retaliatory nuclear response in terms of estimated "megadeaths," or family income levels), but all suffer from imprecision of measurement due to sampling and reporting problems. Moreover, society changes over time for a number of reasons, and the impact of change due to a particular government program is often difficult to identify. As one example, suppose the number of violent crimes in a particular city declines from 3500 in 1976 to 3000 in 1977. What portion of the decline is due to the efforts of police? to a new psychological counseling program? to improving economic conditions? to the weather?

Because societal impacts of public programs are difficult to measure, these impacts, or "external goals," are often transformed into easier-to-measure internal goals. These internal goals may be classed as output goals or input goals. **Output goals** relate to the products of some governmental unit; examples are "pieces of first-class mail delivered," "number of Social Security checks written," "number of clients visited," or "number of reports produced." **Input goals** include numbers of manhours spent on a particular program, equipment purchased, or funds expended. Educators, for example, often use expenditures per pupil as a measure of the quality of education.

Measurement of internal goals is a poor substitute for measurement of an agency's impact on society. As we shall see, however, even accurate measurement of external goals does not solve the problem of allocating government resources among agencies or programs.

POLICY
MAKING

Strategic planning, or deciding on broad courses of action, is termed **policy making**, and is, in theory, performed by the legislative branch of government. In practice, however, senior public administrators from the executive branch also make policy: in the first place, they draft legislation and press for its enactment; and secondly, they fill in gaps in legislation through **administrative regulations**. While such regulations are supposed merely to implement the intent of the legislation, they often create new policy, and take the agency in directions never anticipated by the legislators.

The judicial branch of government also makes policy—through court decisions which strike down legislation, require modification of legislation, or even imply the need for new legislation. For example, the famous U.S. Supreme Court *Brown vs. Board of Education* decision, in which racial segregation in public schools was found unconstitutional, has led to major civil rights legislation at both the national and state levels. Just as U.S. Supreme Court decisions make policy at the national level, state high-court decisions make policy for states.

The importance of policy making in the executive branch has recently led to the development of *policy analysis* as a high-level administrative activity. A **policy analyst** looks for conflicts among different policies and applies various analytical tools to determine the impact and value to society of alternative policies. Policy impacts are often assessed through the use of sophisticated economic and social forecasting tools.

One such tool is the **econometric model**, a highly complex system of hundreds of equations used to predict economic conditions for each of several policy alternatives and several sets of assumptions about the behavior of businesspeople and consumers. The assumptions are called *exogenous variables;* the variables produced by the model are called *endogenous variables.* For example, the effects of a tax cut policy versus a public works program on employment and Gross National Product might be forecast. Or the demands created by a national health insurance program for additional health personnel might be predicted, along with the additional needs for federal and state spending on education. These simulations provide data from which a policy decision may be made.

The **Delphi Technique** is a behavioral tool in which a panel of experts is asked for a prediction of the implications or effects of some policy, frequently termed a *scenario.* Sometimes each expert develops several scenarios, based upon different assumptions about society's behavior. The experts are kept separate from one another to eliminate group social pressures. After each expert has given a scenario, or secenarios, the results are compiled and sent to the other participants, who are asked to revise or maintain their predictions in the light of the others' opinions. The process is repeated several times until a consensus is reached. The consensus may reflect agreement on a single policy or agreement on a set of policy alternatives. An example of the use of Delphi was that by the National Institute of Drug Abuse when it commissioned a study to develop a range of policy options for drug-abuse control.[1]

Another influence on policy making comes from lobbyists: paid representatives of business, labor, and, more recently, consumer and public interest groups, who attempt to influence the content of both legislation and administrative regulations. A recent and continuing example of lobbying at the federal level has been in connection with automobile air pollution standards. Environmental lobbyists have argued for more stringent standards to be applied at earlier dates, while the auto industry has pressed for relaxed standards and delays in implementation. The severe economic recession of 1974-75 and conflicts between energy policies and environmental targets led to some victories for the automobile industry in delaying the imposition of standards from the late 1970s into the early 1980s.

Planning is hierarchical in government as well as in business. The narrowest goals and policies established at one level of government become the broad goals for the next lowest level—which in turn develops its narrower goals and operational plans.

PLANNING AND DECISION MAKING

The disciplines of managerial economics and accounting, quantitative methods, and computer technology are now widely used in government as well as business. Because of the difficulty in quantifying public sector goals, certain specialized technologies—which make use of the disciplines—have been developed for government.

Cost effectiveness analysis, imposed by Defense Secretary Robert McNamara on the Department of Defense in the early 1960s, attempts to compare alternative approaches to goal attainment by measuring the impact per dollar spent on each alternative. In order to make such comparisons, common measures of goals must first be developed. For example,

[1] I.A. Jillson, "The National Drug-Abuse Policy Delphi: Progress Report and Findings to Date," in H. A. Linstone and M. Turoff, eds., *The Delphi Method: Techniques and Applications* (Reading, Mass.: Addison-Wesley Publishing Company, 1975).

suppose you are considering the alternatives of intercontinental ballistic missiles or long-range bombers for a nuclear "second strike" capability. The common measure for each of the two alternatives might be numbers of enemy deaths, and the estimated deaths for each alternative would be divided by the cost of the alternative to determine which was most cost effective. Obviously, if you measured enemy deaths for one alternative and number of factories destroyed for the other, you couldn't directly compare their cost effectiveness. Actual military planning uses many measures of effectiveness, and actual alternatives are based upon complex mathematical models which simulate the effects of various combinations of weapons, delivery systems, and personnel; but the essence of cost-effectiveness analysis is to determine which alternative provides a given level of goal attainment at the least cost.

Management by objectives (MBO) was used as a planning and control tool by the Nixon Administration, and has been implemented in many state government agencies. MBO emphasizes the control function: administrators are held accountable for achieving the goals they themselves established. Suppose you are the Director of a state Occupational Safety and Health Program; you might establish the following goals for your program and yourself for a one-year period:

1. Perform 500 factory inspections (an increase of 10 percent over the previous year) with no additional staff.
2. Hold six informational workshops for businesspeople in each of six principal cities of the state.
3. Reduce the accident rate in each industry to specified levels.
4. Read at least 20 technical articles related to occupational safety and health (a self-improvement objective).

The abbreviated list of objectives contains two output objectives, one impact objective, and one input objective. All of the objectives are measurable, however, and you as the Director could be held accountable for achieving them. Note that there is no quality dimension to objectives 1 and 2—the inspections could be cursory, the workshops dull. If the achievement of objectives 1 and 2 were at the expense of quality, however, it is doubtful that the third objective could be accomplished.

Planning-Programing-Budgeting-Systems (PPBS) are extensions and refinements of cost-effectiveness analysis, in which each governmental activity is evaluated according to what it accomplishes for a given expenditure. In PPBS, governmental functions are classified into a hierarchy of programs, subprograms, activities, and subactivities, which may or may not correspond to the organization of government. For example, C. West Churchman describes A. H. Schainblatt's case of a state government alcoholism program, in which 13 different state agencies participate.[2] Goals are defined for each level of the hierarchy, and goal attainment per dollar spent is the measure of activity and program value. One subprogram in an alcoholism program might be rehabilitation, and the agencies which participate and their activities might include:

1. The courts, which either jail or fine those arrested for alcohol-related offenses (such as drunken driving).
2. A state social agency, which provides counseling to those arrested, as well as to those who seek aid.
3. A state hospital, where people may go or be sent for "drying out."

A PPBS system would attempt to determine the combinations of those agencies and activities which would provide the maximum number of rehabilitated cases at the lowest cost.

Although PPBS is useful in evaluating alternative approaches to attaining the same goals within a single program, it is less useful for comparing programs themselves. How can you compare the impact per dollar spent on higher education with the impact of spending on criminal justice, for example, when their goals are measured in different terms? The answer provided by PPBS is that such comparisons—and the resulting allocation of funds among programs—is a political decision, not subject to the rational approach of PPBS.

The overlapping of programs and agencies in PPBS provides difficulties for governmental accounting. Traditionally, each agency recommends a budget with **line items** for each staff member's salary, for each item of equipment, and for each type of supply, for each classification of travel, and for each capital expenditure. In PPBS, staff members from several agencies may spend part of their time on a given program, so program budgeting must allocate agency expenditures among programs. (Although some proponents of PPBS have argued that government should be reorganized so that agencies coincide with programs, this has proved unfeasible, because programs change much more rapidly than agencies could be reorganized.) Thus two budgets must be created when PPBS is used: a line item budget and a program budget, with **crosswalks** to explain which parts of which line-items appear in each program, and vice versa. Figure 15-1 illustrates the crosswalking problem for a case where five departments from two agencies each contribute time and other resources to a single subactivity.

When President Johnson ordered federal agencies to adopt PPBS, it was also embraced by several state governments and even some cities. But because of the extra paperwork required of the executive branch by

[2]C. West Churchman, *The Systems Approach* (New York: Dell Publishing Company, 1968).

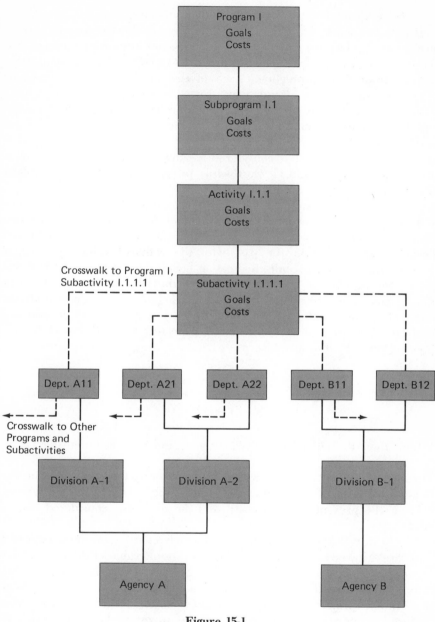

Figure 15-1
Crosswalking in PPBS

PPBS, the need for elaborate information systems to provide feedback on goal attainment, and the difficulty that some legislators experienced in following the crosswalks, PPBS has decreased in popularity in recent years.

Benefit/cost analysis is an economic technique used to evaluate individual projects as well as to decide among alternatives. It is used mainly in the Department of Defense and water resources projects, but has been experimentally applied to programs in education, transportation, and environmental protection. Each of the products and services, or "benefits," of a public program or project is measured in terms of its dollar value to society for each year of the project's proposed or expected life. Benefits are summed for each year, then discounted to present value and divided by total project cost. If the resulting benefit/cost ratio exceeds unity, the project is considered worthwhile. If sufficient resources are not available to fund all worthwhile projects, those with the highest benefit/cost ratios are funded.

As an example, suppose the U.S. Army Corps of Engineers proposes a dam which will provide flood control and recreation benefits. Flood control benefits are measured by comparing the monetary value of actual flood damages done in the past with the reduced value of damages expected if the dam is built. Recreation benefits are measured by multiplying the number of expected visitors to the lake created by the dam times some value for each visit (and netting out the value of former recreation visits to the river). These benefits, expressed in dollars, are projected for each year of the dam's expected life and discounted to present value by the formula:

$$PV = \sum_{i=1}^{N} \frac{Bi}{(1 + r)^i}$$

Where Bi is the annual benefits in year i, and r is the interest rate.

The present value is then divided by total project costs to obtain the benefit/cost ratio. If the ratio exceeds unity, the present value of benefits exceeds the present value of costs, and the project is considered worthwhile.

The interest rate is a subject of much controversy in benefit/cost analysis. A lower rate results in a higher present value of benefits, and a higher benefit/cost ratio. Some people argue that a high rate, such as the rate of profit earned by corporations, should be used, so that investment in a public project will not be justified unless it provides the same "return," in terms of benefits, as private investments do in terms of profits. Others argue that public investments should not be evaluated on the same basis as private investments, and that a lower rate, such as the rate of interest paid on government bonds, should be used. The latter view has prevailed to date.

Zero-base budgeting (ZBB), developed as a governmental accounting and planning tool, has been adopted by both governments and businesses under the impetus of the Carter Administration.[3] Each "decision unit" (generally an administrative unit large enough to have its own budget) develops a "decision package": a set of alternative combinations of activities designed to meet the unit's objectives. Each combination represents a different level of effort and funding, beginning with a minimum level—which is funded at an amount *below* the current budget. Each other element in the decision package includes one or more increments to the minimum level, and is ranked according to its perceived importance.

Information on objectives, activities, costs and benefits, and workload and performance measures is provided by the decision unit for each element in the decision package. Higher-level administrators can then decide (1) whether the benefits of the minimum level justify any funding whatever for the decision unit, and (2) which increments, if any, are justified. The ranking of increments provides a straightforward way of adding or deleting activities if the available budget funds increase or decrease.

Suppose, for example, that you have just made your final monthly car payment of $139.50. Your car is now four years old and in bad shape. You, as the decision unit, establish the following decision package:

1. Buy a stripped-down version of an inexpensive car. After trade-in allowance, your monthly payment will be $109.75 (below your current level of expenditures).
2. Buy the inexpensive car, but add some luxury options such as air-conditioning and a stereo radio. This would require a monthly payment of $139.50 (your current level of expenditure).
3. Buy a more expensive car, but without luxury options, at a monthly cost of 159.50.
4. Buy a more expensive car, with options, at a monthly cost of $179.50.

The first decision to be made—the zero-base decision—is whether to buy a car at all. Do you need a car for basic transportation (the minimum benefit level)? Then you must decide what increments to the basic package are justified by their additional benefits in such terms as comfort, entertainment, and prestige. Your decision might be partially based on whether or not you get a raise (i.e., whether available budget funds increase).

[3]The discussion which follows is adapted from Peter A. Pyhrr, "The Zero-Base Approach to Government Budgeting," *Public Administration Review*, Vol. 37, No. 1 (January/February, 1977), pp. 1-8.

Zero-base budgeting requires that each decision unit justify its very existence in each **budget cycle** (usually a fiscal year; in some state governments, there is a two-year budget cycle). Traditionally, administrators only had to justify additions to their previous budget. ZBB requires a great deal of analysis, communication, and paperwork, however; and many bureaucrats feel threatened by its implications. (The added paperwork is a major cost that can be analyzed using benefit-cost analysis for deciding whether ZBB is worthwhile.)

Table 15-1 summarizes the main characteristics and disciplinary foundations of the policy and planning tools we have discussed.

CONTROLLING AND ORGANIZING

Each of the planning and decision-making tools outlined above has implications for control, because each requires the setting of goals or objectives which can later be compared with what actually happens. Because of the measurement problem faced by government, however, it is sometimes difficult to determine the extent to which goals were achieved in a given period. Thus a public administrator can elude effective control more easily than can a business manager.

Although *effective* control—seeing that an agency's objectives are achieved—can be eluded by a public administrator, public organizations are generally laden with *procedural* controls. The history of public administration is filled with examples of the misuse of public funds; hence along with the professionalization of administration which began in the late nineteenth century has come an ever-tighter system of controlling public expenditures. Moreover, procedural controls have often been extended to all activities of public agencies—not merely those directly involved with spending money. Thus elaborate systems of internal review have developed in many public agencies, which often unnecessarily delay needed action.

These procedural controls are facilitated by an intensely steep hierarchical organizational structure in public agencies. That is, there are many levels in the hierarchy, and thus many "officials." Actions proposed by occupants of lower "slots" in the organization must often be approved and/or modified and forwarded by officials at each higher level—until either the original idea is lost, or final approval comes too late.

Another problem created by the highly bureaucratic form of government organization is the tendency to treat clients as objects rather than people. Hummell[4] presents an illustration of a new-car buyer attempting to register his vehicle and discovering he lacks a necessary form. As he is

[4]Ralph P. Hummell, *The Bureaucratic Experience* (New York: St. Martins Press, 1977).

Table 15-1
Policy and Planning
Techniques Used in Management of
Public Organizations

Technique	Management Function(s)	Disciplinary Foundation(s)	Key Elements
Econometric Modeling	Policy making	Macroeconomics	Many equations; endogenous and exogenous variables; effects of policy alternatives.
Delphi	Policy making	Behavioral science	Panel of experts; independent judgments (scenarios); revision of judgments; consensus or set of policy options
Cost Effectiveness	Planning and decision making	Microeconomics, quantitative methods	Alternative approaches to reaching a common goal; impact per dollar spent
Management by Objectives	Planning and controlling	Behavioral science, information systems	Quantification of goals; self-determination of goals; accountability
Planning-Programming-Budgeting-Systems (PPBS)	Planning, decision making, and controlling	Managerial accounting, economics, and information systems	Programs and activities; measures of effectiveness (impact, output, input); crosswalks
Benefit/Cost Analysis	Planning and decision making	Microeconomics	Project, dollar measures of project benefits; discounting and discount rate; costs; benefit/cost ratio
Zero-Base Budgeting (ZBB)	Planning and decision making	Managerial accounting, economics	Decision unit; decision package; minimum level; increments; budget cycle

shunted about from office to office, his feelings of pride and status turn into anger and frustration.

Nevertheless, bureaucracy is a rational system for accomplishing group objectives and is necessary in both public and private organizations. It attempts to substitute efficiency, scientific reasoning, and value-neutrality for individual whim. Max Weber himself was aware of the dangers of bureaucracy—the tendency for controls rather than objectives to become the administrator's ends, and the dehumanizing both of members of the bureaucracy and of clients.[5]

These problems of bureaucracy are present in any large organization, whether in government or in business, but are probably more severe in government agencies. Why does government seem to succumb

[5]Max Weber, *The Theory of Social and Economic Organizations* (New York: The Free Press of Glencoe, 1964; first copyright, 1947).

to the ills of bureaucracy more than the private sector? Again we return to the measurement of objectives. It is far easier in government to measure compliance with procedures than achievement of societal objectives.

Because of the cumbersomeness of established bureaucracies, newly elected officials often use *reorganization* as a way to reassert executive control over government. Another approach is to simply create a new agency to achieve an executive's objectives, bypassing an existing bureaucracy. For example, Richard Nixon was criticized for encouraging Henry Kissinger and his staff to bypass the State Department in conducting U.S. foreign policy (before Kissinger was made Secretary of State).

STAFFING AND DIRECTING

Government personnel include elected officials, appointees, and professionals or "civil servants." Professionals are usually covered by some kind of **merit system,** which is a set of procedures for hiring, promoting, and discharging employees based upon professional rather than political criteria. Appointees generally serve at the pleasure of an elected official, or are appointed for a fixed term. Elected officials may or may not be legally limited to one or two terms.

Relationships among these three groups are sometimes difficult. Elected officials and their appointees have objectives which may be thwarted by a civil service resentful of change. On the other hand, civil servants object to "political" appointees with little technical knowledge of an agency's activities.

Staffing governmental agencies has three major difficulties. First, existing merit system staff, because of merit system rules, cannot simply be replaced, so officials can only install "their" people in non-merit "slots," generally at the highest levels of an agency. Second, recruitment of new staff must follow detailed procedures, established to prevent favoritism. Often, competitive examinations are required, and/or applicants may be screened by a separate personnel agency. Third, salary levels in government are usually below comparable salaries in the private sector, so top-quality people are hard to recruit. (This is less true in the federal government than in state and local governments—but at the highest levels of management, even in the federal government, pay is lower than in the private sector.)

The contingency theory of leadership—the idea that the correct leadership style depends upon the characteristics of the leader, the subordinate, and the situation—applies to public as well as private organizations. The situation in government, however, is often (although not always) characterized by routine performance of highly structural tasks in an environment of strict rules and regulations. Partly because of this situation, the people attracted to government service tend to be motivated more by security than by the need to innovate. Thus the prevalent leadership style in public organizations is directive rather than permissive.

Government employees must be motivated almost entirely without financial incentives, because salaries and promotions are subject to strict procedural controls. Bonus systems are almost never possible, for example. Thus employers must be either self-motivated (through achievement, affiliation, or power rewards inherent in the job) or motivated with nonfinancial rewards such as praise or increased responsibility. Herzberg's job enrichment concept may prove to be very useful in government—although the steep hierarchy and detailed procedural controls often found in government bureaucracies make job enrichment problematic.

The growing movement toward unionizing merit system employees in government adds a countervailing bureaucracy to existing bureaucratic problems. Although unionization could lead to higher salaries for government workers, thus making recruiting easier, it will not ease the structural rigidities of government bureaucracy—on the contrary, it will probably intensify them.

One promising development, however, is **productivity bargaining,** in which public employees agree to new, more efficient production technologies or increased output in exchange for higher wages or better fringe benefits. Productivity bargaining is most applicable in the delivery of services such as garbage collection, road maintenance, rapid transit, and police and fire protection, where measurement of output per unit of input is clear-cut. It has been most widely used by municipal governments.

**GOVERNMENT
MANAGEMENT
AS A SYSTEM**
Figure 15-2 draws together much of the preceeding discussion and illustrates how government can be viewed as a system which takes internal and external inputs and uses various technologies to process them into outputs for society. (A technology is a way of doing something. It may be facilitating or constraining. Figure 15-2 focuses on management technologies rather than production technologies.)

The major activities of government are viewed as (1) policymaking, which combines external inputs of information about society, lobbying, legislation, and court decisions with internal staff inputs, and operates through the technology of policy analysis; (2) planning and decision-making, which uses many of the technologies described in this chapter to define objectives and alternative ways to accomplish the objectives; (3) processing, which includes organizing, staffing, and directing and which is

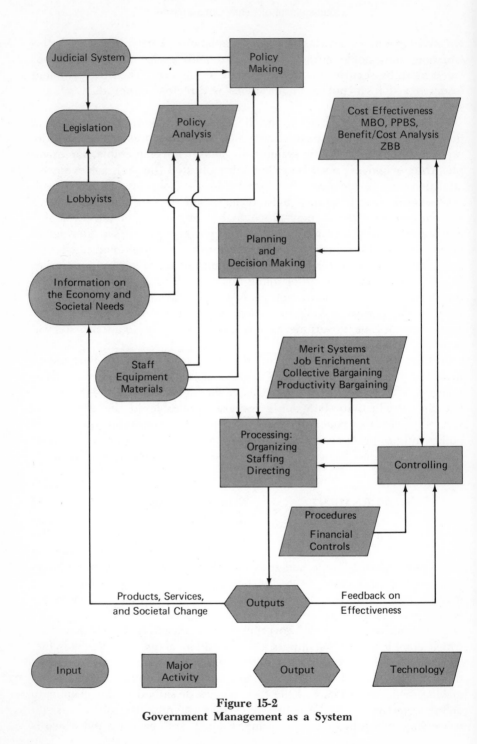

Figure 15-2
Government Management as a System

aided by the technologies of productivity bargaining and job enrichment and constrained by bureaucratic structure, merit systems, and collective bargaining; and (4) controlling, which also makes use of the technologies of planning as well as procedural and financial controls.

The essentials of management apply to public as well as private organizations. Because of the different kinds of goals emphasized by government organizations, however, and because of certain unique constraints on measuring objectives, organizing, and motivating employees, government managers have developed specialized technologies and adapted other technologies used in the private sector. Still, like any organization, a government agency must ultimately produce a product or service that is valued by society.

The penalty for not producing an output valued by society is extinction. In the private sector, declining profits are a signal of unsatisfactory performance. If performance does not improve, the firm will exhaust its financial resources and go bankrupt. In the public sector, the signals of poor performance are less clear and slower to be perceived. Eventually, however, a public agency which does not perform will be denied funding—the equivalent of bankruptcy.

REFERENCES

The American Academy of Political and Social Science, *Theory and Practices of Public Administration: Scope, Objectives and Methods*. Monograph 8. Philadelphia: The Academy, 1968.

BUCHELE, ROBERT B., *The Management of Business and Public Organizations*. New York: McGraw-Hill Book Company, 1977.

GULICK, L. and L. URWICK, eds., *Papers on the Science of Administration*. New York: Augustus M. Keeley, 1937.

MCCURDY, HOWARD E, *Public Administration: A Synthesis*. Menlo Park, Calif.: Cummings Publishing Company, 1977.

SHARKANSKI, IRA, *Public Administration*. Chicago: Markham Publishing Company, 1972.

STARLING, GROVER, *Managing the Public Sector*. Homewood, Ill.: The Dorsey Press, 1977.

WALDO, DWIGHT, ed., *Public Administration in a Time of Turbulance*. Scranton, Pa.: Chandler Publishing Company, 1971.

PART

5

DYNAMICS OF MANAGEMENT

This concluding part looks to the future and emphasizes the dynamic nature of the field of management. Part 1 summarized the past development of the subject; Part 2 identified the functions of the managerial process; Part 3 introduced the contributions from related disciplines to the managerial functions; Part 4 concentrated on operational areas in which management has applications. In short, this book has provided in a capsule the past and present topics important for a manager.

If the process of management were static, the first four parts would present a fairly complete picture, but a principal characteristic of the subject is that it is undergoing rapid changes. Thus there is a need for this final part to emphasize the necessity of the reader's focusing on an approach to change.

Increasingly, managers must understand their role under conditions of rapid change. In certain situations they will find themselves facing conditions that change as a result of forces outside their own control; they must in these situations learn to *adjust* to new developments. On the other hand, they will find that their role in society is to *promote* change and to *create* progress; they thus are involved in initiating and directing change. Modern society offers numerous opportunities that require either adjustment or creation or both.

This part does not attempt a summary, since the book itself is a summary; it will not attempt to look into the crystal ball and forecast specific developments of the 1980s and 1990s. It will provide a foundation for facing change and will encourage readers to contribute their own addenda to the single chapter in this part. Not only this part but the entire book should be treated as a point of departure for continued learning.

16

MANAGEMENT AND CHANGE

by John Douglas, Miami University (Ohio)

<== **IDEAS TO BE FOUND** ==>
IN THIS CHAPTER

- Changes in management concepts
- Ecological issues facing managers
- New managerial attitudes
- Change agents
- Sensitivity training
- Model for change—systems approach
- Survival management
- Changes in management jargon

Change is one of the most characteristic features of management. Leadership can be seen as an attempt to implement change. Much of the preceding discussion in this book testifies to continued change in management. Thus change is not new. What *is* new to managers is the recognition of the complexity and inescapability of change. This last chapter is organized around two questions: (1) What are some of the significant changes in the management field? (2) What are some possible management responses to change?

CHANGES IN THE MANAGEMENT FIELD

*Changes in
Knowledge, Information,
and Techniques*

Many of the past chapters in this book offer concepts and language unknown to the manager of the small factory in the last part of the nineteenth century. The profession of management had its roots in the engineering problems of production. Thus the technical aspect of the management field has advanced greatly and will probably continue in its contribution to the engineering-type problems of the future.

The growth and use of economic concepts was a feature of the development of management in the first half of the twentieth century. Attention to the microfeatures of economics and theories of economic growth and allocation of scarce resources has come primarily since the end of World War II. Cost effectiveness studies developed not only in private firms but also in governmental and nonprofit organizations.

The field that received most attention during the last two decades has been the behavioral sciences. The marketing manager, controller, quality inspector, personnel director must interact with others; they must try to coordinate the efforts of people in performing the operations of the firm. Wherever a manager must relate with other persons, some aspect of behavioral science comes into play. The behavioral science applications to the management field have had top priority in the programs of management in the past; however, expectations should not be abnormally high. Machines are usually more predictable than people, and the advances in the technical areas of management over the past 100 years will not be so easily matched in the behavioral field. Even when scientists can identify the significant factors in individuals, groups, or societies, the relative weight of the factors constantly changes. Group identification and belongingness may be important in one period but not in another. People and their environment continually change, and the difficulties facing the behavioral scientist are great. Perhaps all that can be expected for the next few decades is a better understanding of the problem rather than a specific model which improves the predictability and control of behavior.

Changes in
Scope of Management

There was a time when the field of management spoke primarily to the managers of industrial plants. Because the dominant problems of the factory system were production, the men who joined together were engineering types. The early journals, professional associations, research, publications, and participants from the universities and colleges were oriented toward technical problems and solutions. Recently managers in the public sector, managers of educational institutions, medical clinics, employment agencies, consulting firms, and staff units of religious organizations have found that they have many common problems. Thus the application of management concepts and techniques to varied types of organizations spreads and will continue to spread as the makeup of organizations changes.

The broadening of the scope of management should bring greater demand for specialization of the application of management knowledge. There will be more research studies dealing with the management of organizations concerned with poverty, voluntary groups, political units, etc. The early statements about the universality of management will find expression in specific applications and interpretations of insights in differing new contexts.

The increased scope of management has been accompanied by new social pressures to increase the utilization of groups previously under-represented on the management team. Affirmative action programs are now directed toward improving the opportunities of minority racial groups. In the 1970s, management recruiters increasingly sought qualified blacks as managers. The American Management Association has focused research on greater utilization of women as a new source of future managers.[1] Congressional relaxation of the age for compulsory retirement has enabled older managers, with their valuable experience, to continue longer to provide useful service to society. The result is that management has become more important to a much larger proportion of society.

Changes in the Issues and Problems Facing Managers

A pronounced trend in the American management scene is the *growth of educational preparation and training programs*. Each year, beginning persons at all levels of the organization (machine operators, secretaries, supervisors) enter their careers with higher levels of formal education. More companies and universities offer training programs for advanced study.

This educational trend has caused an *increase in the career mobility* of the work force. Each graduating class is expected to make an increasing number of job or career changes during the lifetime of its members. A graduating senior may expect to make at least seven changes in career or company, not including changes in geographical location *within* the company.

Another change in the workforce under the manager is a *change in composition*. Fewer jobs are available to the traditional blue collar worker. Automation and technological changes in the nature of work have stimulated growth in white collar positions. Each year the ratio of white to blue collar changes, which means that today's manager must deal with a more educated and mobile subordinate. Furthermore, managers themselves have become more educated and mobile. Companies are finding that traditional motivational techniques no longer yield the expected results and inroads are being made into the once "loyal" members of the organization.

---

[1]The concern for women as managers can best be felt by noting the great increase in number of books written on this topic in the 1970s. For example, see Rosabeth Moss Kanter, *Men and Women of the Corporation* (New York: Basic Books, 1977); Margaret Hennig and Anne Jardim, *The Managerial Woman* (New York: Anchor Press/Doubleday, 1977); Laurie Larwood and Marion M. Wood, *Women in Management* (Lexington, Mass.: Lexington Books, 1977).

The white collar workers and public service employees will be a challenge to the skills of management. The question of legitimacy of organization has not been clearly defined for many of the new groups seeking or contemplating some form of collective representation. Teachers went on strike in the 1960s and will continue to use the strike as a means of power equalization. New groups have considered taking some form of collective action against what they think are autocratic institutions and practices. Groups that contemplated action in the 1960s (ministers and priests, for example) may express themselves if changes do not meet their expectations.

The future holds much uncertainty in the relations between organizations and individuals. The security derived from educational training and the mobility of the labor market give rise to a situation where subordinates no longer automatically yield to hierarchical authority. The question of **governance** (who has rights) will continue to be crucial in interpersonal relationships.

Changes in the Environment

The world is changing. Population changes are becoming extremely significant to management personnel in organizations. These changes can be viewed as changes in (1) consumers, (2) factors of production, and (3) participants in society. The increase in the size of consumer markets and the segmentation of markets into strata (age, ethnic) are obvious changes. Consumption patterns vary and are in constant states of change, and the manager continually searches for market information to help in making sound decisions. Values, expectations, and aspirations are continually being transformed.

Population increases are favorable when viewed as expansion in consumer markets and greater availability of human resources. There are many instances, however, where the population changes are not seen as positive aspects of societal growth. When the increase in numbers increases density, unemployment, poverty, there is a question about the value of increase. The population explosion, as a problem to society, varies among countries, but in the future management must be aware of the impact of urban concentrations of people in all areas.

Some environmental changes relevant to management are pollution and social changes in the cities. Pollution (air, water, land, noise) seems to be the cost of industrialization and the exploitation of the resources of the country. What makes the topic critical in the last quarter of the twentieth century is that many **ecologists** (scientists who study humanity's relationship to its environment) foresee the possible destruction of irreplaceable resources. Managers in organizations as well as the professional and academic communities are now starting to show interest in the subject.

The crisis in the cities and urban centers increasingly affects management. The interdependence of the many factors of society make one problem the problem of many. Thus management in the 1980s may become more oriented to its sociological dimensions.

RESPONSE OF MANAGEMENT TO CHANGE

As a result of the changes discussed, the managers face a dilemma. They live in a dynamic, changing world filled with uncertainty. The change in the body of knowledge in the disciplines of engineering, economics, behavioral science, operations research, and systems (to name only a few) continues unabated. Individuals and groups surrounding managers constantly demand consistent and firm action from them. Are there any models or approaches that help managers cope with the world in which they find themselves?

In the past few years the scientific community has spent more time and effort in descriptive studies of organizational life *as it is*, not as it necessarily should be. The reality models to follow cover the broad areas of the manager's *attitude* toward using the information from the academic disciplines, the manager's *processes* in dealing with the human and non-human factors, and the manager's *priorities*.

A Modifying Model for Dealing with Changes in Knowledge and Information

This first model describes a type of mind or attitude that managers need in facing the changes in the substantive knowledge in their field. Professor Charles Summer[2] believes that for managers of organizations to become professional, they must learn to use and modify the knowledge of others. But the knowledge has to be applied in the manager's world rather than in the scientific or academic world. Thus the orientation for the manager is toward action and the payoff comes in results and problem solving. How does a manager approach the ever changing knowledge bank? What intellectual qualities does the manager need? What is the modification process for the manager? Table 16-1 shows the characteristics of the managerial mind.

This simplified but useful "modification model" views knowledge and the scientific world in a way that does not require polarization; as a manager you are not forced to have your head in the clouds or your hands in the grease. You must modify the one world to fit the other world.

[2]Charles E. Summer, Jr., "The Managerial Mind," *The Harvard Business Review* (January-February 1959), pp 69-78.

Table 16-1
Basic Intellectual Qualities and Modification
for Management

Basic Qualities		Management Modification
The Factual Attitude:		
The manager demands and seeks facts before making decisions	BUT	must use reasoning and judgment if lack of facts or time prevents the complete researching of a problem.
The Quantitative Attitude:		
The manager attempts objectivity and collects "measurable" facts	BUT	does not worship mathematical systems and thus doesn't postpone or shun judgments when action is called for.
The Theoretical Attitude:		
The manager develops an interest in searching for concepts that help catalog events into the same meaning; develops an interest in reasoning out laws to explain the relationship of one concept to the other	BUT	realizes that reasoning and quiet thought, as well as the use of theory from others, can be valuable in professional practice, provided one maintains a healthy distrust and a willingness to abandon theoretical concepts if they do not fit the specific problem.
Predisposition for Truth:		
The manager would like every word tested and traced to the abstract characteristics that connect the word to the object it represents in the real world	BUT	realizes that one cannot shrink from the problem because some statements are impossible to define precisely.
Consistency:		
The manager tries to be sure that the arguments in reasoning are valid—that premises are consistent among themselves rather than contradictory and that the statement of conclusions and decisions is also consistent with the statements of premises	BUT	cannot expect to discover scientific laws in every decision through strictly valid arguments, and sometimes finds it necessary to substitute "reasonableness" for syllogistic precision in thinking.

*Change Models
for Dealing with
Process Change*   Machines, markets, and products rarely resist change. However, when a human being is asked to change rates or procedures, the possibility of resistance to the change is created. Among the methods developed to deal with resistance and other aspects of human behavior, three models will be described in this section: the planned change model with behavior as the major ingredient; a decision-making model; and a systems model.

The Planned Change Model.   Many changes discussed in management are conceived of as planned change. In planned change, there is a definite goal or objective in mind, and the problem is one of moving or directing all the efforts of resources to the prescribed goal. The concepts and language of planned change come primarily from anthropologists and sociologists.

Although managers have modified the concepts, the idea of planned change has a definite connotation. Warren G. Bennis, Kenneth D. Benne, and Robert Chin[3] have concentrated on the deliberate and collaborative idea of planned change. For change to be planned and deliberate, there must be an effort by some party or parties, called change-agents, to affect the client system.

The **client-system** is usually the person or unit in need of and desiring the change. The person with communication problems or the department with high personnel turnover would be examples of client-systems. The **change-agent** is the person or unit brought into the system to help resolve the conflict, induce change, diagnose problems, etc. In the original thinking of the process in planned change, the change-agent was conceived as a "free" agent from outside the system. A personnel director called in by an engineer who was having difficulties with a boss would qualify as a change-agent, because of not being part of the client-system's world. The most obvious change-agent for organizations is the outside consultant. The manager interested in change within a unit might turn to the consultant or change-agent, identifying a subunit as the client-system.

The need for collaboration or involvement by the client-system and the dependency on the client-system grow out of the position taken by social scientists that requires recognition of the ethical questions behind change. To the social scientist, the person required to change must participate in the process and must desire the change. Induced change is somewhat frowned upon, for even in planned change there is the necessity for the client-system to be aided in identifying the problem and developing solutions.

One development in management training, sensitivity training, illustrates the concepts behind planned change. **Sensitivity training** deals with human learning and behavioral change and usually occurs in groups. The leader or trainer is from outside the immediate environment of the participants and through discussion and feedback the persons are encouraged to understand the impact they make upon others and are given support if they want to make any behavioral adaptations. In many instances the changes require changes in attitudes through a three-fold process suggested by Kurt Lewin.

In a training group, commonly called a **T-group,** conditions exist for individual behavior change by first focusing upon *here-and-now* situations. In other words, the group creates experiences which are shared by all

[3]Warren G. Bennis, Kenneth D. Benne, and Robert Chin, eds., *The Planning of Change* (New York: Holt, Rinehart and Winston, Inc., 1961).

members, thus forming a common bond. The experiences are reality-type and personal. The trainer adds a second ingredient to the here-and-now experiences, the idea of *feedback*. Participants are encouraged to respond (i.e., feed back) to the experiences, stating how they view them and their impact on them. Eventually the reality as perceived by the other group members becomes the behavioral benchmark for each participant desiring change. The third condition for human learning in the group situations is unfreezing. **Unfreezing** is a period of unlearning or shaking up that usually takes place before change can occur.

In the 1970s, many organizations broadened their approaches to planned change. They moved from approaches that had been highly individualistic, such as sensitivity training, T-groups, and supervisory development, to approaches which involve the whole organization. **Organization development (OD)** is the term given to a planned change in the organization involving the total system and directed toward creating total organizational effectiveness.[4]

Another planned change model and one that is simple to use is proposed by Arnold S. Judson in a short book, *A Manager's Guide to Making Changes*.[5] Using his experiences in line management, staff management, and consulting, Mr. Judson discusses how people are affected by and respond to changes and why their resistance is primarily based upon attitudes. One of the manager's first jobs when contemplating the introduction of any change is predicting the extent of the resistance from the people who will participate or be affected. Changes in methods of operations, products, organization, or the work environment will be met by some form of worker response. Will the response be a resistance or an acceptance of the change? What are the measurable risks and specific gains? From analysis in tabular form a manager can identify the areas of greatest gain and those of greatest loss. This identification is helpful in developing what Judson calls a systematic approach to making changes, with the following steps:

1. Analyze and plan the change.
2. Communicate the change to those involved.
3. Gain acceptance of the required changes in behavior.
4. Maintain control during the transition from the status quo to the changed environment.
5. Consolidate the new conditions and follow up to insure the success of the change.

[4]Glen H. Varney, *Organization Development for Managers* (Reading, Mass.: Addison-Wesley Publishing Company, 1977).

[5]Arnold S. Judson, *A Manager's Guide to Making Changes* (London, New York, Sydney: John Wiley and Sons, Ltd., 1966).

Changes in Decision Making   Not all changes are behavioral, although when changes are implemented the behavioral factors become of prime importance. A second change in a traditional management process is the change in the method of decision making. Chapters 5 and 12 have discussed the traditional approach from the past to the present. All managers, however, face the framing of the problem, and here some new concepts and approaches have also been developed. The idea of **suboptimization** (a state where one or more goals are in conflict with each other so that maximization is impossible), the idea of making marginal decisions, or even the unsophisticated statement of "muddling through" are products of the post-World War II period.

In a valuable article for managers,[6] "The Science of 'Muddling Through,' " Charles E. Lindblom compares two approaches to administrative decision making: the rational-comprehensive method and the successive-limited comparisons method. He says that the first method, the most common today, must give way to the second when the manager is faced with complex problems. Lindblom distinguishes between the two with the terms root and branch. A comparison of the two in Table 16-2 shows the differences. The picture coming from this comparison is clear. The decision world of the manager calls for adjustments, adaptation, and comparisons of alternatives emerging from the specific environment rather than decisions structured from static goals and objectives. The reality is change, and the management posture is response. The forcing of situations into predetermined and perhaps superficial models will probably give way to a more reality-oriented approach.

Systems Change   The application of systems theory and process to the manager's job marks a significant change in the field of management. The concept of work flow, once limited to machine-type operations, now is applied to the manager's work, which is defined in terms of the input, throughput, output, and feedback of the system involved. Where the inputs and outputs that link two subsystems converge, an **interface** is established, and much of the manager's behavior and time is spent on interface points. One constant demand upon the manager is to monitor the system, to keep the system at a state of *dynamic equilibrium*, and to make *continuity-type* decisions. Change is anticipated, expected, and even necessary for the continuing growth of the system so that the manager's response to change is somewhat different from that described in earlier sections.

One of the best descriptions of the reality of the manager's job, the notion of systems and the manager's job, and the relationship to change,

[6]Charles E. Lindblom, "The Science of 'Muddling Through,' " *American Society for Public Administration*, 19, No. 2 (Spring 1959).

Table 16-2
Decision Making Model for Change

Root (Rational-Comprehensive)		Branch (Successive Limited Comparisons)
1. The administrator identifies values, objectives, or ends, and then seeks the means (policies) to reach the ends	BUT	this is almost impossible to do since determination of values and objectives is usually intertwined with the empirical analysis of the alternatives. Often a means-end analysis doesn't apply or is limited.
THUS		
2. A "good" policy is one most appropriate for meeting the desired ends	BUT	the real test of a "good" policy should be whether there is agreement among analysts that the policy is good in itself (workable), not that it is the most appropriate means to an agreed objective.
AND		
3. All important factors are considered, analyzed, and evaluated. The process is a comprehensive one	BUT	in dealing with real, complex problems, all important factors cannot be known, analysis must be limited, some alternative policies will be neglected, and important values will be overlooked.
AND		
4. Theory is often used; goals and values are maximized by selecting the best solution	BUT	in reality and dealing with so many limitations, theory would be restrictive and inappropriate in most cases. The administrator gives up the search for the "best" solution, and makes marginal and incremental comparisons between policies and/or solutions and finds the better one.

comes from the work of Leonard Sayles.[7] In this work Sayles speaks of a second Industrial Revolution. The first Industrial Revolution was technological. In the second revolution the insights and lessons of machine technology (e.g., interchangeable parts, development of special purpose machines, planning of operations by sequence, and the interdependence of subunits) are applied to the work world of the contemporary manager. Change, when viewed in the systems sense, is an expected event and often beyond the direct control and influence of the manager.

Sayles describes what managers actually do on their jobs during an eight-hour day. It was found that a great deal of a manager's time is spent

[7]Leonard R. Sayles, *Managerial Behavior* (New York: McGraw-Hill Book Company, 1964).

outside the assigned task. The manager was a participant, for example, in many **external work flows** (i.e., giving advice to another manager at the same level, discussing problems with community leaders, responding to the manpower budgets from the personnel department, speaking with a customer about product complaints). In these two-person contacts, the manager cannot always function through traditional organizational hierarchy; it is not feasible to use the channels of legitimate authority. Rather, the manager provides the connective tissue or link between one subpart and another subpart of a larger system, and operates, therefore, at the interface where the job with its authority and responsibility meets the jobs of others.

Another time-consuming activity of the manager, in addition to spending time in the external work patterns, is the time spent on monitoring the system. In dealing with subordinates and with others outside the manager's authority field, it is necessary to know when and where to change behavior or to encourage change in others. **Monitoring** the system tells the manager when administrative action is required. It is possible to find out how things are going by initiating contacts with other members, making use of the contacts initiated by others, observing performance, and reviewing numerical records.

The similarity in the process change models can now be seen. The modifying model of Summer, the planned change model of Lewin, the "muddling through" model of Lindblom, and the systems model of Sayles all reflect an interest in reality. The orientation is toward operating in the world as it really is rather than in a prescribed, artificial world. Change is not worshipped but is seen as a necessary ingredient for maintaining the growth of the system. Innovation, the introduction of change into a system, becomes more than a luxury for organizations; it becomes an integral part of an organization's growth. There is a clearer picture of the interdependence of all related parts and a better insight into the nature of systems. Table 16-3 not only summarizes the ideas from Sayles but also incorporates many of the ideas from previous process change models.

Changes in Priorities

Developments in systems theory and their application to organizations have caused managers to have renewed interest in the world about them. Inflation, unemployment, poverty, and energy shortages have significant impact upon all organizations regardless of orientation, public as well as private, profit-centered as well as service-centered. The new managerial perceptions are central to the recently emphasized area of **ecology**, the study of humanity and its environment. For this reason considerable attention was given to this approach in Chapters 3 and 4.

One of the most common terms in the popular literature is the concept of **survival**. We are being told that time may be running out for

Table 16-3
The Manager's World

	1st Industrial Revolution	2nd Industrial Revolution
Time Period:	1850s	1950s
Management Level Involved:	First level: supervisors, plant superintendents	Middle and upper level managers
Nature of Manager's Job:	Supervise subordinates using authority and organization control	Views job as part of work flow system. Monitors the system to get feedback
Scope of Job:	Primarily works on small jobs and with subordinates	Deals in external work flow; minimal interactions with direct subordinates; performs monitoring function of system
Type of Decision Approach:	Identify problem, apply analysis and make decision	Makes marginal adjustments to maintain continuity and movement of the system
Attitude toward Change:	Desire for stability, predictability, minimize change	Expect, welcome, and innovate change into dynamic system

the survival of the human race. For years the topic of our survival and possible elimination from our planet was always thought of in terms of military holocaust—nuclear warfare. The survival problem now facing societies on this planet deals also with the destruction of the resources necessary to maintain life. Will we be able to reverse the onrushing deterioration of our environment? Will the costs overwhelm us? (Costs of technological advances; costs of air, water, noise, pollution; costs of the polarization of society into ethnic groups and economic haves and have nots; costs of lifting aspirations and desires for change.) The change in the environment has been occurring for eons, but it is the rate of change that worries the scientists. Temperature changes in the earth, for example, are artificially stimulated by smog, and unless we innovate to restore natural balance, another ice age may befall the world. The contemporary literature is filled with other examples of what will happen to our lungs because of the deficiency of oxygen, to the fish population from polluted streams, and to the human nervous and hearing systems from noise pollution.

Administrators of organizations should not miss the readings of Galbraith, Drucker, Heilbroner and others on this topic. Each calls for change—for innovation. Robert Heilbroner[8] in a popular article briefly

[8]Robert Heilbroner, "Priorities for the Seventies," *Saturday Review* (January 3, 1970), p. 174. See also Richard H. Viola, *Organization in a Changing Society* (Philadelphia: W. B. Saunders Co., 1977), and Clarence Walton, ed., *The Ethics of Corporate Conduct* (Englewood Cliffs, N.J.: Prentice-Hall, Inc., 1977).

described what he believes *are* the national priorities: military goals over civilian goals, private desires over public desires, and affluent wishes over wishes of the poor. He then turns his attention to what sets of priorities *should be* for a decent nation-state:

First set (within man's power to achieve in the immediate future):
1. The demilitarization of the national budget.
2. The rebuilding of cities.
3. The elimination of poverty.

Second set (potentially within man's power but a distant goal):
1. Overcoming a racist culture.
2. Reducing the alienation between the young people and their society.

Third set (examples of the kinds of priorities to move from mere survival toward ultimate salvation):
1. Improve the treatment of criminality.
2. Make efforts to contain and control the police arm.
3. Rescue the environment from the impact of unregulated technology.

Even though the rape of the environment was done by man's misuse of technology, Heilbroner does not want technology destroyed. Rather, he wants more technology of a different kind. If man applied his technological skill to the environmental problems, there might be "an exhaustless automobile, a noiseless airplane, a reliable method of birth control suitable for application among illiterate and superstitious people, new methods of reducing and coping with wastes—radioactive, sewage, gaseous, and liquid, and new modes of transporting goods and people within and between cities."[9] Thus, a major priority is for *technological research*.

The 1970s saw a revival of the "conservation theme"—only this time the idea of survival had a note of urgency to the issue. Professional organizations have responded to the popularity of the topic by endorsing seminars and conferences on man and his environment. Congressional subcommittees are active and proposals are being submitted to make a "clean environment" an inalienable right of man. Managers as administrators or as citizens will be involved in this movement. The decision making world of the future manager will be changed as our governmental agencies respond to the cries for action.

The response models described in this section are but a few of the examples possible. They do show, however, that managers and adminis-

[9]Heilbroner, "Priorities for the Seventies," p. 174.

trators live in a changing world, a world in need of responsible innovation as well as responsible response. There are other priority models for not all persons agree on what problems of a nation are to be given first attention. What is important, however, is not acceptance of a specific set of priorities but a recognition that change in priorities, decision making approaches, and processes is inevitable in a dynamic, growing system. A manager of a small establishment may not have the resources to sponsor technological research in air pollution but can innovate responsibility in the work environment and can sponsor growth and change within the methods and processes of a firm.

Changes in Management Jargon

A revision of a book on *Essentials of Management* brings into focus a final type of change that a manager faces—the continual process of inventing and introducing new terms, acronyms, and jargon to emphasize old and basic concepts or principles. If the original edition of this book on essentials satisfactorially summarized the underlying fundamentals and principles of management, the need for continual revision of the book would seem to be unnecessary. Fundamental truth is certainly long-lasting. Yet, while the essentials do not change, this final part has shown that problems and the environment do change. Thus, updating of illustrations, refinements of analytical tools, refocusing on new problems, and reporting of new research on the essentials are needed periodically. Furthermore, a manager needs to keep up to date on the current usage of new terms, often referred to as buzz words, in order to understand modern expressions. In short, the language of management undergoes rapid changes with the introduction of new words, acronyms, and styles of expression.

While most of the essential concepts of management have roots in historical developments, the jargon of management is dynamic; "old wine is placed in new bottles." From a practical viewpoint, modern managers must continually adjust their vocabularies to new methods of expression. Often an old idea is rediscovered and given a new name. Since management is built on a number of disciplines, new terms emerge from each of these disciplines and other terms emerge that serve as gangplanks between disciplines. Therefore, it is necessary for the well-informed manager to keep current through continual reading of the professional literature. Table 16-4 has been added to this edition to help the reader translate some of the basic, essential concepts into current language—the language of new research, new practices, and new analytical approaches.

SUMMARY

Part 5, "Dynamics of Management," has purposely been left unfinished. Managers of organizations must always face an unfinished world. Rarely do they have all the information to make a perfect decision; rarely do they

Table 16-4
Changing Terms Identifying Essential
Concepts of Management

A Layman's Guide to the Current Managerial Jungle of Buzz Words and Jargon

Current Buzz Words	Essence of Term's Meaning and Usefulness	Durable, Related Essential Concept
Contingency Approaches	Organization structure and leadership styles are contingent on the task, technology, and environment. No universals will fit all situations.	Follett's (1930) law of the situation. Harvard's case emphasis indicating diversity in practice.
Systems Approach	Viewing a subject as a whole composed of interdependent parts and delineated by clear boundaries.	Synthesis of elements of knowledge. Integration of component parts.
Management by Objectives (MBO)	A systematized idea for setting clear and definite objectives for each individual at all hierarchical levels, usually through joint participation of superior and subordinate.	Control elements of targets, measuring performance, flagging variances, and taking corrective action; feedback by participation of those concerned.
Management Information Systems (MIS)	An all-inclusive system for providing management with information for effective decision making	Use of all available data, e.g., accounting data library, and primary collection, before making a decision.
Organization Behavior (OB)	The study of the behavior of individuals in organizations through emphasis on behavioral sciences, i.e., psychology, sociology, political science, anthropology.	Organizations involve people; thus managers must adjust to individuals and groups.
Organization Climate (OC)	The total of the degree and quality of environmental factors that influence participants, usually measured by their perceptions.	Humanity has evolved in civilizations through responses to challenges from outside; esprit de corps; morale.
Organization Development (OD)	A planned, organizationwide effort for participating in continuous rethinking (unfreezing) and changing beliefs values, and structure to adapt to new challenges.	Groups need not get stuck in a rut; animals (human) must adapt. Creativity is basic to progress.
Organization Effectiveness	The measurement of whether the organization is attaining the goals which it has chosen.	Organizations should actually obtain results.

Table 16-4 (cont'd.)

Current Buzz Words	Essence of Term's Meaning and Usefulness	Durable, Related Essential Concept
Zero-Based Budgeting (ZBB)	The identification of the irreducible minimum (zero) of program costs and renewed justification for each extra program, thus providing the framework for rethinking priorities and replacement of new programs for old programs having lower value.	Incremental decision making; opportunity costs; trade-offs; continual review of present programs; "cut out deadwood."
Delphi Technique	A group decision-making technique involving an iterative process for securing independent recommendations and support, in writing, without feedback from others except for sequential knowledge of positions until a solution is reached. (Avoids face-to-face distortions.)	Consultations with independent experts is valuable, especially when judgment must be used (no empirical facts available); pooled, independent judgment.
Time Management	A technique for allocation of one's time through setting goals, assigning priorities, identifying and eliminating time wasters, and use of managerial techniques to reach goals efficiently.	Work improvement, scheduling, and concepts from scientific management. Ideas from Benjamin Franklin.
Operations Research (OR)	A scientific approach for solving problems, usually using quantitative approaches, in which an optimum is sought but where a team of diverse specialists contributes.	Utilization of quantitative models and methods whenever the subject can be stated mathematically or statistically.
Planning/Program/ Budgeting (PPB)	An integrated system for rational ordering of inputs and outputs of an organization, with focus on identifiable goals. Interrelates separate budget elements and long-run goals.	Planning involves interrelating outputs (goals) with budgeted inputs (costs) or each component of a unit's activities.
Satisficing	A term coined by H. A. Simon to contrast with optimizing; an attempt to find a satisfactory solution which need not be the exact optimum.	Realistically, an approximation of reasonable solution where the theoretical optimum (e.g., an economic man) is not of practical importance.

Table 16-4 (cont'd.)

Current Buzz Words	Essence of Term's Meaning and Usefulness	Durable, Related Essential Concept
Cost/Benefit Analysis	The quantitative examination of alternative courses of action where benefits are directly related to their costs.	Allocation of resources (costs) to the satisfaction of goals (benefits).
Program Evaluation and Review Technique (PERT)	A quantitative method of scheduling activities in which a network of activities must be performed in a definite sequence but uncertainty is faced. The optimum path is referred to as the critical path.	Planning and scheduling require precise description of activities and times required but actual completion is affected by uncertain factors.
Male Chauvinist (sexist) undertone in the English language	The movement by some groups to "desex" writing and speaking in English in order to further reduce discrimination against women in management circles.	Male and female of the species are different; tolerance of differences; also, Man, Homo sapiens (mankind), differs from lower animals.

have the full authority to implement the best one of their solutions; and rarely can they predict specific human responses to events.

Essentials of Management gives managers a perspective to view their present environment. They can see the past, present and future developments of the field. They can identify the managerial processes and the techniques in the related disciplines to applications in business operational functions and activities of public agencies. But most importantly, managers may sense the need for an appropriate posture.

No matter how large or small the organization, the problems, decisions, and responses emerging from one environment have an impact upon other environments. As one of the principal characters in life's unfinished but continuing drama, the manager has the potential of determining the destiny of our society.

REFERENCES

BENNIS, WARREN G., KENNETH D. BENNE, and ROBERT CHIN, eds., *The Planning of Change* (3rd ed.). New York: Holt, Rinehart and Winston, 1976.

BENNIS, WARREN, *Organizational Development: Its Nature Origins and Prospects.* Reading, Mass.: Addison-Wesley, 1969.

BRADFORD, L. P., J. R. GIBB, and K. D. BENNE, *T-Group Theory and Laboratory Method.* New York: John Wiley & Sons, Inc., 1964.

Chamberlain, Neil W., *Enterprise and Environment*. New York: McGraw-Hill Book Company, 1968.

Churchman, C. West, *Challenge to Reason*. New York: McGraw-Hill Book Company, 1968.

Drucker, Peter F., *The Age of Discontinuity: Guidelines to our Changing Society*. New York: Harper and Row, 1969.

Jacoby, Neil H., *Corporate Power and Social Responsibility: A Buleprint for the Future*. New York: The Macmillan, Co., 1973.

Judson, Arnold S., *A Manager's Guide to Making Changes*. New York: John Wiley & Sons, Inc., 1966.

Kahn, Herman and B. Bruce-Briggs, *Things to Come*. New York: The Macmillan Co., 1972.

Moffitt, Donald, *The Wall Street Journal Views America Tomorrow*. New York: Dow Jones & Company, 1977.

Steiner, George A., ed., *Changing Business Society Interrelationships*. Los Angeles: Graduate School of Management, UCLA, 1975.

Tarnowieski, Dale, *The Changing Success Ethic*. New York: American Management Association, 1973.

Viola, Richard H., *Organizations in a Changing Society*. Philadelphia: W. B. Saunders Co., 1977.

Walton, Clarence C., The Ethics of Corporate Conduct. Englewood Cliffs, N.J.: Prentice-Hall, Inc., 1977.

INDEX

257

Uncertainty, conditions of, 158
Unfreezing, defined, 246
Unity of command, 68-69
Urwick, Lyndall, 18

Valuation methods, 207-208
Values:
    dominant American, 33
    moral, 30-33
    price representing, 210
Variable costs in breakeven
        analysis, 110-11
Variables:
    endogenous, 223
    exogenous, 223

Varney, Glen H., 246
Vertical flow of communica-
        tion, 97
Vertical integration, 64
Vroom, Victor, 144-46

Watson, John, 141
Watt, James, Jr., 14
Weber, Max, 23, 33, 73-74,
        231
White, Maunsel, 16
Whitney, Eli, 14
Whyte, William F., 32-33,
        137

Wiener, Norbert, 187
Women in management, 4,
        241
Woodward, Joan, 76-77
Work flow, external, 249
Work improvement, 196-98
Work sampling, 199
Work standards, 198-200

Zero-base budgeting, 222,
        229-30, 254
Zone of acceptance, 97
Zone of indifference, 34